MW00439799

The KARANKAWAY COUNTRY
and ADJACENCIES

Miles 0 5 10 20 30 40 50

VICTORIA

GOLIAD

PORT LAVACA

OLD INDIANOLA

PORT O'CONNOR

ARANSAS
NATIONAL WILDLIFE REFUGE

REFUGIO

Blackjack Peninsula

MATAGORDA I.

Copano Bay

50 miles to
Camp in the Brush

ROCKPORT

ST. JOSEPH I.

ARANSAS PASS

CORPUS
CHRISTI

Corpus Christi
Bay

MUSTANG I.

Corpus Christi Pass

PADRE I.

NORTH

WEST EAST

SOUTH

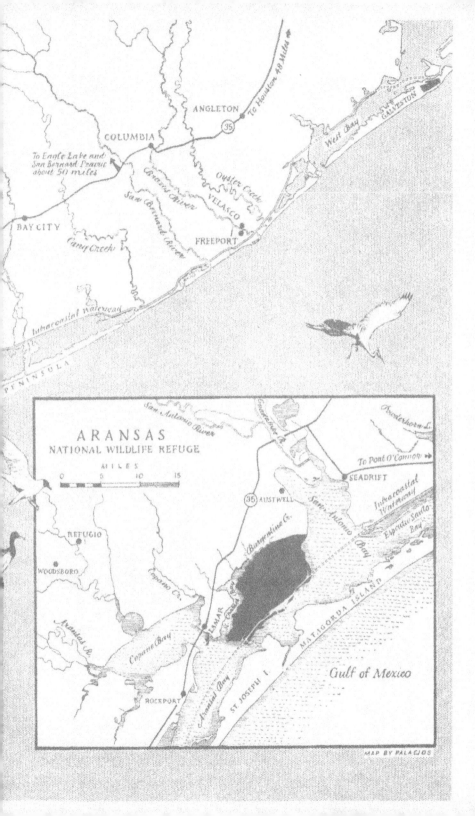

ARANSAS
NATIONAL WILDLIFE REFUGE

MILES
0   5   10   15

MAP BY PALACIOS

Karánkaway Country

BY ROY BEDICHEK

Foreword by W. W. Newcomb

Karánkaway Country

UNIVERSITY OF TEXAS PRESS, AUSTIN & LONDON

ISBN 0-292-74304-1
Library of Congress Catalog Card Number 74-3537
Copyright 1950 by Roy Bedichek; Copyright © 1974 by the estate
   of Lillian Greer Bedichek
Printed in the United States of America

Second edition

TO MY WIFE, LILLIAN GREER BEDICHEK

CONTENTS

Maps of Texas

FOREWORD

Roy Bedichek came late to the writing of books; his first, *Adventures with a Texas Naturalist*, was published in 1947 when he was almost seventy, and his second book, *Karánkaway Country*, appeared three years later. An author's age may not be necessarily pertinent to the content of his writings, and certainly the spirit and exuberance that mark Bedichek's books are those of a youthful and questing mind. But it is difficult to imagine that his books could have been written by a younger person, for they are the distillates of a lifetime of rambling a beloved land, of searching observation, of discussion, debate, wide reading, and reflection.

Bedichek, though born in Illinois, grew up on the edge of the blackland prairies of central Texas, and, after attending the University of Texas, he became something of a vagabond, wandering the United States, tramping Europe one summer, and holding a variety of jobs. Some fifteen years later, with a family to support, he settled down to newspaper jobs in New Mexico and San Antonio, finally becoming director of the University Interscholastic League of Texas, a position he held for over thirty years. The history of the League and his beliefs about rivalry and competition as an educational force were set forth in his third book, *Educational Competition: The Story of the University Interscholastic League of Texas* (University of Texas Press, 1956). Original and charming, though the least known of his books, was *The Sense of Smell*, published in 1960 in the year following his death.

This stark outline of Bedichek's career gives little hint of Bedichek the man—his penchant for camping out, his appetite for food cooked in or over the campfire, his deep knowledge of Greek and Latin philosophers and poets, his predilection for quoting long passages of Whitman, and his familiarity with Shakespeare, nineteenth-century English poets, Russian novelists, Browning, and Thoreau. Bedichek's life and writings also were intimately bound up with those of Walter P. Webb, the eminent historian, and J. Frank Dobie, the widely known and respected storyteller of the Southwest. They were the two other members of what Frank Wardlaw has termed the "incomparable triumvirate who were at once the conscience and the directing force of many aspects of the intellectual life of Texas." Though each was a singular, unusual, independent-minded man, pursuing his own star, the strange alchemy of a broadly shared outlook and mutual affection brought them together in an enduring kinship. Bedichek's literary works surely would have been very different had the fates not thrown this trio together—stimulating, influencing, and reinforcing one another. Luckily for those of us who never had the good fortune to share a steak or a campfire with Bedichek, his character and career have been searchingly portrayed by his friends and colleagues in *Three Men in Texas: Bedichek, Webb, and Dobie* (edited by Ronnie Dugger, University of Texas Press, 1967).

While *Karánkaway Country* is focused on that strip of coastal prairie lying roughly between Corpus Christi and Galveston and once inhabited by the poorly known and much maligned Karankawa Indians, it also serves as home base for excursions to other sections of Texas, for a discussion of the flood and erosion controls practiced in Coleman County in central Texas, for example. It also provides a convenient local setting for richly tailored essays on wildlife, soil, human skin, goats, and the other topics suggested by a wide-ranging intellect. In a broader sense, *Karánkaway Country*, like its predecessor, *Adventures with a Texas Naturalist*, is not so much about a place as it is an exposition of a philosophy—an attitude and a conviction about the proper relationship of man and nature. Though the diverse chapters, from diseased rivers to coons and from open skies to prairie chickens, may be read simply as a collection of entertaining and informative essays, they are related building blocks in the edifice of his convictions. Bedichek's philosophy, if it can be reduced to a few words, is essentially that man must learn to live on peaceful and conciliatory terms with his natural environment. It has, of course, a number of facets: men have an obligation to the animal world to perpetuate its diversity; natural systems, such as rivers, should be treated as units, not as piecemeal problems; land, in the Jeffersonian sense, is held only in usufruct by the living; and so on.

Though disguised by what might be taken to be the provincial ramblings of a gifted storyteller and essayist, *Karánkaway Country* might better be regarded as a regional expression of a theme that has an old and honorable history. It has occupied a number of America's most gifted minds, from Thoreau to Rachel Carson, Jefferson to Justice William Douglas. Occasionally, America has listened and taken heed of these wise people; often, their words have been half-heard or maligned, and quickly forgotten. The American conscience, it seems, is fickle, now inflamed with the rape of modern or primeval America, more often supine and torpid under the devastating onslaught of ignorant or greedy exploiters. That the theme should find such able expression by a Texan, raised in a land but a few years removed from a frontier where "contempt for wild life" was "almost beyond belief" (to quote Bedichek), is remarkable. It attests to the genius of the man and the dogged persistence of a civilized, rational, and critically important way of viewing and living in our earthly home.

Foreshadowing the ecological and environmental concerns that were to haunt the American consciousness in the sixties and seventies, in the decade following the Second World War a number of writers besides Bedichek became concerned with the extermination of various animals, the destruction of forests, the pollution of rivers and oceans, and the human population explosion. Rachel Carson's compelling *The Sea around Us* was, for example, a product of these years. It was also the era of the "Neo-Malthusians"—William Vogt, Fairfield Osborn, and others—gloomily prophesying impending world-wide overpopulation, hunger, and starvation, sometimes prescribing radical and, to many, repulsive corrective measures. Though motivated by the shared awakening to ecological perils, Bedichek's works are unique in approach and spirit and stand alone. He was no doomsday prophet in the Neo-Malthusian mold, nor was he given to sermons studded with exhortations about what America and the world must do to extricate itself from decline and ultimate effacement. Much of what Bedicheck, a moralistic conservationist tinged with a mystical veneration of the benefits to be derived by man from nature and the outdoors, points out may properly be interpreted as desperately sad. But it is tempered with understanding, gentleness, and an even humor that often transmutes itself into optimism and hope for mankind and the earth. It might be argued, then, that Bedichek, though an outstanding ornithologist and naturalist, in important ways perceived and understood humanity—and that breed called Texans—as well as or better than he did whooping cranes and wolves. In this sense he was more philosopher than naturalist, as much anthropologist, in the classical sense, as philosopher.

Dobie has quoted Bedichek as saying that it is a waste of time to read a book that has not stood the test of time—uttered perhaps in jest, though an accurate statement of his reading preferences. One cannot help but believe that Bedichek would have modified his judgment had he lived to contemplate a second edition of *Karánkaway Country*. For the problems faced in these pages are as current as they were almost a quarter of a century ago when the book first appeared. It is a strong statement, perhaps more needed now than then; it is timely, perhaps timeless.

W. W. NEWCOMB

TEXAS MEMORIAL MUSEUM

xii

ACKNOWLEDGMENTS

In the preparation of this book I have been assisted by friends and well-wishers to whom acknowledgments are due:

For the freedom of the Aransas National Wild Life Refuge during my early visits there, I am indebted to C. A. (Bud) Keefer, Manager; and, later, to Julian A. Howard, his successor.

I. V. Duncan, of Eagle Lake, set me up in the middle of the old and famous Coushatte Ranch, under lease from David Wintermann, who offered no objection to my camping there. This ranch includes the Bernard Prairie, one of the few remaining haunts of the Attwater prairie chicken. As will be noted in the chapter on this disappearing species, Tom Waddell, Game Warden, gave me much firsthand information.

Sam H. Cooper, Secretary-Manager, Central Colorado River

Authority, and R. G. Hollingsworth, Vice-Chairman, took the trouble to show me work of such great promise in soil-water conservation that it has confirmed me in the belief that in Texas, at least, the control of the so-called "little waters" is of the first importance.

G. E. Colbath, Trapper for the Texas Game, Fish, and Oyster Commission, told me about the trapping profession generally, and gave me a new insight into the ways and wiles of some of those animals which he makes it his business to capture. He studies animals to outwit them. In his study and experience, however, he has come not only to respect his prey, but to have genuine sympathy for all wild life. In the excision of certain elements—a necessary measure if we are to have "refuges" at all—he performs after the manner of a surgeon who causes his patient as little pain as possible.

J. Frank Dobie accompanied me on a camping trip to his native Brush Country, background of some of his most important contributions to the culture of the Southwest. He read the brush chapters of this book, as well as several others, and I profited by his criticisms.

Another good friend, Glen Evans, Assistant Director of the Texas Memorial Museum, criticized for my benefit certain portions of this book dealing with soil-conservation problems, to which he is extremely sensitive and upon which he is unusually well informed.

The University of Texas Research Institute favored me with a grant to help defray expense of field trips and to provide clerical assistance in the preparation of this book.

The assistance of Katherine Blow, Reference Librarian in the University of Texas Library, has been of great value to me. She has genius for guiding ignorance in the ways of recorded knowledge. Furthermore, and finally, I followed the pattern set by the more cautious writers who undertake a paragraph or a book touching seriously any phase of Texas history, persuading E. W. Winkler, Librarian (Bibliography), in the same library, to read the chapter entitled "Karánkaway Country," and I forthwith adopted his emendations.

THE AUTHOR

which the satisfaction of the apelike curiosity of another species far from justified? With rats I might have succeeded; but with foxes, no.

The experiment died prematurely, failing to add its mite of fact to the mass of *Vulpes* data—which by this time has doubtless become a library of experimental minutiae, checked, rechecked, and verified by generations of investigators, eventually to contain every scintilla of dependable information concerning the genus, chemical reactions, and all except, perhaps, "the silence that spoke and eloquence of eyes" by means of which three certain foxes once on a time stirred an emotional response in a boy, making him quite uncomfortable in the belief that perhaps these particular individuals understood him and his kind better than the best authorities in animal psychology considered at all possible. Nor will that record ever contain a statement of the satisfaction I have felt several times since then upon seeing the farewell wave of an escaping tail flashed momentarily from some open space in the lawless chaparral.

But such sentimentalism does not go with science. The "love-is-all-in-all" stargazers of the last century are out of date. They are rarely mentioned now except to ridicule, while most of them are forgotten. Poor Goethe is mercilessly lambasted by present-day scientists, in spite of the fact that he discovered a new bone in the human skeleton and perhaps foreshadowed Darwin himself in some of his more or less poetic speculations.

Science has moved on over the hill and far away from Goethe's excitement at finding a robin feeding and taking care of a couple of motherless baby wrens. It has left behind, also, the religiosity of Büchner, who began what he meant for a scientific work in 1885 with a hymn to Love. It stands now on the other pole. It has become the fashion to account mechanistically for the phenomenon we call life. It is even asserted that all life processes may be explained by laws of physics and chemistry. All disharmonies in human behavior, from spanking a child to the abolition of war, will be resolved by Positive Science when it has had time finally to analyze Man in its laboratories, correlate the results, and so find out exactly what he is made of, what it is that set him going in the first place, and what it is that keeps him going. Anything "idealistic" is anathema to a large section of the new priesthood.

Be that as it may, I do not regret abandoning the experiment and finding out thus early that such research was not for me. Since then I have learned something of foxes from men who have studied them in their natural haunts, and from running across them casually in the woods, where they stay not to be questioned, and rarely do anything notebook-worthy; but, frisky in their freedom, give a certain tone to the out of doors as grateful to the spirit as woodsy odors are to a city-jaded sense of smell.

The fact that I have no taste for mathematically dominated investigations of an analytical sort does not mean that I have no taste for their results. Far from it. I marvel at them and am insatiable in areas whose terminology I understand. Positive science is a world in itself, or, rather, it is a certain way of looking at the world. Whether or not one joins this great, patient army of truthseekers is a matter of individual preference and natural bent or talent. The souls of some men thrive on the relentless pursuit of truth, or what they firmly believe to be "truth." Other souls do not.

One is almost tempted at this point to ask the classical question, "What is truth?" The anatomical facts which constitute *Vulpes* a genus present a kind of truth and very valuable in any sensible person's thinking. And still the sympathy one feels for a penned fox is truth too. Your suspicion that his intent eyes plead, perhaps accuse, is truth about *you*, as well as an item worth noting about the fox. You have a feeling, if not a conviction, of guilt as you see the delicate nose rubbed raw from thrusting it through the wire netting. And why does he still press that ring of raw skin through a mesh? There are motions of the "sniffing" muscles which tell you plainly that he is inhaling air from the outside—ravenously tasting it before it becomes polluted. Animal prisons stink just as human ones do, each with its characteristic odor, however. If the smell of his own prison is revolting to the dull nose of man, it may be that the imprisoned fox is enduring a revulsion utterly beyond human comprehension, since his olfactory sense detects a dozen odors to man's one, and experiences each noisome effluvium with a far greater intensity of disgust. All this is "truth," too, of a certain kind.

There are—there have always been—the tenderhearted, scorned by their more rugged brothers as "chickenhearted." Pandarus, whose name, associated in later literature with love intrigues, has come unjustly to have a disgusting connotation, was such a sentimentalist, whose "truth" concerning horses is just as valid as that of Diomedes, tamer and trainer of horses for battles in which they were to be slaughtered. Homer's account of why Pandarus came to Ilium empty-handed, except for his bow and arrows, is a charming bit of humanism inserted (perhaps as dramatic relief) between descriptions of the spearing out of eyeballs, the cracking and crushing of skulls, the spilling of entrails, and other blood-and-guts details of how this hero or that met his fate.

In dialogue with Aeneas, this Lycian youth tells why he didn't bring his chariots. "In my father's stables there are eleven excellent chariots, fresh from the builder, quite new, with cloths spread over them; and by each of them there stands a pair of horses, champing barley and rye. My old father Lycaon urged me again and again when I was at home and on the point of starting to take chariots and horses with me that I might lead the Trojans in battle, but I would not listen to him. It would have been much better if I had done so, but I was thinking about the horses, which had been used to eat their fill, and I was afraid that in such a great gathering of men they might be ill-fed, so I left them at home and came on foot to Ilium armed only with my bow and arrows."[1] And once in the chariot with Aeneas, he refuses the reins, saying, "Aeneas, take the reins and drive. If we have to fly before the son of Tydeus the horses will go better for their own driver. If they miss the sound of your voice when they expect it, they may be frightened, and refuse to take us out of the fight." This is horse wisdom which cannot be gainsaid.

Homer, poet of a ruling caste in a barbarian society, may have

[1]Gustav Schwab, *Gods & Heroes, Myths & Epics of Ancient Greece,* translated by Olga Marx and Ernst Morwitz. Introduction by Werner Jaeger, Pantheon Books, Inc. New York, 1946.

been holding this boy up to ridicule for the purpose of inciting in his hearers contemptuous laughter for such excessive consideration of horses. Nevertheless, irrespective of the poet's purpose or partisanship, there is here presented a case, or type, of not uncommon occurrence in human society—savage, barbarian, or civilized. The further implication that Pandarus, while entering battle, even side by side with a great hero, still has his weather eye on means of escape, is clearly invidious. So we may have here something of that naïve contempt that our contemporary hunter, of heavy jaw and bulging brows, feels for the modern lad who, for some obscure reason, does not take enthusiastically to the business of bloodletting among the lower animals.

The born nature lover is sometimes as ashamed of his love as he would be of a minor physical deformity. Among his more insensitive brothers and playmates he feels soft, unmanly, left out, and nourishes his strange affection in secret and apart. We find the gentle Jeffries confessing, as to a theft, his habit of stealing off for a look at the dawn. "So long since," he says, "that I have forgotten the date, I used every morning to visit a spot where I could get a clear view of the east. Immediately on rising I went to some elms; thence I could see across the dewy fields to the distant hill over or near which the sun rose. These elms partially hid me, for at that time I had a dislike of being seen, feeling that I should be despised if I was noticed. This happened once or twice and I knew I was watched contemptuously, though no one had the least idea of my object."

Just the other day I saw a 4-H boy at the conclusion of a competition with a one-hundred-dollar-prize check in his hand, crying like his heart would break as they led the calf he had nurtured for a year away to be slaughtered.

There are many kinds of truth. Folklore contains truth concerning beliefs of people, although the beliefs themselves may be erroneous. Hence, here is truth about untruth, and since it is everywhere evident that men are apt to act and react as much upon the emotional content of untruth as upon truth itself, it may well be that truth *about* beliefs is of great importance—at least, in the field of human relationships.

Had I turned out to be a poet or an artist of any kind, I should believe that an incident of my tenth spring was a dedication, for then it was that for the first time I became acutely conscious of natural beauty and felt for some moments an elation which has been repeated with such intensity only at rare intervals since.

Freedom had come to me in the way of a bridled and saddled pony. A bird denied wings until he was old enough to become conscious of their function might feel something of the thrill on his first flight that I felt when, booted and spurred, I turned my pony's head southward while a great star still "blazed in the forehead of the morning sky."

My father's final directive was to keep the sun to my left in order to reach a certain homestead six miles across the almost fenceless prairie for a day's visit with two brothers, my chums and playmates. As I rode forward, keeping an eye on the dawn, I noted that the great star was being gradually consumed in the light of the still unrisen sun, which obliterated one by one all stars of lesser magnitude and touched up gaudily a few filmy clouds—skirts of the fleeing night.

As the sun cleared the horizon, I was riding along a stretch of level grassland bordering a creek margined by rows of deep green trees about two hundred yards to the left of my course. Flowers were blooming; dew glistened upon the grass. My pony felt that the time had come to frolic. He danced, snorted, and tossed his head up and down against a tightened rein.

I became conscious of birds singing in chorus, hundreds of them, filling the little valley to the brim with music, as the recent sun had poured it full of mellow light. I tried to make my mount stand still so that I could better hear this song, evidently intended for me alone. But the saddle squeaked as the impatient animal fretted, jingling the rings my vanity had hung for ornament on the cheeks of the bridle, along with a brilliant red tassel I had paid twenty-five cents for at the general store in preparation for this particular trip. The cheerful chorus continued.

Over the meadow among the flowers stalked (they didn't hop) hundreds of birds, turning now and again their yellow breasts toward me, each expansive front adorned with a crescent, velvet-black. They strode about, stretching their necks, opening their long, sharp beaks, singing toward the sky, casually—very casually—picking up an insect now and then. It was apparent that their chief business was with the song; eating was a minor matter.

My whole world was green and blue, except for the flowers and the bicolored breasts of those proud and joyous birds. And the chorus was also green and blue out of which shot skyward bursts of individual song, like the brilliant flowers springing up here and there in sudden rapture out of the communal happiness of the level, grassy meadow, bordered by trees of deeper green.

My pony became quiet at last and I know not how long I sat and looked and listened, consciousness merged in the general ecstasy of that April morning.

If this experience was not, indeed, a dedication, it was at least the beginning in me of a transition between a barbarian and a civilized culture, telescoped or epitomized, as Herbert Spencer says it is, in the life of one individual. "Ontogeny repeats phylogeny." Until that memorable morning, I had, on occasion, trailed along with other boys armed with limber willow flails, seeking in grassy places these very birds and killing them with one sharp blow across head or back. Blinded in the light of our lanterns, they fell an easy prey. When a sufficient number had been taken, we roasted our victims upon spits over coals of a dying campfire. We called these birds "dikes," a name which must have been our own invention, for I have never heard it used to designate them since; and the bird books contain no record of it. Distaste for "dike hunts" dated from my accidental attendance upon that festival of song held just at sunrise upon a stage of April-flowering meadowland.

The meadow lark is not of the herding kind, but rather a creature who simply enjoys associating with his fellows. They never fly in close flocks, all wheeling at once in one direction or another as their cousins the redwings and starlings do. This bird never quite surrenders his own individuality to the regimented mob. He resembles in his manner of association another cousin of his, the grackle, but he is not so pompous nor so funereal. On the other hand, he is never solitary, as another cousin, the oriole, is. He is a betwixt-and-betweener. He associates with his kind but demands a reasonable isolation. Hundreds of them may be seen stalking about the meadow feeding, but never in close, greedy clusters. Each individual demands elbow room. Presently a scattered group takes off to an isolated tree and, thus gathered, they sing for an hour or two in concert. They are brought into this close association apparently as a choir is, from love of hearing their own voices rhyme and chime together. This is not mere gregariousness, but genuine sociability.

These characteristics are typical, also, of the human beings we find living in the American Midwest: a fierce individualism and an unconquerable sociability. Nowhere else in the world are people generally and spontaneously more sociable, more touchy to crowding, or more rebellious of regimentation. Is not this an explanation of why so many of the Great Plains states have adopted the western meadow lark as the "state" bird? In Montana the selection was made, so the legislative enactment reads, "as preferred by a referendum vote of Montana school children." Wyoming, Kansas, Nebraska, and North Dakota have all adopted this sociable individualist of the bird world as their "state bird," and Oregon joins in honoring the meadow lark by a similar adoption. The sovereign state, main business of which is always war (euphemistically, "defense"), nearly always adopts as a part of its official insignia a predator of great physical prowess or cleverness, or both: qualities useful in war. The nonwar-making political unit is permitted wider totemic choice, including the peaceful genius of the people—for example, a civic virtue or character trait held to be especially admirable in man's everyday dealings with his fellow man.

The meadow lark is awkward on the ground, earthbound as a quail, and, with back turned, drab as a sparrow; but, facing you, he displays a color contrast as violent as it is pleasing. Pouring or gurgling out that splendid song of his, how accurately he translated for me that hope, as yet undifferentiated from the child's reality of reverie, and the unclouded joy of those precious morning hours, when life was in its morning too: "O thou brilliant bird!"

So, Pandarus and his horses, Jeffries stealing a look at the dawn, the 4-H boy weeping over his check, my own emotion-charged memories of meadow larks—all represent a way of looking at the world—one of the avenues to reality, if you will.

I believe no literate person will identify the attitude toward nature herein suggested as a species of nature faking. If such there be, his ways and mine are so far apart as to be unarguable. To misrepresent an observation by even the slightest twist in order to make it support one theory or discredit another is not a venial but a mortal sin, since "it involves spiritual death and loss of divine grace." Once an observation is set out clearly and honestly, however, the observer has a certain freedom of interpretation. Decent newspapers sharply differentiate news from editorial matter. Every competent and conscientious editor knows that editorialized news is faked news. Likewise, slanting the record of an observation of a natural occurrence to bolster a preconception or nourish a prejudice, or simply to be entertaining, is nature faking.

Many observers are content simply to make the record. Library shelves are crowded with valuable books which one may classify as *news* from nature. It is a special kind of nature writing, now the prevailing fashion. The record is all-in-all. Hudson may have had this type of literalist in mind, rather than the true scientist, when he called them "people who do not believe in what doesn't exist, they having first made the rule that nothing exists which they can't explain or which does not conform to the natural laws known to them," thus making their own understanding the measure of what is possible. The more philosophic Whitman, however, far from exhibiting Hudson's impatience, makes obeisance to this type of research:

Gentlemen, to you the first honors always!
Your facts are useful, and yet they are not my dwelling,
I but enter by them to an area of my dwelling.

It is to the necessary seclusion of this "area" that such men as Hudson resort to muse and meditate, and to indulge their speculations, thus, as he himself says, saving his own soul. Facts are the approach or entrance to the walled-in area of the true nature lover's dwelling, where he may analyze and "remember in tranquility" his reactions to what he himself sees or senses in Nature firsthand, as well as ponder those valuable volumes of fact which he keeps ever at his elbow. Gentlemen, to you the first honors, not always, but generally: I am not as critical as Hudson nor yet as generous as the good gray poet.

Karánkaway Country

I KARÁNKAWAY COUNTRY

My interest in the Texas coast began at the
age of fifteen with an astounding glimpse of the Gulf of Mexico
off Galveston Island from a point where the Buccaneer Hotel now
stands. Until that overwhelming moment, an acre pond was the
largest body of water I had ever seen.

There were no droughts on the prairies of central Texas as severe
as those further west where, according to local humorists, bullfrogs
are often three years old before they learn to swim. Nevertheless,
in our community in the northwestern corner of Falls County, fear
of water scarcity was one of the big, dominating fears of the people;
and I heard often and often all during my childhood, especially at
religious revivals under brush arbors in the dry months of July and
August, long and fervent appeals to "Almighty God" for rain.

The Missouri, Kansas & Texas railroad, known as "The Katy," ran, in the summertime, Sunday excursions to the coast—a romantic region of islands, bays, sand dunes, wide, wide beaches, stunted trees, and thundering water. The round-trip ticket cost $2.50, or about a half a cent per mile—surely the cheapest tuition per unit of education I have ever been required to pay. For the first time I saw far-out breakers and waves advance, dwindling as they came up the beach—starting with a roar, as if determined to invade and devour the land, but weakening as they approached, and finally lapsing into a harmless little lisp and licking at your feet, returning to the sea; advancing anew, only to be baffled, again and again, forever and forever—or so I thought, never having heard of a hurricane.

These occasional Sunday glimpses of the sea, the new odors of salt water and the life thereof; the sight of strange birds and of weird, aquatic forms dragged out in fishermen's nets; the ocean-going vessels, alien and mysterious—all made up a new world to think upon and dream about. It brought to me, a drought-frightened boy, a sense of security in the knowledge that really and in truth there was that much water in the world. The school geography said that the earth's surface was roughly one fourth land and three fourths water, but I didn't believe it until I looked out over the apparently illimitable Gulf whose charging waters were in some way miraculously held in place by a fragile bar of sand. I am now told that the sea contains 330,000,000 cubic miles of water; but, to the unmathematical imagination in a thirsty land, one glance at the ocean is far more reassuring.

Upstate boys accustomed to playing about in the placid waters of ponds and inland streams here got the surprise of their lives. How well I remember the first rude embrace of the sea! With a number of companions far out on "West Beach," joyously naked, I rushed forward to meet the landward-racing waves. I was slapped roughly, as if by a giant whose temper was ruffled at the familiarity of an impertinent midget. Not only slapped—I was knocked down, ducked, rolled, tossed about, strangled, until I learned to accommodate myself to the waves. Then came the thrill of being lifted, rocked, and, gently wavering, like a falling leaf, let down, up and down again and again, in slow, pulsative timing. I experienced with the whole body that original rhythm from which, some say, the very sense of rhythm in animal creation was derived, based back in the very beginning, before life left the sea. For hours, in the new-found delight of complete resignation, I yielded, body and soul, to the lift and subsidence, the heave and fall of vast suspirations, to the huge breathings of the great monster, now grown tolerant, even kindly.

Since that period when "The Katy," for so small a fee, gave me my first experiences with the land of salt water, until the present moment, I have missed few opportunities, and made many, to visit not only Galveston Island but many other good camping places, strung along all the way from Sabine Pass to the mouth of the Rio Grande, from pine forests of heavy rainfall northeast to droughty areas of cactus and mesquite four hundred miles (as the crow flies) to the southwest.[1]

The pendulum of my original interest, swinging through this four-hundred-mile arc, has of late years settled down to the central portion of the Texas littoral; roughly, to that piece of it lying between Galveston and Corpus Christi. This middle section is typical of the whole coast, except for the lower Rio Grande Valley, which would seem to belong more to Florida or southern California than to Texas. Moreover, it is rich in Texas history. Indeed, this middle section probably contains more units of historical interest per square mile than any other area of the state. The great French explorer, La Salle, touched here tentatively and by accident in 1685 and left a few men to hold a fort, who were eventually liquidated by the Karánkaways. Not, curiously enough, on the site of this fort, but on a shifting sand bar of old Indianola, there has been erected a giant statue of La Salle, sturdily facing the bay whose waters are eating up the sand, as if determined to undermine the memorial and take it into its bosom, as it has already taken the other works of man on this fateful bar. Uprooted cement cisterns are now the most obvious remains of a city which once contained six thousand souls.

[1]Following the meanderings of the tidewater coast line, the Texas coast measures 624 miles, while the length "measured in steps of one mile is 973 miles for the mainland and 709 miles for the islands."

3

Antedating La Salle by a century and a half came the Spaniard, Cabeza de Vaca. Shipwrecked on Galveston or on St. Joseph Island (?), he spent six years as slave, trader, and medicine man among the Karánkaways, leaving to us a thrilling narrative of his experiences. Along this coast the privateer, Luis Aury, operated nefariously; and a little later it was the scene of the piracies of Laffite, including the occasional abduction of Karánkawan women.

Nearby the grounds now occupied by vast chemical works engaged in making magnesium from seawater, the Battle of Velasco occurred. And shall one forget to mention Austin's Colony, or the Battle of San Jacinto itself, final triumph in the War for Texas Independence? A month later the Treaty of Velasco was signed at Velasco, by the terms of which the invaders were bound to retreat beyond the Rio Grande. Texas histories all call attention to the fact that Texas is the only state in the Union which fought a foreign power individually and singlehanded to win its freedom.

On the civil side, this area entertained the two Audubons and Edward Harris in 1837, and the younger Audubon again in 1845–46. Thomas Drummond, a Scottish botanist, whose name now identifies many Texas species, collected great numbers of specimens here; and the pioneer naturalists, Berlandier and Lincecum, lived and worked less than a hundred miles up the Brazos River from historic Velasco.

The Mexican Government brought a colony of Irish to the mouth of the San Antonio River to serve as a buffer against further encroachments of American colonists to the southwest. They doubtless brought to Texas valuable new elements of old world culture, although the erratic Gideon Lincecum, the botanist, disapproved of them in a vitriolic entry (March 8, 1855) in his *Journal:* "Powell's [Power's] colony of Irish immigrants lies on the seacoast and the San Antonio River, south of the town of La Bahia. They are a captious, discontented, quarrelsome, drunken, riotous, bigoted, fanatical, ignorant set of Roman Catholics, incapable of self-government and possessing none of the material for making good citizens."[2] But if the author of this splenetic estimate of the sons of Erin were

[2]*Journal of Gideon Lincecum,* edited by T. N. Campbell.

alive today, he would find difficulty in distinguishing the citizens of Irish extraction of San Patricio County from the descendants of other elements of colonial Texas now resident in that and in adjoining counties, so far as civic or other virtues are concerned—or vices, for that matter. The contents of the melting pot seems not to be any the worse for its Irish alloy.

There is, however, still a noticeable Teutonic flavor in those communities fed into Texas in the 1840s through the ports of this same section of the Texas coast. There were more German immigrants—many more—than Irish, and apparently less assimilable. Early Texas science, especially botany, is charged with German names. In an appendix to his *Naturalists of the Frontier*,[3] Professor S. W. Geiser lists 153 names of naturalists and collectors known to have worked in Texas from 1820 to 1880. A good fourth of these names are German.

One of these university-trained colonists, Jacob Kuechler, proved with data taken from a cross section of a 130-year-old post oak that "moisture is the only cause of variation in tree-rings." This innocent bit of scientific research came in handy during the disastrous drought of 1856 and 1857, for with it Kuechler was able to persuade a discouraged and disintegrating colony to hang on a little longer and give the new land a further trial. Sure enough, his prediction of the cyclic character of rainfall in the New Braunfels section turned out to be accurate, and lean years were followed by fat ones. He published his findings in the *Texas Staats-Zeitung* (1859), and again in the *Texas Almanac* of 1861.

This "clearly anticipated the classic tree-ring work of A. E. Douglass," says Dr. T. N. Campbell in an amply documented article in the January (1949) issue of the *Tree-Ring Bulletin*. And, according to the same authority, Pechner, ten years earlier, saved a drought-stricken colony near New Braunfels by fortifying its courage with this same tree-ring evidence. There is a folk saying widely accepted that only a fool or a stranger predicts weather in Texas; but here is a long-distance prognostication made and recorded a hundred

[3]Southern Methodist University Press, Dallas, 1937.

years ago concerning the cyclic character of rainfall in this region that is now found to be borne out by the United States weather records of almost a century.

Early German immigrants, trekking northwest, followed roughly the windings of the Guadalupe River, still, in spite of the erosions in the uplands of its drainage area and the pollution of its waters, the most beautiful river in Texas. Colonies were dropped here and there along the way clear to New Braunfels. "On the proud, clear, swift-flowing Guadalupe," writes one of these immigrants, "we have founded a city." Alas! this stream, after a hundred years of cultivation in the lowlands and goat raising on its headwaters, is neither so clear nor so proud as of yore. Its current, however, is swifter and its floods far more disastrous. Colonists pushed on up the river from New Braunfels, and, at last, jumped the divide to settle Fredericksburg on the headwaters of the Pedernales, the second most beautiful river in Texas.

These colonists had an eye for the picturesque in landscapes. The scenic setting, the old world architecture, as well as the very physiognomy of its people, combine to give Fredericksburg, even after the lapse of a century, an aspect as German as the Rhine.

One of the present features of these Guadalupean settlements, often remarked in financial circles, is their uninterrupted solvency. During the depths and throes of depression in the thirties, when municipal credit was cracking all over the country, the bonds of city corporations along the Guadalupe generally maintained a Teutonic stability—so much so that bond buyers referred humorously to that succession of communities as the "Hindenburg Line."

Two cultures coming from opposite directions advanced to within shouting distance of each other in the Galveston–Corpus Christi arc of curving coast line. From the northeast—that is, from the Old South—came the slave-cotton-sugar cane economy, while from the southwest, also following the coast line, came institutions of Spanish descent. The peak push of the cane-cotton culture ended in Brazoria County, where ruins of sugar mills and plantation homes evidence a departed glory; while from this county on southwest to the Rio

Grande many of the extensive cattle ranches still exhibit features of the Mexican hacienda culture.

It has been said (I know not how truly) that the Texas coast represents the richest accumulation of natural resources ever found anywhere in the world in so limited an area, not excluding gold fields and diamond mines. Whether statistics bear out this statement or whether it merely effervesces from the general optimism of the region, I cannot say. It is a fact, however, that the wealth represented by oil, gas, sulphur, harbors, rich coastal prairie lands, metal made from sea water, grandiose schemes for tourists, such as the multimillion-dollar one now materializing on Padre Island—all these elements of Nature's bounty (including climate and the now imperiled fish and oyster industry) taken together form an amazing aggregate, a massing of heterogeneous wealth, a storehouse of natural riches, diverse and abundant, for which it would be hard to find a parallel anywhere else in the world concentrated in so little room.

Interests engaged in the exploitation of these natural riches sometimes get in each other's way. In some quarters great concern is felt at the invasion of coastal waters by oil drillers. Wells eight-, ten-, fifteen-thousand-feet deep are being completed, and still deeper penetrations are predicted. Wild gushers (of not unusual occurrence in large oil fields) would here spread incalculable death and destruction over wide areas now occupied by other thriving industries, especially those engaged in taking shrimp, oysters, and fish from coastal waters. Already under the impact of river silt (much of it due to river dredging), industrial wastes, oil "slicks," and whatnot—under these smotherings, greasings and poisons—oyster production has dwindled to one fifth of what it was a few years ago. Oil is an extractive industry: when it's done, it's done, leaving wrack and ruin and poisonous rubbish behind for later generations to clean up. On the other hand, the fish-and-oyster industry, like agriculture properly practiced, is self-renewing, a profitable investment going on and on forever, yielding steady and dependable returns, living and letting live. Fundamentally considered, oil is the prodigal,

7

spending his patrimony in riotous living, while the fish-and-oyster industry is the other, and less appreciated, brother in the parable who stayed at home to raise swine. One squanders, the other conserves; one consumes his capital, the other lives on periodical increase.

But whatever may be the long-distance views and apprehensions of certain economists, there remains the unimpeachable evidence of ancient oyster production along this coast which staggers the imagination. Great reefs and banks of shell are a geologic feature, and form an inexhaustible mine of material for paving roads along the coast far into the interior.

Anyway, Indians lived mainly on fish and oysters here for countless generations; and, departing (via bullets and bayonets), left the white colonists an unimpaired source of wealth. Certainly from 1536 to 1821 the tribes known to history as the Karánkaways[4] lived mainly on fish and oysters all the way from Galveston Island to the northeastern tip of Padre Island. They came up this coast from Mexico long before Columbus and were found well established in this area when the first white man sighted these shores.

Giants of industry now huddle where the Karánkaway once roamed. When one of these giants steps on the toes of another, legal or political battles ensue. Triumphs of technology are made here and recorded in technical journals; research foundations are established; and the romance of these vast developments is told over and over in newspapers and in popular magazines. But by far the most spectacular resource is oil, a "problem child." It is always in some kind of lawsuit, or being accused by one political faction or another of "running the state," or being praised as "the backbone of the state's economy." It is even now, at this writing, an issue between state and nation in the Supreme Court of the United States. Gushers make headlines; oil millionaires are always performing newsworthy stunts. The very genius of oil is spectacular, so much so that when the Texas coast is mentioned in any part of the coun-

---

[4]The name comes from "Comecrudo" (a Coahuiltecan), and means "dog lovers," whether on account of an emotional affection for the dog as a pet, or delight in his roasted flesh, is not clear.

try visions arise of forests of oil derricks by day and of gas flares by night, and the far-flung odor of the heavy, soiling, greasy, ground-loving smoke of carbon black assails the nostrils. A distorted picture, badly out of focus!

The old Indian-fighter, trail-driver, cowboy tradition is, in a meas-ure, being supplanted, or supplemented, by oil-field heroisms which are quite as thrilling as anything the elder culture can supply. If one cares to hazard an excursion for a day or a week out into the waters of the Gulf to witness an offshore installation of an oil derrick and oil-drilling machinery, he will find a new environment of physical danger in which prodigies of valor and prowess are performed and "men are men," much as one finds them recorded in song and story of cowcamp and cattle trail. The inherent, everyday hazards are no greater in one employment than in the other, and, in the extremes, a hurricane in one case will pretty well balance a stampede in the other. And illuminating parallels may also be drawn between the pioneer enterprisers of the open range and the modern ones of the open sea (at least, as far out as the edge of the continental shelf), proving the lengths to which rugged individualism will carry men when the predatory impulse is given free rein, where stakes are high, and the emulative instinct toned up to the peak of its ferocious capabilities.

In Texas a curious affinity develops between the new and the old. Many pioneer cattle families are forced into oil by the simple physi-cal fact of oil underlying the land they own. Occasionally, of course, one finds a rancher who refuses to permit any oil prospecting on his land, saying proudly that he is in the cattle business and "wants no truck with oil." But he is the exception. On the other side, oil money often seeks ranching investments with no economic motive visible, or even possible. The new culture invades the old, not for profit, but for the prestige which the pioneer industry holds in the public mind. Castles of magnificence may now be found for only week-end occupancy on ranches that had become so impoverished as to be incapable of supporting an owner in even modest squirelike compe-tence.

9

In many cases the flow of oil money is joining estate to estate under one ownership. Emulation sometimes occurs in restoring range conditions of the golden age, so much so that one may find extensive pastures undergrazed, or without a single grazing animal, held vacant until the native grasses thrive again, "belly-deep to a horse." Deer raising becomes fashionable, and deerproof fences around immense acreages are constructed at enormous cost. In one conspicuous case, called lately to my attention, the oil owner fenced not wisely but too well. His deer inbred, producing a mangy, runty lot of progeny. When a game-management man suggested the cause, miles of expensive fencing were demolished to permit the captive animals wider contacts with their kind.

The most generous estimate that I find of the Karánkaways was made by Father Pena (1722): "It was seen that they [the Karánka-ways] were very docile and would enter readily upon the work of cultivating the earth and their own souls, the more because they live in greater misery than the other tribes, since they subsist altogether upon fish and go entirely without clothing." Subsequent history shows that they never cultivated the earth or their own souls in a manner pleasing or even tolerable to the white man, and Father Pena, says Dr. Herbert E. Bolton, thus "proved himself either igno-rant or defiant of history, a bad sociologist, and a worse prophet." Maybe the pious Father was merely issuing a prospectus as a basis for solicitation of funds for establishing missions; and the literature of a prospectus, as has been proved in this country generally, should not involve the author's status as prophet, historian, or sociologist. Criteria for judging the excellence of this type of literature are de-rived from other considerations—chiefly the pragmatic one, "Does the prospectus sell the prospect?"

The white man's estimate of the Karánkaways gets darker as contacts with them enrich and embitter his experience. Says one: ". . . inhabiting along the coast from Galveston westward is a tribe of cannibals, noted for their gigantic stature and hideous aspect. All of them [all males, I suppose] were over six feet in height, and each man carried a bow as long as himself, from which they shot arrows with great force and precision. Their language was an almost inarticulate guttural, impossible of imitation, and the lowest form of human speech." Spanish captives complain of the cruelty of the Karánkawan children, especially of the boys, who "pulled their beards every day by way of pastime . . . and scratched them in such manner that many times they brought blood, because they had long, hard fingernails." . . . Pioneers report their bodily odor so atrocious that horses and cattle ran away from them, "sometimes for three miles from the stable." Certainly this was an inconvenient odor for a horse thief to have, or for a hunter, either.

Later commentators continue their animadversions: ". . . one of the fiercest of Texas tribes," we read. ". . . convincing evidence that they were cannibals" . . . "their notorious inconstancy" . . . "they remain in the bonds of native brutality." A chronicler of 1750 reports a triumph of missionary work in that fifteen Karánkaways were baptized at the mission *in articulo mortis;* and that the missions succeeded mainly with infant baptisms and deathbed conversions, inspiring that scornful remark by a twentieth-century investigator, "These Indians were left in paganism only in that narrow span of life which lies sandwiched between thumbsucking and senility."

Despite the good—nay, the holy—intentions of missionaries, and notwithstanding our admiration of those heroic lives devoted to the service of their respective religious faiths, still these efforts have often resulted in the unmitigated corruption of the morals and, not infrequently, in the physical annihilation of tribes in whose behalf spiritual regeneration is undertaken.

Taking only the history of the colonization and conquest of the New World, including the Pacific Islands, as a basis, is not the evidence overwhelming, not of a conscious policy, but of an uncanny instinct in the white European for conquest and imperialism generally, that he so often first attacks the primitive on his spiritual side? His native religion is made sick; his gods are dethroned. The rest, then, is easier: social organization deteriorates, ancient rituals and usages which gave unity to the tribe are abandoned, and an alien, and therefore meaningless, morality is imposed. Thus weakened, it is time for the trader to enter, along with the soldier re-

11

inforcements. Missionary, trader, soldier—thus many native cultures have been destroyed.

Among the traders who followed priest and soldier in this case were smugglers who sneaked into the harbors of these shores with kegs of whisky which they bartered to the Indians. Sometimes their vessels were wrecked in a storm and the sea delivered the cargo direct to the customers. The simple Karánkaways had a profound reverence for the sea and faith in it, since it furnished them with fish, oysters, birds' eggs, and other great blessings. It was natural, then, for them to believe that this new drink which came up out of the sea had the approval of the Great Spirit; and it was quickly substituted in religious ritual for yaupon tea, their hereditary drink. At the end of an all-night session, drinking to the Great Spirit with this new concoction, they were found to be "quarrelsome and dangerous, and they stole and begged from the whites," according to pioneer reports. Hence police, rather than priestly, measures were in order.

Happily, twentieth-century missionaries are more and more taking cognizance of the wide differences in culture patterns, and are using more effective approaches. The new science of Applied Anthropology is making headway, not only with the Church, but with administrative agencies of various governments which have to do with primitive peoples and even with advanced cultures differing essentially from their own. Chapter VII of Professor Clyde Kluckhohn's *Mirror of Man*[5] teems with specific examples of the humanizing contributions which Applied Anthropology is making in this field.

Any wild life, including human wild life, yields easily to pauperization. Pelicans, deer, gulls, Karánkaways—all are corrupted by artificial feeding. Parasitism ensues. It was not so much spiritual as corporal nourishment which kept these savages hanging around the missions and the homes of charitable pioneers. We hear of considerable numbers of Karánkaways frequenting the settlements, availing themselves of periodical supplies; and, in another case, "a thousand

[5]McGraw-Hill Book Co., Inc. New York, 1949.

pesos in private funds had been spent for maize, meat, cotton cloth, tobacco," etc., to lure them into the Christian fold.

On the spiritual side, during four years in the 1750s, twenty-one souls—twelve adults and nine children—had been baptized *in articulo mortis.* All during this period the Karánkaways robbed, stole, killed, alternating parasitism with piracy. Good Father Solis reports the heroic work by Father Joseph Escovar of no avail: "He [Father Escovar] aids and succors them as best he may in all their needs, corporal and spiritual, giving them food to eat and clothing to wear," etc. But the Copanes (the Karánkawan tribe for which Copano Bay was named) have for some reason melted away from the mission, "for the most part of them are in the woods or on the banks of some of the many rivers, or with another nation also Karánkaways, their friends and confederates, on the shore of the sea . . . They are all barbarous, idle, lazy; and although they were so greedy and gluttonous that they eat meat almost raw, parboiled or half roasted and dripping with blood, yet rather than stay in the mission where the padre provides them with everything needed to eat and wear, they prefer to suffer hunger, nakedness and other necessities, in order to be at liberty and idle in the woods or on the beach, giving themselves up to all kinds of vice, especially lust, theft and dancing."[6] The incorrigible Karánkaways!

It is an old story, this imposition upon a primitive people of what is to them a brand-new set of values, an alien schedule of proprieties. When they balk at accepting our own way of life, we become furious. We declare them outside the pale, guilty of the most odious abominations in the sight of God and man. Angered, we proclaim a Holy War, the end and aim of which is not so much conquest and conversion, or the saving of souls, as extermination, after which their immortal souls may make what shift they can, so far as we are concerned. For illustration, take the simple matter of the Karánkaway stealing a few cattle. Individual ownership of good-to-eat animals roaming loose about woods and prairies could not in the Karánkawan mind be conceived of at all. The animal belonged to the hunter

[6]From *Diary of Father Solis* (Inspector), quoted by Herbert E. Bolton, *Quarterly of the Texas State Historical Association,* Vol. X, pp. 138–39.

or group of hunters who gained possession of it alive or dead. Yet "stealing" cattle was one of the most heinous charges preferred by early settlers against these few surviving, often starving, savages. Neither could these primitive people conceive of land except as a common hunting ground; and I must myself confess to a personal sympathy with this view, especially while abroad with my binoculars, since I experience a Karánkawan impulse to anger and violence every time I am confronted with a "posted" or "keep-out" sign, or an especially difficult fence, or padlocked gate.

Still, one of the De Leons of Victoria, claiming that the Karánkaways had stolen his cattle, decided to poison the whole tribe. He ordered from a druggist a large quantity of arsenic, but the druggist, "divining his purpose, gave him cream of tartar instead." He boiled the corn, made hominy of it, added what he supposed was the arsenic, and presented it as a gift to the Indians. ". . . Next morning to the astonishment of the hospitable [and doubtless devout] don, the Carancawas came begging for another supply of boiled corn."[7]

So, too, our fathers in dealing with remnants of our Indians resorted to a practice which we of this generation have severely condemned—i.e., transplanting populations, "bulldozing" them, root and branch, out of their native soil. How terrible a thing this has become since the German Nazis began doing it, and the Russian Communists! We now lose breath in pious rage at the mere mention of such a mass atrocity. Yet a pitiful remnant of the Karánkaways was moved only a hundred years ago into Mexico, and a final note on them is made by J. H. Kuykendall, as follows: "In the year 1855 the once formidable tribe of Karánkawas had dwindled to six or eight individuals who were residing near San Fernando, State of Tamaulipas."[8]

Early explorers, as well as pioneers of this section of the Texas coast, report a curious habit of the Karánkawan warrior. At times he was apparently fascinated by the sight of the sun submerging itself

[7]"Reminiscences of Early Texans," J. H. Kuykendall, *Quarterly of the Texas Historical Association*, Vol. VI, p. 253.

[8]Ibid.

in the sea. The wonder of sunset over water was too much for the mind of this simple savage. He became still as a statue, oblivious to his surroundings, gazing spellbound at the point on the horizon where the waters had closed over and quenched this great ball of fire. I can imagine a seven-foot Karánkawan standing thus, magnificent in his nakedness, the tight braids of his coarse hair reaching nearly to his waist, each braid interwoven with bits of colored cloth and terminating with the rattles of a rattlesnake which "made a faint ringing as the wearer moved." Now, for the period of the seizure, these barbaric trophies sleep, since the head is stone-still, and no corded muscle of the massive shoulders twitches to awaken them. Finally, in the deepening dusk he stirs. The fire has gone out. The sea is gray again. The rattles awaken as he moves away toward his camp behind the dunes.

"The Creek Indians regarded it as a divine favor," we are told, "when they could travel at least once during their lives to the Bay of Mobile to see the sun disappearing in its waters"; but there is no mention of the Creek being paralyzed at the sight of it.

I cannot but regard this "Karánkaway trance" as some kind of religious exercise or observance. Overcome by contemplation of "Powers" which are at once more obvious and more mysterious at the junction of land and sea than in any other natural environment, something analogous to "freezing" or "playing dead" among certain animals and insects attacks this stalwart primitive. Perhaps the profound emotional disturbance excites some glandular secretion which annuls all thought and power of motion, throwing the subject into a cataleptic state, or something like it, for an hour or more, rigid and staring steadfastly out over the sea. Early observers say it attacked only the men, which I can readily believe, since, in savage cultures, women can spare little time from the dismal, down-to-earth drudgery of camp and travel to speculate or wonder about anything, or be concerned about how, when, or by whom the world was made, how operated or what is going to be done with it finally, or any human responsibilities connected therewith.

One must himself live for some little time out of doors in this littoral environment before he can give sympathetic consideration to these strange seizures. It is only after wandering about among the lakes and lakelets; walking across moist flats pricked about the knees at every step by drooping, needle-pointed marsh grass; skirting lagoon meanders; prying into dense, fragrant growths of scrub oak and sweet bay, leg weary in the dunes from the drag of un-resistant sand—it is only after a period of such discipline that you are prepared for this Karánkawan devotional. Then, at the close of an autumn day, you emerge from the brush and find yourself on a wide, smooth beach, lately wet by the tide, offering firm but springy footing. The wind has died down, and the great stretch and spread of placid water, the easy walking, and unobstructed horizon relax the tensions and tediousness of brush, sand dunes, and swamp which have so far throughout the day disputed your every movement.

Once, after a period of this kind of struggle, I found myself in just such a situation. It was near sunset and there was a haze lying upon the water which vastly enlarged the sun and subdued its brilliance to easy visual tolerance. The huge disk sank, flattening out on the horizon, disappearing so rapidly that I sensed, or imagined with sensual intimacy, the actual eastward turning of the earth itself. Suddenly the great fire went out, and I found myself motionless, as if hypnotized, conscious but powerless for a moment to break the spell, gazing steadily at the still glowing horizon, thoughtlessly, but with a sense of immense distance, of the mystery of universal motion in endless space throughout unending time. Maybe by dwelling too long on the reports of pioneers of how the savages of these shores suddenly became rigid and maintained for a long time an unaltered posture, gazing out over this very bay—maybe my interest had become morbid and I was myself seized and experienced on this occasion an abbreviated Karánkawan trance.

The Karánkaways are gone. Only bitter memories of them remain. In the minds of our people they are eternally damned, largely because they refused a culture we offered, resisting our proffered blessings to the last gigantic male and squatty female. We won the material war, exterminating the enemy. We also won the war of words, that is, the propaganda war, establishing them as fiends in human form and ourselves in posture of nobly extending a succoring hand which they obstinately refused.

Our weapons of propaganda were as superior to theirs as the machine gun is to the bow and arrow: pen, paper, printing presses; a facile language of richest heritage against a few grunts of pain and protest and sighs, sobs, and wailings of despair, which died out on the wind of these beaches more than a century ago. No careful Karánkawan historian ever documented the case against the white man. We have left of them, bequeathed to us, only a few place names—names of bays, inlets, points of land, straits, and creeks—modulated to our ears by the soft-voiced Spaniards, but still retaining in their vocalization a primitive flavor, like the lisp of waves or wind among fallen leaves.

"I pronounce," says the poet, "what the air holds of the red aborigines . . . natural breaths, sounds of rain and wind, calls as of birds and animals in the woods, syllabled to us for names, Okonee, Koosa, Ottawa, . . . Natchez, Chattahoochee . . ." and, I may add, Karánkaway, Copano, Cujanes—"leaving such to the States they melt, they depart, charging the water and the land with names."

When I began refreshing my memory by reference to notes made in former years on camping trips to the Texas coast, I found that I was more familiar with that section of it which lies between Galveston and Padre islands than with any other—the region of the Four Great Rivers of the ancient explorer, viz., the Brazos, Colorado, Guadalupe, and Nueces. On one prospecting trip I ran across a professor of archeology with a group of his students busy sifting the material of an immense shell mound for Karánkawan relics, which gave me a renewed interest in these people.

I was told by Dr. George Williams, of Rice Institute, that there are more different species of birds found from year's end to year's end in the vicinity of Rockport than in any other on the whole coast. Vast concentrations of migrations occur here, for which he gave me reasons: geographical and meteorological, and I am sure he is right. I didn't suggest to him that another reason might be that this area contains the most reliable, energetic, persistent and long-time amateur observer of bird life that I have found anywhere else on the whole coast in the person of Mrs. Jack Hagar, of Rockport. Her list to date (or to the date I took it a year or so ago) includes four hundred and thirty-six species, half the number recorded for the whole state of Texas.

Near Rockport is a wedge-shaped peninsula of bays, lakes, inlets, marsh, dunes, dense brush, and prairie, lying between San Antonio and St. Charles bays, which is the last stamping ground, dancing ground and whooping place of the few whooping cranes left on earth. The Audubon Society and the U. S. Fish and Wildlife Service saw eye to eye on the importance of this strip of littoral, and it was purchased as a reservation—*with* reservations. However, of this more later.

In charge of a station for the Texas Game, Fish, and Oyster Commission, I found J. L. Baughman, Chief Marine Biologist, interested not only in game and commercial fish, but in all wild life, and promoting widely attended semiannual seminars on conservation problems. I found G. E. Colbath, in charge of trapping on the Refuge, not only hospitable but extremely helpful—a trapper, but a humane one—and an acute and reliable observer of wild life. Also, I was welcomed by C. A. Keefer, the then Manager of the Refuge, whose interests extend over and beyond the game-preserve orbit. This Refuge is especially attractive as an example of the co-operation of three diverse agencies to one end: the Texas Game, Fish, and Oyster Commission, the Audubon Society, and the U. S. Fish and Wildlife Service.

Rivers intrigue me. I can sit on a log and look upon a flowing stream for an hour at a time without feeling those twinges of conscience which come while idling in other environments. The two longest rivers in Texas empty in the Karánkaway Country only fifty miles apart. Their drainage basins spread out to a width of 250 miles to take in the very heart of the state, and finally come again within shouting distance of each other at their sources, six hundred miles as the crow flies from the Gulf. Each delivers an immense burden of silt; and extensive impounding and hydroelectric developments have been completed along their courses, with others in progress, and much more on paper.

These are my reasons for selecting this Karánkaway country for observation and the Refuge as a center or base from which to make excursions here and there. And the reason why I reasoned myself into this particular locale is that I like it. I thus follow the approved psychological pattern, invoking reason to justify a decision already determined by emotional preference—a not uncommon hypocrisy.

2   LAST OF THE "WHOOPERS"

Extensive marshes are a feature of the Ka-
ránkaway Country as far west as Port Lavaca, and recur at intervals,
mainly near the mouth of streams, all the way to the Rio Grande.
"These brackish, sedgy, tide-washed marshes," says Vernon Bailey,
"are inhabited by rice rats, rails, water snakes, and great numbers of
crustaceans."[1]

In the beginning—at least, a very long time ago—the Marsh was
given a Decoration and a Voice. But I doubt that the Karánkaways'
god had any hand in this, for he concerned himself mainly with the
affairs of the belly, leaving refinements—that is, appearances, or the
subtler harmonies of an environment—to another Power with greater
interest in the spiritual well-being of man.

[1]North American Fauna No. 25, Biological Survey of Texas, U.S. Department
of Agriculture, 1905.

Disdaining adornments, the Karánkawan deity directed vocational education, teaching his hungry hunters how to carve the bow of red cedar, six or seven feet long, twist smooth the quarter-inch bowstring of many fine strands of deer sinew, how to fashion and feather the infallible arrow, and how to stand poised like a heron in the transparent water of the bay, spearing fish which in those days swarmed in from the ever-bountiful waters of the Gulf.

And even after the winds of March had lashed the bay to make it turbid, still "the arrow flies and the fish dies," for the submerged naked legs of the Karánkaway were sensitive to the approach of fish through subsurface undulations, as the heron's legs are said to be. A fish rarely made off with an arrow; and, if the bowman missed his mark, the missile, point plunged in sand, stood up in plain sight with the feathers above water. This economy, in a handicraft culture, was one of great importance. For there was no profit in the manufacture and sale of this primitive ammunition, hence no fund from which to finance advertising campaigns popularizing mere slaughter under the guise of sport. On the other hand, the savage lad was brought up in the belief that it is noble in man to kill only as other decent predators kill, that is, to satisfy immediate need.

Besides finny fish there were several species of shellfish, especially oysters and clams, which the Karánkaway scooped up by the boatload from rich beds unravaged by machinery, unsullied by oil, and not yet buried under drift, silt, and the polluting waste of poisoned rivers. Indeed, a tribe of Karánkaways with their simple hunting skills and weapons would now starve to death along these oil-rich, civilized, i.e., impoverished shores. But that is another story.

When Cabeza de Vaca was shipwrecked on St. Joseph's Island (or on Galveston Island) in 1528, fish and oysters were there in abundance, so why should the Karánkaway have risked his yard-long arrows with shaft half an inch in diameter and scraped to a jadelike finish, fledged with three feathers from the wild goose and tipped with costly flint—why should he have risked this splendid weapon in the open marsh at the whooping crane which had learned almost to a yard how far the shaft would carry? Evidence that he didn't hazard many shots at this magnificent winter visitor is found in kitchen middens, acres upon acres of them, left by these gigantic Indians, strung along the bay shores all the way from Galveston Island to Corpus Christi. Tons upon tons of oyster shells, which form the great bulk of Karánkaway mounds, have been sifted, but no bone of the whooping crane has yet been identified, although the skeletal remains of smaller birds and mammals, especially of deer, occur in considerable quantities.

Thanks to the periscope towering above that breast of delicate meat (so prized by our pioneers), the bird can see far and away across flat, treeless areas, while the sentinel on duty has a voice[2] that carries under favorable conditions at least three miles. The bird's weasand is a wind instrument of amazing construction, five feet long. Half of this incredible length is coiled about the breast bone, with a reverberating voice box located in the lower end of the trachea. Thus equipped with lookout from which to see and with a voice to trumpet a warning miles across the level lands, and withal a wary disposition and an especial distrust of man, the Decoration and the Voice have managed to survive the impact of a machine civilization, but narrowly—balanced on the wavering margin of extinction.

In the autumn of that year 265 years ago when La Salle, having missed the mouth of the Mississippi, landed near Cavallo Pass on Matagorda Bay, the Karánkaways, who had lately displaced a still more brutish people, saw vast migrations of whooping cranes materializing in the hazy northern sky like clouds that had suddenly decided to become birds. Still as stone, in rapt exaltation, the more mystically inclined individuals, men and women, but more especially men (who have always had and still have more time to wonder), gazed awe-struck as these great white birds came sailing majestically to earth on wide extended wings, black-tipped to emphasize their enormous spread, which measures by modern tape

---

[2]Robert Allen describes the "whoop" as "a high note somewhat like the blast from an open cornet, a rolling note on a high register and then a lower trumpet note." *Audubon Magazine*, May–June 1947, p. 138.

seven and a half feet, or near the height of certain Karánkawan warriors as they appear in the pioneer descriptions of this "ignoble savage."[3] In April they were gone again. How in his dark mind did this aboriginal fisherman account for these startling apparitions, materializing in October and vanishing in April? Did the medicine-men supply their devotees with clarifying, or at least simplifying, theories to ease the strain of wonder, a refuge and relief not unknown in our own day and generation? Maybe so, maybe not. At any rate, they came in autumn and left in spring, age after age, in an October-to-April cycle which, in the geologist's time telescope, appears as rhythmical as the half-second beat of the vast wings which bring them along stainless highways to their winter home.

I had looked many times upon these marshes and found them wanting. They are vast and flat and green, rimmed with a curving coastline on one side and hedged about with low, brush-covered dunes on the other. Moreover, they are cut into curious curlicues by serpentine lagoons containing little pancake islands which some tourists amuse idle moments by making into "hearts" and "spades," "trapezoids," and other more fanciful designs. I am told that the imaginative eye of a pioneer cowman chose the pattern of a meandering stream in one of his many marshes for a cattle brand, and thereupon proceeded to sear its intricate and decorative outline into the smoking flesh of ten thousand bawling calves.

These marshes are so extensive that they literally swallow up features which elsewhere might be striking, or reduce them to the incidental or the trivial. Even the great blue heron and the American egret, two of this coast's largest waders, shrink almost into insignificance, while individuals of lesser species dwindle down to mere dots.

Although hardly conscious of the deficiency, I was always looking for something else to complete the picture—something commensu-

---

[3] Anthropologists have not yet verified this estimate from the few skeletal remains so far recovered, and go only so far as to say that the men were unusually tall and the women rather squatty.

rate with the background or with the general scene, and at home here, something to fill up the measure of a want and make the completeness which the nature lover has learned to look for in nature, as a golden eagle flying down a lawless gorge in the Rockies, or a condor among the "sheer chasm's utmost crags." Look seaward and the white pelican satisfies, or, in summer, a soaring man-of-war bird, but turn your gaze back to the marsh and something is missing.

On a sunny morning of early spring (1949) I accompanied C. A. (Bud) Keefer, then Manager of the Refuge, on one of his crane-census trips over the lower end of the Blackjack Peninsula in a jeep. The moment my eye fell on a family of three whooping cranes looming up in magnified outline (due to the peculiar atmospheric conditions of the moment), I realized that I had found what was missing. Here was the figure which gives authenticity to the marsh. Here is a double completion, for bird and marsh emphasize and enliven each other. I had seen this bird once before in a zoo where he looked like a monstrosity; but here he literally "walks in beauty." Nothing less than such a marsh can frame a whooping crane; nothing less than a whooping crane is adequate for such a marsh.

Those rich cultured Englishmen of the last century must have felt something of this oppressive vacancy in their marshes, for we find in the record that the whooping crane was frequently imported by the gentry to adorn the marshes of their landed estates.

Too bad the Karánkawan artist had no such genius for tapestry as the Japanese artist of that period had, for he would have left us woven designs of these marshes upended on many a gigantic wall hanging; and what other animal form, pray, than this stately crane could he have chosen to complete and adorn his representation?

The census that morning yielded eighteen whooping cranes, and we had seen half of all that were left in the world!

Twice yearly for a quarter of a century this nearly extinct species has made headlines in newspapers throughout the country: once in October when he arrives at his winter home in the Karánkaway Country and again in April when he takes wing for a mysterious destination in the far north. As yearly their numbers dwindled, their

24

headlines grew bigger; and the more imminent their extinction,[4] the more details of their lives and behavior were fished up out of bird books to pad the accounts of their semiannual migrations. Skilled reporters were occasionally assigned by metropolitan papers to "cover" the whooping cranes; magazine writers, ornithologists of great fame, and no end of bird-loving tourists visited the pitiful remnant in its winter home.

This narrow strip of Texas littoral, comprising 47,000 acres, was selected as a wild-life refuge largely because the last of the cranes favored it. But even with this area set apart and available, the whooper population continued to dwindle. Statistics gathered over an extensive period indicate that the species is unlikely to survive. The Refuge itself is not enough. Something must be done, else the stage is all set for the final act.

Hedged in, this magnificent bird is making its last stand on earth. Farming areas on one side of the Refuge edge in closer and closer; on the other, the everlasting barrier of the Gulf. Slashing through the whole length of littoral, and even invading a part of the Refuge itself, runs the Intracoastal Canal, on which mile-long lines of oil barges trail their oil and filth every few hours from one end of the crane territory to the other. County road builders are making mud-shell excavations at this writing, tearing down a protective reef on one end and perhaps opening the way for hurricane waters. But worst of all, and as a final debauchment of these virgin marshes, are the oil "developers" pushing in for the final squeeze, making their seismographic surveys, which involve earth jarring, subterranean peals of artificial thunder as well as terrific underwater explosions, occasionally blowing out a deadly "oil slick" to mess up the waters of a bay—deadly, I mean, to all avian life. Besides these "thunderers," there are spotted (sparsely at present) over the whole area colonies of drillers boring five, eight, fifteen thousand feet for oil and

[4]Writing in the winter of 1947, Robert Allen says: "Over the last nine years an average of 57.6 per cent of the adult whooping cranes have failed to reach the Gulf Coast with young. Last winter [1946] this figure was at an all-time low of 82 per cent. This year [1947–48] it is 73 per cent. Of twenty-two adults on the Texas wintering grounds this season, sixteen did not raise young, or were unable to bring their young safely to this hereditary wintering area." Ibid.

gas. Moreover, the grazing rights are leased to cattle interests whose employees ride horseback or "jeep" around the whole place, calling their cattle, not as of old from the melodious throats of cowboys, but (loyal to the machine age) with an ambulance siren! Fleets now of bombers, now of jet fighters, from the great naval airbase only forty miles away, occasionally drone overhead or shriek across the sky.

The ear of wild life is attuned to Nature's voices. Each sound means something—something different, perhaps, in the specialized ear of each species: something significant affecting its welfare, favorable, unfavorable, or neutral. Each natural sound is a kind of musical language in these myriads of listening ears, and especially is this true of birds. They hear vibrations full of meanings to which our own ears are deaf. Really, with all this clangor, medley, mixture and meaningless melange of weird and outrageous disturbances bursting upon these wild creatures, one may ask in their behalf (no matter with what beneficent intentions this Refuge was created and *then leased out*)—is this a *Refuge,* or Pandemonium?—literally the abode of all the demons. I mean, of course, from the standpoint of a wild wary bird, tottering on the edge of extinction. To a human being accustomed to the clangor of city traffic, to the sour odors of alley garbage cans, to bright lights blotting out the stars, to huge buildings day and night constricting the sky itself—to such a one this place does in truth and in fact seem to be a haven of peace. But to a bird fresh from tropic jungles or from the silences of arctic snow, it is something else. After all, everything is relative.

In season, around the edges on both land side and water side hover the hunters to take advantage of game which has become somewhat tamed by the protection afforded within the confines of the Refuge.

Inside the fence, however, gunners are held at bay and all trapping is under scientific direction. In a certain sense, it is a wild-life refuge, despite what I have said about oil and noises and marginal massacres. It holds more than crumbs of comfort for the nature lover, and it is certainly the only and last hope for the preservation of the whooping crane. So, in the spring of 1948, those interested in the survival of the species undertook desperate measures.

It was a gamble, a hundred-to-one shot, a measure *in extremis*. The keen eye of Bob Allen noticed that nearby and in clear view of the Refuge Headquarters a lone crane selected and defended as his "territory" a stretch of salt and freshwater marsh along Mesquite Bay, spending an entire winter there. This area, 150 acres in extent, was fenced with hog wire eight feet high to receive and protect two pinioned birds. The Corpus Christi *Caller-Times* (May 8, 1949) quoted C. A. Keefer, as follows: "Two whooping cranes on the Aransas National Wildlife Refuge, nesting in captivity for the first time in history, are on 'loan' from the National Audubon Society and the Audubon Park Zoo of New Orleans. The whole idea was dreamed up by Bob Allen of the Audubon Society and me when Bob was here observing the cranes in the spring of 1948. He agreed to do what he could to get the birds; and I agreed to see what I could do about getting the Fish and Wildlife Service to give me enough money to build a fenced enclosure. We both succeeded."

This wild-life idyl occurred during one of my prolonged visits to this part of the coast. The courtship, mating, nest building, and brooding of a pair of whooping cranes is something no naturalist of this generation had ever witnessed. And what better luck could happen to a tyro in crane-lore than to be able to observe this unique show from daylight to dark atop a thirty-foot observation tower in the company of the two greatest crane authorities in the world: (1) Dr. Lawrence H. Walkinshaw of sandhill crane fame, and (2) Robert S. Allen, *the* authority on the "whoopers."

One of the birds secured for the experiment had been wounded in capture, an eye shot out, left for dead, wings tangled in a barbed-wire fence. Rescued by a boy on a bicycle and taken to a nearby Nebraska town, the bird's wounds were healed by a surgeon, and "Pete"—so he was named—was turned, pinioned, into an enclosure owned by the Nebraska Rod and Gun Club. Fourteen years passed. In addition to the fare provided by his keepers, he was permitted to eat whatever the sight-seers tossed to him through the wire meshes of his prison. His feathers became soiled, and the parasites on his body multiplied. Years of misery these must have been for Pete.

27

(A special parasite, by the way, uses this crane as host and will expire, also, if and when the whooping crane becomes extinct.)

Far away in Louisiana another crane was caught (some say) in a muskrat trap. He, also, was placed in solitary confinement, and the huge wens on the bottoms of his feet bear testimony to months of treading the unyielding cement floor of a cage, an especial hardship, since the crane's feet are fashioned for the cool, oozy floor of the marsh. He was named "Joe," and Joe also missed the wide choice of animal and vegetable food which his native marshes supply. His feathers lost their luster, were dingied with the smoke and dust of the city. Upon these two bedraggled specimens—Joe, doleful and forlorn, and Pete, "one-eyed and seeming ancient"—hopes were pinned for the survival of the species.

It was no "fool" experiment, although the chances were all against its success. In the first place, the sex of the birds was unknown and undeterminable at the time, since, as Allen says, "there are no bird anatomists." The age of the birds was another hazard. It is known that this crane lives normally about forty years, but how long he could remain sexually efficient caged in a zoo no one could tell. No expiring species was ever bred successfully in captivity, although it has been tried time and again. There were, indeed, Cajun rumors that this species had once bred in Louisiana. So, it was not definitely known that the birds could, even under the most favorable conditions, ever be induced to nest as far south as the Texas coast.

However, great faith was placed in the rejuvenating effects of freedom, a natural habitat, normal crane activity, food and those food combinations Nature made exclusively for the whooping crane, the wholesome exercise necessary in gathering it, the sexual excitation of seeing other cranes going about their amours and of hearing, even though distantly, their love whoops—all these influences were taken into consideration. It was no "fool" experiment.

Nevertheless, when Joe and Pete, stained and nervously excited from their long journey, were finally brought together and released in the enclosure prepared for them it was a quite dismal betrothal. The birds drooped, they fed listlessly, they rarely whooped.

The newspapers published merry remarks about the "courtship," the "wedding," "crane nuptials," speculated obliquely on the prospects of progeny, and "carried on" as is the journalese fashion when news concerns the mating activities of elephants, hippos, or other huge creatures, which the public for some reason considers funnier than the same activities in lesser and less unusual species. But despite these journalistic pleasantries, the whole affair was rather tragic, and the dance these long-immured creatures performed at that time was far from the "joy visible" of the Greek phrase. It seemed, rather, only the natural calesthenics which followed freedom from an irksome restraint, from being caged and cooped up and escaping from a depressive situation.

The experimenters now increased the chance of having male and female in the same enclosure by introducing another crane, a cripple, which had been unable to follow the migration of the others to their breeding grounds. "Old Crip," as he is called, had already spent one breeding season on the Refuge along with a companion, maybe a mate, maybe a son or daughter. He is the largest whooping crane that any Refuge employee has ever seen. The introduction of Old Crip was the signal for an immediate and desperate battle. Pete tried to expel the intruder from the enclosure. Morning, noon, and into the dusk, he pursued Old Crip, until finally Old Crip got out and was making for another part of the Refuge when he was discovered and driven back. After some days of this he was removed, since the keepers were fearful that the birds might injure each other. The behavior of Pete during this episode strengthened the belief that he was a male, while the indifference of Joe seemd to indicate the opposite sex.

And who knows but what this introduction of a possible rival stimulated the hormones and was perhaps the final fillip of incitement which set the birds to nesting among the cattails? Meantime, their plumage had grown lustrous, their bearing more stately, their "territorialism" more vindictive, their dances more lively, spontaneous, and joyful. The experimenters' reliance on natural food, exercise, and the response of health and instincts to a natural habitat seemed in course of being justified. Here were two live captive cranes, not mere candidates for the taxidermist, to which state their former life in captivity had reduced them. Meantime, Mrs. C. A. Keefer had kept the two birds from going completely native by a little feeding once a day. They responded to this treatment by singling her out as the one human being in the world worthy of trust. They finally ate out of her hand, even out of her shirt pocket. This shyest, rarest, wildest of wild birds yields readily to human kindness. A factual account of the taming of one of these birds is published in *Audubon Magazine,* July–August 1948, under the title "A Whooping Crane Called Bill," by I. W. Oliver.

Then it happened. The birds were nesting! The Associated Press reported May 5, 1949, that "Two eggs and the nest of two captive whooping cranes were found Wednesday [May 4, 1949] by C. A. (Bud) Keefer. . . . Before he found the nest, Keefer spent four days of intensive observation on a watch tower built at the edge of the 150-acre enclosure in which the captive cranes were placed last October."

Eggs meant that one of these birds was female: the most skeptical raised no objection to this deduction. It was thought that Pete had laid the eggs and "she" was promptly renamed "Petunia." Joe remained maleish, if not male, spending only about half as much time on the nest as the faithful Petunia. He preened himself for hours (perhaps male vanity), he danced, or plunged fiercely at deer which happened to browse by, and gobbled up a too venturesome snake now and then. About once a day he took it upon himself to drive every other sizable marsh bird out of the enclosure, including herons, egrets, white ibises, and roseate spoonbills. Hopes for the fertility of the eggs grew with the apparent maleish activities of Joe and the femaleish demeanor of Petunia. From a 100-to-1 shot, the odds dropped to 50-to-1. Ornithologists from far and near came flying in. The great sandhill crane authority, Dr. Lawrence H. Walkinshaw, arrived from Battle Creek, Michigan; Robert Allen forsook for the present his investigations in the Everglades and began a dawn-to-dusk vigil in the watchtower; the Cruickshanks, famed photographers, arrived; and throngs of visitors drifted in until it became necessary to bar the general public in order to maintain quiet which the brooding birds seemed to demand.

Day after day during daylight hours every action of the nesting birds was recorded, since no record of the kind had ever been made before and, in all probability, no opportunity to make such a record would ever occur again.

Then suddenly and dramatically the "dream" ended. About 5:30 A.M. on the twenty-third day of incubation, Allen and Walkinshaw noticed from the watchtower Joe pecking at the eggs, and concluded that he was breaking up the nest. When he finished, both birds walked off a little way from the nest and performed a brief dance. Then they emerged from the cattails, coming directly to the tower, whereas heretofore they had always come separately, each one sneaking from the nest for twenty yards through the cover of cattails before showing himself. All this change of front the watchers considered ominous.

Examination of the shells showed material in them dried down to a yellow residue sticking to the inside surface. There was no trace of blood or other indication that either egg had contained an embryo. Obviously, they were infertile.

Thus the supposition that both birds were female was strengthened. However, Walkinshaw said that 30 per cent of the eggs of sandhill cranes are normally infertile. It may be the same with whooping cranes. It is true Joe acted maleish, Petunia femaleish. But it was known that birds deprived of association with the opposite sex frequently reverse behavior. A few days after the breakup (May 25), in company with R. W. Clapper, member of the Refuge staff, I saw Petunia mount Joe. Joe crouched exactly as a willing female would, showing no sign of impatience or of displeasure. There was no sexual contact, however. Thus the matter of the sex of these birds remained confused.

About three months later (July 22) Petunia died. Joe wailed from about 1 A.M. on until daylight, according to Mrs. R. W. Clapper, residing in one of the Headquarters cottages. Next morning the body of Petunia was found lying in shallow water, somewhat mutilated by coons. Indications were that death came from natural causes, and that the coons, as is their custom, were merely scavenging. The remains were sent to the Patuxent Research Refuge where an autopsy was made to determine the sex and the cause of the bird's death. Petunia was found to be male, and hence the first supposition concerning his sex was correct, his violent attacks upon Old Crip explained on the basis of sex rivalry, and his mounting of Joe, later witnessed, was in the natural order of things. Hence, "Petunia" now becomes "Pete," and "Joe," "Jo," or, more formally, "Josephine."

Mrs. Clapper describes the "wailing" she heard from Jo deep in the night as lacking the vibrant note she was accustomed to hear in the "whooping" of the cranes. It was monotonous, she says, continuing on a single note, and was still going on when daylight came. Indeed, it was repeated intermittently throughout the day.

Old Crip, meantime, had been occupying in solitary grandeur a great marshy area in the lower end of the Blackjack Peninsula, some ten miles or so from the 150-acre enclosure set apart for the breeding experiment. He was now brought into the enclosure as a companion, if not a mate, for Jo. Although his sex was not absolutely determined, still measurements made just prior to his release in the enclosure compared favorably with those of other males on record.

Was the Bud Keefer–Bob Allen try at mating two old bedraggled cranes, sex unknown, in a latitude nearly two thousand miles from the normal nesting range of the species, in the face of the fact that no expiring species had ever been mated successfully in captivity—was all this expensive effort under such handicaps an irresponsible or harebrained adventure? By no means. Consider what it proved, irrespective of the 1950 sequel, of which more later.

It demonstrated that a natural environment, natural food, the freedom of a large enclosure, the whoops of amorous cranes in the distance, rivalry, et cetera stimulate sexual and nesting activities. If these two specimens, old, worn, and debilitated by years of captivity, could be restored to mating and nesting, even in nesting grounds far away from the hereditary ones, the chances of bringing about a productive mating between two young and vigorous birds under similar conditions would be greatly enhanced. And why not build an enclosure in a suitable terrain in their ancient nesting grounds—in Iowa, Minnesota, or southern Canada? And if one enclosure produces young, why not a dozen enclosures, and so on until the species is again established on a stable basis? We should have here something new in the world.

And this courageous enterprise opened the news channels of the world—newspapers, magazines, radio, and motion pictures—to the whooping crane. Every school child in America now knows this splendid creature, how many of them are alive, their spectacular flights, from the warm coasts of Texas to be lost in the cold mists and winds that beat about the pole, and back again.

Meantime, Old Crip and Jo fed peacefully through fall and winter in the 150-acre enclosure. They became accustomed to new masters, since C. A. Keefer was assigned to a refuge in Nebraska, and Julian A. Howard took his place as Manager of the Aransas Refuge. Mrs. Howard undertook the chore of feeding the birds specially prepared "vitaminized" food thought to promote successful mating. About this time another crane, sole remnant of a Louisiana colony, was discovered and transferred to the Refuge.

April 22, 1950, Jo and Old Crip were reported nesting. Presently one egg was laid. All the papers hoped for two, but throughout the month that followed a second egg was not definitely reported. Press and radio were alerted for hatching time, and on May 26 the big news came. "The first whooping crane ever hatched in captivity" made the superlative for which all newspapers yearn.

"The sex is not known," said Mr. Howard, "nor is anyone sure just when the bird was born. But it was two days ago that the routine of the nest underwent a radical change. Jo took over the sitting. Before that she and her crippled mate had alternated." This thirty-eighth whooping crane in the world was dubbed "Rusty" from his dingy buff color.[5]

Mr. Howard placed the probable date of the hatching May 24 or 25. All observations were made from atop a thirty-foot tower, and since the nest was hidden in the cattails, and no one allowed in the enclosure, the more intimate details of this newsworthy event will forever remain in obscurity.

[5]Even as this is written (May 30) Rusty is reported missing, perhaps dead. But, dead or not, the demonstration is valid.

When you enter a competition, consider the prize. In this case it was nothing less than the salvation of a species, and the most desperate methods were justified. When the mold we call a species is destroyed by the hand of man it is a cosmic tragedy greater far than any conceivable slaughter of individuals for, in the annihilation of a species, life itself has been denied one of its chosen avenues of expression. It is no reassurance to be told that

The Eternal Sákí from that Bowl has poured
Millions of bubbles like us, and will pour,

since here it is not the bubbles but the Bowl that concerns us.

When the divine mold is broken by the interference of Man, Nature, "so careful of the type," has been thwarted; an impudent hand inserts a period before the sentence is complete, and the veritable Word of God is scorned and silenced. No court will pardon a criminal on plea of his attorney that the person he murdered would eventually have died anyway; and certainly Nature doesn't pardon man his wantonness because in the course of time a given species either dies or merges by imperceptible degrees into another form as the deft hand of the Maker may alter the mold itself—all in good time.

A species is a mold from which flows an endless procession of individuals, each and every one initialed inimitably. No substitution, no deceptive copy, no forgery is possible: the word "unique" here acquires a special significance above and beyond its relative meaning in discussions of the work of human hands. Ages have gone into the making of this mold. It summarizes a cumulative experience of unimaginable amplitude. "Cycles ferried its cradle." Launched midst violent flux of materials, now becalmed, now tossed in the turbulence and disasters of blind physical forces, spirit-piloted it comes, serenely arriving at last on this bank and shoal of time.

Our own species is, so far as we know, the only one which has been provided with the mental power and with the emotional sensitivity to recognize and appreciate the miracle of species creation. Man, of all earthborn creatures, has attained to a knowledge of good and evil in his contacts and communications with other works of the Creative Will. And although the brother's-keeper feeling of responsibility for his lowly kith and kin is so generally diffused as to be felt but vaguely by the great majority of mortals, we have here, in the saga of the whoopers, a case introduced with such fanfare of publicity, presented on so vast a stage in so grand a manner and spotlighting so spectacular a species that, all in all, our own accountability in the drama is stirring depths of public opinion rarely disturbed by any question of human obligation to the animal world.

3 WILDLIFE REFUGE

The sanctuary idea, like so many other civilizing influences, comes to us from the ancient Greeks. When timber cutters, sheep, goats, and brush fires had made barren the land, once richly verdured, native vegetation in pristine state was preserved here and there in plots which had been set apart as sacred to one divinity or another.

They were ever a source of inspiration to Greek poets. Here nightingales sang in shady coverts; tangled vines in great masses were token survivals of native jungle; flowers unknown elsewhere bloomed, "narcissus and the golden beam of crocus" looked forth; perennial springs fed sounding waters heard distantly within. Species eradicated elsewhere thrived under the protection of the god. No wonder

The quiring Muses love to seek the spot
And Aphrodite's golden car forsakes it not.

When the Chorus in one of the old Greek dramas hears a blind man stumbling about in a sanctuary, it is horrified and calls to him to come out of there at once. It is a "verdant dell where running water, as it fills the hallowed bowl, mingles with draughts of honey," and is no place for the polluting touch of human feet. The unseen and unseeing trespasser had in his blindness trenched on soil "forbidden human tread," consecrated to the "All-seeing Gentle Powers," while the "region all around . . . is guarded and possessed by dread Poseidon." The great comic poet of the same period lets us in on the fact that there were even in those days poachers, killers, skulkers sneaking about the confines of such sanctuaries to take nefarious toll of wild life harboring there. In a popular farce, or extravaganza, an actor, dressed up as a bird, is made to say to an assemblage of his fellows in feathers,

Now they treat you as knaves and as fools and as slaves:
Yea, they pelt you as though ye were mad.
No safety for you can the Temples ensure,
For the bird-catcher sets his nooses and nets,
And his traps, and his toils, and his baits and his lure,
And his lime-covered rods in the shrine of the Gods![1]

In another connection we are told that a wreath for the altar of Artemis is gathered from one of these sanctuaries, in a green and virgin meadow,

Where never shepherd leads his grazing ewes
Nor scythe has touched. Only the river dews
Gleam, and the spring bee sings; and in the glade
Hath Solitude her mystic garden made.

Thus, with a commercially despoiled land before them, the most distinguished Greek poets, in the final fruiting season of Greek literature, were possessed of the "wilderness" idea, which has now in our own land and time happily attained enough following to begin exerting some little political influence. Automobile roads and airstrips are being banned from a number of the larger national reservations, for the benefit of that growing clan of nature lovers who

[1]Translated by Benjamin Bickley Rogers, *Fifteen Greek Plays*, Oxford University Press. New York, 1943.

want their nature "straight." As Regional Forester R. H. Rutledge aptly puts it, referring to the two-million-acre Selway Bitter Root Primitive area: "We wish to hold and maintain frontier conditions such as our forefathers met, with mystery, romance, freedom of use, and inspirational qualities unimpaired and preserved for future generations."

But the average wild life refuge is still another matter. It represents merely the best the Wildlife Service, or the philanthropist, or such organizations as the Audubon Societies can do under the circumstances. Being practical men, they bargain and haggle and make as favorable deals as possible with other practical men who are just as much absorbed in getting whatever they can out of it.

There are even refuges, I am told, whose boundaries are gerrymandered to provide cozy nooks for hunters to take advantage of animals unable to comprehend this crooked business; and it is well known that a hunting lease adjacent to a refuge derives additional value from the fact that game there is not only more plentiful but less suspicious. Thus, in a sense, some refuges ensnare and beguile, as well as protect, certain forms of wild life.

Accidentally, here and there over the surface of the earth, a genuine sanctuary is created even in a limited area, under conditions which permit natural life to go on much as it did before the interposition by man occurred. Such, for instance, is the spectacular case of the Barro Colorado sanctuary. Here are 3,100 acres perched on a tropical hilltop in the middle of Gatun Lake, formed during the construction of the Panama Canal by letting water into the area which inundated every point less than eighty-five feet above sea level. The rich and various tropical life thus entrapped was left undisturbed; and, through a wise United States administration, it was put in care of the Institute for Research in Tropical America. These three thousand acres have become a veritable mecca for biologists, ecologists, and other scientists. Not a single form of life is disturbed except for strictly scientific purposes. This is sanctuary with Science enthroned therein instead of a whimsical Greek god. It is ideal from a dozen different points of view. But this is a happen-so and no chance assemblage of chances will provide a comparable windfall for wild life and science in another millennium—perhaps never again. However, the title of Science to this biological Eden is even now being clouded by serious talk of a sea-level canal which will drain Gatun Lake, put a period to research now under way, and leave a great devastated area round about.

Ordinarily, refuges are grabbed up here and there, catch-as-catch-can, in the scramble and melee with alien and unsympathetic interests. Not as yet fully conscious of the handicaps of such enterprises in conservation, I was a little disappointed to find extensive trapping in progress on the Aransas National Wildlife Refuge when I visited there in March of 1949. One thinks of a wild life refuge as a sanctuary, a sacred place, wherefrom Artemis and her clan have been forever barred; and where every species is guaranteed life, liberty, and the pursuit of happiness. We like to think of it as an animal Eden where Earth, unimpeded—indeed, uninfluenced in any way by man—may bring forth the living creature after his kind. I find this to be a naïve view of the so-called refuge. In these necessarily small areas set apart by law as sanctuaries, Nature cannot be allowed to take her course.

In any restricted area carved out of a natural wild-life province, Nature begins to show great partiality, and the species so favored eventually swarms over the face of the earth, extinguishing those handicapped by the artificially imposed restrictions. And then what? Inanition, disease, death. Too much prosperity proves to be as deadly for any form of life (man included) as too many hardships. Excess of either, as in the old Greek tragedy, attracts the attention of Nemesis, the Great Leveler, who evens the score, humbles the mighty, exalts the meek. Nature permits nothing too much. The cards are reshuffled and every species gets a new deal.

This method applied to a limited area, however, defeats the very purpose for which man sets up this artificial situation. If one might have a refuge as large in extent and as varied in natural environment as the whole state of Texas, for example, Nature might be allowed to do her worst or her best therein. But, after all, man himself is a part of Nature and is entitled to his own little nook or corner, so we cannot have refuges of continental size and still reserve for the lord of creation a place in the sun.

To get down to particular cases, consider the status of the deer. This charming animal thrives on the Aransas National Wildlife Refuge, which comprises about 47,000 acres of marsh, salt- and fresh-water lakes, brush-covered sand dunes, savanna, and coastal prairie. On the sixth day of the eventful week of creation, deer were told to be fruitful and multiply, and multiply they do. A refuge is a microcosm in which the theory of Malthus that population tends to increase faster than the means of subsistence is demonstrated suddenly and with catastrophic results.

Since a prudential check on the deer population is not practicable, consider a predatory check: say, wolves, pumas, and bobcats, all fond of fawns. A sufficient number of these predators permitted free range could probably cope with the fecundity of their prey, but they would also, in passing, snap up tidbits of wild turkey, quail, prairie chicken, and other species which are already teetering on the edge of extinction in this particular habitat. Nor would they stop there. Provided with a home breeding place and sanctuary in the center of a rich farming area, they would soon range far afield, varying their menus, as occasion offered, with calves, chickens, goats, pigs, and other succulent domestic species. Of course the farmers wouldn't put up with this.

The great horned owl is in bad repute here. This magnificent (and, on occasion, magniloquent) night bird was bringing nightly to the nest I had under observation, coots, pack rats and cottontailed rabbits. Sometimes, I am told, he mistakes a teal for a coot and a bobwhite for a pack rat. He is fond of young turkeys, also, and this lessens his prestige among the hunters. Hence, he is shot on sight. Coots swarm over the lakes and rob the glorious canvasback of his hard-earned celery as, out of breath from a long dive, he rises with a root of this vegetable in his bill. Coots are said to interfere with the mating activities of ducks, and they certainly consume an inordinate amount of good duck food. It would seem that the killing off of owls and of other predators feeding on coots will make it necessary eventually to kill the coots; thus the story goes, the problem getting bigger and more complicated at every step. So far as this Refuge is concerned, the ideal "balance" seems to favor the hunter rather than the naturalist or nature lover.

I found a generous naturalist here who was quite disturbed over trapping, shooting, and otherwise interfering with what he chose to call, with great reverence, "the balance of nature." The trouble is that the "balance of nature" is a false figure of speech, and we find little in reality corresponding to the popular conception of "a balance." Nature red in tooth and claw, that is, competitive; or Nature at peace, that is, co-operative; or Nature in alternating moods, or, at one and the same time, competitive *and* co-operative (her normal condition), is only in rare instances in balance for any extended period. Her so-called balance is shifting, precarious, and stays put only long enough for a quick glance to read the scale by pounds and ounces. Geologically considered, an even balance is of only momentary duration. The evolutionary process itself is only another name for an ever tilting of the scales up and down between and among the infinity of forms in which life chooses to express itself. The arrangement in time order of fossils of any species has written the Q.E.D. to this theorem.

If, for convenience, we speak of this constant imbalance as "a balance," then the rude intercession of man disrupts the scales, such as they are, and forever after they register false weights; and no accuracy of computation on the basis of what they show is possible again. When man takes over it becomes man's balance, if any—not Nature's. Thus the refuge becomes a problem of selection, of maintaining man's balance; that is, of course, an artificial balance, because, forsooth, the whole situation is artificial.

Deer, well enough protected, soon overpopulate a restricted range, become undernourished and eventually (experience shows), one disease or another sweeps away the excess. Since there is great demand for these animals as game in various parts of the country, it has been deemed advisable to limit the population on this Refuge by trapping and distribution to ranges that can maintain them in health. This service has been undertaken by the Texas Game,

41

Fish, and Oyster Commission, which supplies personnel and para-phernalia for doing the job, by and with the consent of the U.S. Fish and Wildlife Service, the agency which administers refuges of this kind. The man whom I found in charge of trapping is G. E. Colbath, who has taken ten thousand live deer in the last nine years, making his score slightly in excess of a thousand animals per annum, a world's record.

Now this trapping happens to provide an opportunity to observe the reactions of various animals to the experience of being caught, for the type of deer trap now in use catches other animals as well as deer. It is a cagelike contrivance with two doors, one at each end, which, sliding in grooves, are closed down by contact of the animal with a trigger concealed in the dirt floor. He steps on it and *click*, two doors fall simultaneously, one before and one behind him.

Aside from certain curious variations in behavior, the individual trapped responds ordinarily to this sudden calamity with actions and devices which may be said to represent the genius of his species. It is, of course, a life-and-death matter and the tension upon the emotions, mentality, and sheer physical strength and endurance is terrific.

What does the deer do when, startled by the thud of falling doors, he finds himself abruptly and neatly stalled in, with little room for maneuvering of any kind? Nature formed him to flee from enemies with which he cannot cope, but his superb legs are now useless. There is no living, moving thing to stand up and fight with horn or hoof. He is at once dumfounded, and after a frantic jump and bump or two against the ends and sides of the cage, the captive deer quits kicking against the pricks, subsides, chews his cud and awaits patiently whatever destiny has in store for him, even lying down if the wait is a long one.

When, however, the men approach to transfer him from trap to truck, he flies into a panic, dashes futilely against the walls, bruises his lips to bleeding and occasionally knocks a few front teeth out in his desperation. He exhibits no intelligence in meeting the novel sit-uation—only fright and the madness thereof. A man enters the trap, flanks the animal, and holds him struggling while the other trapper brads a metal identification tag in his ear and saws off his horns (if any) even with his skin. He is loaded through an unbelievably small hole into a truck. The company of his kind quiets him—he is that gregarious. With the truck bumping along over pasture roads, crooked and pockmarked with chuck holes, a single deer shows great excitement, but calms down when another is put in with him. As the truck proceeds along the "trap line" and the number of prisoners increases, all panic subsides and confidence is restored.

As I enter an open glade, a dozen deer bound away in long leaps which suggest the lightness of some flying animal, but stop, tense, fear struggling with curiosity, before entering the safety of a thicket, bodies quartering and each neck curved as if posed delicately by some sculptor who knew exactly what he was about. Each animal lifts his nose to give the air a free sweep up the nostrils, and each ear is funneled to catch an identifying sound from the disturber of their peace.

With binoculars focused on the stately buck, leader of the group, in air so transparent that a wink of the fringed eyelid and the slight sniffing motions of the nostrils are visible, I derive not only an aesthetic enjoyment, but the additional pleasure of that sympathy which the very nearness of almost any form of warmblooded wild life awakens in the average human being. This is the affectionate impulse which moves the child to reach out his hand to stroke an animal, especially a furry one, even a caged tiger. I wonder how long this magnificent buck will hold his pose, and decide to try him out. I am really taming these deer for the hunter's rifle. This trusted leader is finding the human form, posture, and odor harmless. One can hardly expect that he is learning to distinguish binoculars from a gun. His curiosity is being satisfied and his suspicions dulled. Suddenly I make myself as frightening as possible and the leader plunges into cover, followed by his polygamous family. I have often seen curiosity and suspicion wage doubtful war in this animal's consciousness.

His curiosity often betrays him. He is not satisfied with the testimony of eyes and ears. It is only his sense of smell which seems to bring overwhelming conviction. Mr. Colbath tells me that he was perched atop a forty-foot windmill tower looking for turkeys one morning when a deer came to drink of water running from the vent of a pipe which happened to be exactly below where he was seated. He dropped his hat just in front of the animal. The deer, he said, jumped about four feet high, kicked viciously at the hat, and bounded away. After running about twenty steps, however, he stopped and looked back. Curiosity overcame him and he gingerly approached the hat, sniffing. As soon as he got the wind from it, he turned and plunged into the woods. When his nose caught the man odor, he had no further doubt, and acted appropriately.

The deer of the Refuge, and of many of the large ranches, follow the cattle to the feeding troughs, develop a fondness for cottonseed cake (especially when the mast is scanty), become accustomed to the fences, barns, and dwellings of man, and other man-made devices, learning to tolerate even man's odor anciently so offensive, and, finally, to stand and be shot, or walk into traps like a milk-pen calf.

Indeed, he is threatened with complete domestication. I see them nibbling about the dwellings of men, beguiled by caressing gestures and coaxing tones. In some sections of the state they are pastured for eleven months of the year with tame stock to the end that they may be "harvested" at so much per shot by hunters. This is a step toward domestication, degradation, parasitism, as well as an oblique attack upon sport as sport, since the zest of difficulty is removed.

So-called sporting interests are constantly hammering at the gates of this Refuge, pleading that a short period be set aside for hunting within its borders. Even the goose soon comes to know when he is on sacred ground. I have seen flocks, wild and wary on the outside, become fairly gentle once they are on the inside. This trusting attitude of wild life within the Refuge makes the treachery of the "sportsmen's" proposal particularly offensive. The true sportsmen repudiate such suggestions. After all, if mere killing is to become the be-all and the end-all of hunting as sport, the "sportsman" eventually becomes a butcher, which is a perfectly honorable calling so long as one is frank and open about it.

The prestige of sport is a survival from the time in the evolution of human society when certain powerful predators preyed on man and had to be killed in self-defense, and man, himself a predator, preyed on weaker species in order to supply himself with necessary food. The "protector" and the "supplier" naturally attained great preferment. With the passing of the original incitements to the chase coupled with a curious persistence of the prestige, numberless contradictions and illogicalities present themselves. In certain cases, the seriousness of the effort, contrasted with its obvious futility, invites humorous treatment. For illustration, the demand for trout in some sections of the country is so great that the only practicable way to meet it is for the fish hatcheries to grow trout to legal size, and, just a few days before the season opens, dump them by the truckload into the streams where this demand is most vocal. Thus one set of men breed and rear trout and deliver them en masse to streams, where other men suddenly line the banks with their curious contraptions and extract these same fish laboriously, one by one, until the day's limit is reached. This reminds one of those elaborate, tedious, and often expensive preparations which the elders of the family undertake at Christmastime to amuse the children for a brief, delirious period.

I am told by the late Judge Leroy Denman, of San Antonio, life-long experimenter with catching and domesticating wild species, that our deer trappers make a conspicuous failure of trapping really wild and "uncontaminated" deer. These children of the forest or the open range, he says, simply refuse to go into the traps. Trappers generally deny this.

So deer trapping offers a warning to parasites. These Refuge deer become corrupted, in a manner of speaking, in their human contacts. They feed with domestic animals and gradually acquire a little of their complacency. They forsake the wild ways of the the forest and forget their forest wisdom. They have no seers or prophets, none to tell them that man, no matter how kindly he may for the moment appear, is eventually, inveterately and forever their enemy; none to cry, "Beware of man bearing cottonseed cake. See what domestication has done already to Bos."

Man began molding certain species of this genus to his own uses before the dawn of historic time. Egyptian monuments of 3000 B.C. contain representations of oxen; and bones of them are found mixed in with the neolithic remains of Swiss lake dwellings. Millennia of study and ingenuity have gone into the making of domestic breeds, some of which are now caricatures of the wild species from which they came. The prize Hereford, for instance, looks like a mechanical structure built up with geometrical blocks of steaks and roasts mortared together mission style with sheer fat. The Brahma has so far lost least of natural beauty in yielding to the demands of domestication, retaining still a great deal of the dignity as well as the superb style of Bos in the wild. This is the more remarkable since the Brahma is one of the oldest breeds on earth. Marco Polo remarks upon the beauty of the Brahma. Probably he was the first European who ever saw this splendid animal.

The Brahma's ability to take care of himself under any reasonable conditions has made him a favorite in the coast country. On the other hand, many of those fat, lumbersome specimens of certain other breeds, which we see taking prizes at agricultural fairs, can't even take care of their own calves. Their legs have difficulty in bearing up the enormous weight—indeed, they are physical monstrosities—while mentally they tend to become a mere mass of benumbed instincts. We hear them called "beautiful," as one says a steak is "beautiful," but this is mere metaphor, since the appeal is obviously gastronomic rather than aesthetic.

Really, the dog, so far as I have been able to observe, is the only species that has profited by domestication. Its number has increased a thousand or a millionfold. Generally, the dog enjoys more creature comforts than the wild species from which he came, while still maintaining a certain amount of independence. Except for the comparatively few apartment lollipops, the dog has maintained his four freedoms: freedom of range, freedom to fight and mate promiscuously, and freedom to associate with his peers, much as he did in a state of nature. He has gained greatly on the spiritual side. His appreciations have been widened, his wits sharpened, and his affections warmed and deepened by his intimate contacts with man.

Particularly is this true of the cur, which so far outnumbers the gentle breeds as to swamp them completely in statistical calculations. Neither are work dogs and edible dogs, occurring for the most part on the fringes of civilization, considered. The great mass of the dogs of the world are either taken into human society on a purely affectionate basis or as copartners with man, serving as guards, hunters, herders, and assisting in other vocations, training for which is in direct line with the native canine instincts. These are the influences which have set the dog apart among all domestic animals. It is another of those miracles worked by love.

Francis Bacon goes even further and deduces the "fact" that God is necessary to man from the analogy of the dog's dependence upon man. It is only in the wholesome atmosphere, he says, of this relation of dependence that the dog is lifted out of himself and onto a far higher plane, that is, it is only by resting his confidence in a superior being. In like manner is man's nature lifted up and glorified, says Bacon, only by the trust and confidence which he reposes in a higher being, namely, in God.

The dog-man relationship and the analogies based upon it permeate literature and philosophy. Plato's Socrates, speaking in half-humorous vein, makes the dog out to be a true philosopher because he growls suspicion and hatred at the presence of a stranger (i.e., against that of which he is ignorant), and beams love and affection upon his acquaintances (i.e., upon that which he knows): *ergo,* the dog obviously loves knowledge and hates ignorance, the first mark of the true philosopher.

But to return to the deer: does this animal learn anything from all those harrowing experiences—trapped, tagged, dehorned, forced into a rolling, bouncing truck and hauled for hundreds of miles to be released in a strange environment? Does he henceforth give this type of trap a wide berth? By no means. He has learned exactly nothing, if you judge him by his subsequent behavior. There are no "spoilt" deer as there are "spoilt" wolves. I asked a trapper what he meant by a "spoilt" wolf. "One which has been trapped, and hence has become wise to traps," he replied. Two or three trap lessons so educate a wolf that he often becomes the trapper's despair. We have what we call "quantity trappers," men who enter a section with many traps which they work industriously and are able to show quantity production. But after the quantity trapper has moved on to pastures new, it is sometimes necessary to bring in the expert trapper, wise in the ways of the "spoilt" wolf, to clean up the range. Trapping literature abounds with the drama of these special cases. Indeed, they *make* trapping literature.

The wolf quickly learns his lesson, but not so the innocent soft-eyed doe or majestic buck. They are deceived by the same clumsy contrivance as easily the second time as the first time, and the third time as easily as the second.

On one occasion a couple of young trappers amused themselves in the boss's absence by roping deer as they bounded out. One of the young men stood on top of the trap with his lasso ready while the other opened the door. It was great fun to see a vigorous buck "change ends with hisself" as he dashed headlong against a rope, the other end of which was securely tied down. But they grew careless, as boys will, and one morning a fine eight-point buck got loose with a thirty-foot lasso looped over his horns. The next morning on their rounds they found this buck trailing his rope in the identical trap. "Tagged" deer, which means deer which have been caught on this Refuge and a metal identification tag bradded in the ear, released far away occasionally return and are caught again.

But the deer has a wisdom of his own. He finds his way in the pathless wilderness; and, what is still more difficult, these trapped deer often hew to a homing line for hundreds of miles from the point of their release, threading their way among farms, ranches, villages, and cities alive with their human and canine enemies. This has been demonstrated by the return of a number of "tagged" deer to the Refuge.

In the spring of 1942 a doe released near Goliad, ninety miles due west of the Refuge, was trapped again in twenty-one days. In the spring of 1944 a six-point buck was trapped and trucked four hundred miles west before being released near Sheffield, Texas. In the fall of 1945 he was again caught on the Refuge in a trap of the same type as the one in which he was originally taken. Pathfinding wisdom comes to the deer early in life: a fawn caught in Trap Number 14 in the autumn of 1946 was loaded into a truck with many other deer and driven one night to San Angelo, Texas, 390 miles away; and from there, after a short stop, to Nolan County, 77 miles north. Three weeks thereafter this fawn was caught in Trap Number 15, only about 125 yards away from the scene of his first experience with traps.

These returning deer do not all arrive. One, en route back "home" from near Albany, Texas, 375 miles northwest of the Refuge, was killed by a hunter at Cuero, 100 miles northwest, showing that the animal was making a line straight as the crow flies from the point of his release back to the Refuge when the casualty occurred. Indeed, there is only one record of a Refuge deer being retaken while he was moving away from his old home. This one had been trucked to Armstrong, a far western county in Texas, and was shortly thereafter killed further west in a New Mexico village into which he had strayed.

Something draws these wanderers back. One observer may call it "Providence," another "instinct," but whatever it may be called, the mystery remains. A rancher friend of mine found a litter of seven pigs in the wilds and took them home with him. During the night one escaped and made his way back to the maternal nest across miles of rugged country.

Jean Henri Fabre records but does not explain prodigies of home finding on the part of his numerous and beloved cats while he is being bumped from one domicile to another in Paris and environs.

This so-called "homing instinct" in many animals is really more difficult to account for than migrations, upon which there is so much scientific speculation and as yet so little light.

We guess the creature has a sixth sense, and that there is a magnetic current with which the "homing instinct" is in tune; that he has a "feel" of the earth's rotation east-west, which, taken with the north-south pull of the magnetic current, places him in latitude and longtitude. We say that birds, especially, remember landmarks and are guided by them; and Carl Axel Anderson, of Dallas, the nation's closest student of the monarch butterfly, says these gorgeously winged creatures seem to migrate by a radioactive beam, to stay on which "they'll fly through a building, in one window and out the other," or, "if no windows are open, then up and over the roof and down again until they get back on the beam."

But I find it difficult to attribute any of these means or accessories to a little grunting pig making his way in the night through sand hills and marshlands and semitropical underbrush on and on with little deviation from the true course to the nest where his mother bore him only six weeks before.

And a deer, jammed with fifty others into a truck, boxed in with only inch-wide peepholes between the slats, whisked along winding highways at forty-five miles per hour in the night—this timid creature, dazed and frightened, turns homeward and, after backtracking two hundred miles, is killed exactly on a beeline between the point of release and the Refuge from which he had been removed a few weeks before. This is mystery, deep mystery! Until better explanation offers, and at risk of being called "idealistic," or "sentimental," I shall prefer the poet's reverent and melodious surmise:

There is a Power whose care
Teaches thy way along that pathless coast . . .

There is in the brush and swampy river bottoms of this part of the Texas coast a large, vicious wild hog. Some twenty years ago a gentleman introduced the European boar. Ranchmen of the region say that this animal interbred with the semiferal razorbacks already on the range. The progeny were neither game hogs nor animals which might be penned and satisfactorily fattened for meat, but huge, rangy, ugly, untamable beasts. This unfortunate cross, it is said, spread up and down the coast wherever the environment was favorable, and the Refuge still contains a number of them. The foregoing account of the wild hog is generally accepted along this part of the coast. Judge Leroy Denman, of San Antonio, who brought these animals in, told me that the European boar and our domestic breeds of hogs produce sterile offspring. Judge Denman's breeding experiments, however, were conducted in confined quarters, and it is possible that when the animals gained the freedom of the open range, with a more varied food and more opportunity for the expression and exercise of natural instincts, crosses became more successful. The official view follows:

"In about 1928 and the years immediately following, Leroy Denman of San Antonio bought approximately forty European wild boars from zoos and kept them in a pen on St. Charles peninsula near Austwell [present site of the Aransas Wildlife Refuge]. Some of these escaped from the pen into the wild, where, according to Denman, they did well, but did not thrive in the pens. He reported that they crossed readily with domestic hogs in the pen but that the third generation was sterile. Because of the mixture with domestic swine, the boars lost much of their wildness. At present [1944] Denman has about forty-five on his Powder Horn Ranch in Calhoun county where he hopes they will become completely wild because no tame hogs are there with which to cross-breed."[2]

When one of these boars is caught in a deertrap, it is just too bad. He doesn't bang about and then quit as the deer does, nor root out as the javelina, nor dig out as the wolf or raccoon, nor does he take his imprisonment lying down as the soporific opossum, but proceeds at once to make kindling wood of the slats which bar his freedom. After one of these animals has finished with a trap, it is easier to build a new one than to try to repair the wreck. His rage is unconfined; he gnashes, smashes, splinters the one-by-four material, and tears joint from joint, leaving the structure, as a trapper expressed it, "lookin' like a cyclone had hit it."

Other animals have still different reactions.

When the javelina, an animal of dim vision, wanders into a deertrap, what does he do about it? Well, generally he sets to rooting under a wall of the enclosure and soon excavates himself out of the

[2]*Principal Game Birds and Mammals of Texas,* Texas Game, Fish, and Oyster Commission. Austin, Texas, 1945.

difficulty. On one occasion a javelina entered, ate the bait, and found the rear exit barred by the wire netting which is stretched across the end opposite the entrance in order to give the animal entering the impression that he can walk right on through. This javelina investigated no further, but dug himself out, although he had never sprung the trap and the door behind him was wide open. He could have turned and walked out, but chose the hard way. Actually caught, however, his attack upon the trap is severely logical. He simply roots himself to freedom.

The deer, as we have seen, of greater intelligence but less stable emotionally, makes little or no effective effort to escape, is dumfounded from the beginning, and returns again to be caught in the same trap. To match this stupidity, the javelina goes to great pains to dig out of a trap the door of which is not closed.

Opossums, skunks, and raccoons are caught on this Refuge in "live" traps, so called since they are designed to take the animal alive. Identical bait attracts each of these "vermin." I even found a swamp rabbit in one, with his skull cracked. In turning about to leave the trap, his hind foot had evidently touched the trigger, releasing the door, which struck him on the head. Thus poor, bungling bunny got himself killed in a "live" trap.

The opossum snoozes away the time, showing little excitement and no anxiety about what is going to happen next. It is not unusual to find one curled up in the sunniest corner of a coontrap, out of the wind, and sound asleep. On one occasion I undertook to arouse a large, fat opossum in order to make him realize the gravity of his situation. He responded to a gentle punch in the ribs with an angry snarl, showing a few of his fifty teeth. No other mammal, by the way, except a few moles, has as many teeth as this sluggish marsupial. A broken tooth gave his grin a grotesque quality. He blinked, but his eyelids didn't work in concert, the left lid winking about six times to the right lid's once, affording a kind of comic relief from the deadly seriousness of his broken-toothed grin. In a few minutes he closed his mouth as slowly as he had opened it, twisted himself a bit like a sleepy child, and settled down again into profound slumber. Why worry?

The trapped skunk is quite another sort. You find him alert and often threatening you by stamping about and hoisting his tail, always a danger signal. The trapper releases him, gingerly lifting the door and stepping back a safe distance, rifle in hand, while the little fellow makes an unhurried exit, as if he had the whole day in which to make his escape. He is killed by a rifleshot at some distance from the trap to keep him, the trapper says, from "stinking it up." If released in a roadway, he ambles down it for a distance of twenty or thirty yards, pausing as he turns to quit the road and seek cover. This pause is fatal. The trapper knows the habit, so waits for the moment of hesitation in order to shoot at a still, wide target instead of a narrow, moving one. They distinguish varieties of coastal skunk by the stripes, calling one "narrow-striped," another "broad-striped," and a third "short-striped," which illustrates a folk habit of naming a natural object by its most spectacular, and therefore most memorable, feature.

I very much doubt if this animal is as harmful to game birds as he is here believed to be. I find his percental dietary listed as follows on the basis of examination of stomachs and feces of 1,700 specimens taken in Michigan: insects 57 per cent, rodents 10 per cent, birds and poultry 2 per cent, fruits 17 per cent, and grain 12 per cent.[3] Neither do I believe that coons are half as harmful to turkeys on this refuge as the authorities assume. The same University of Michigan investigation, covering two years and study of five hundred coon stomachs, records his diet as follows: birds, .43 per cent, insects, 5 per cent, grain, 20 per cent, fruits, 12 per cent, crawfish and crustaceans, 59 per cent, leaving only 3.57 per cent unaccounted for. Since turkeys make such a poor showing on the Refuge and coons are under suspicion, this animal is trapped furiously, more than a hundred traps being set for him throughout the season. He can hardly walk without walking into one. As between turkeys and coons, I agree with my trapper friend, Emmett Smith: "There's only one day in the year when a turkey is more interesting to me than a coon, and that's Thanksgiving." I think the respective dietaries of 1,700 skunks and 500 coons taken on this Refuge would not show a great variation in

[3]University of Michigan, School of Forestry and Conservation, Bulletin No. 1.

53

the percentages given for skunks and coons in the Michigan report.

"Running the trap line," as they call it, we found, one morning, a bobcat tethered by a chain in a clump of sweet bay with a hind leg nearly pinched off at the second joint in the viselike jaws of a steel trap. He had mutilated every shrub within reach of his claws and teeth. Driven into hysterics by the terrible pain, he had apparently spent the whole night biting and clawing the insensate vegetable growths round about. He was killed and the stomach cut open, the contents of which revealed that this particular bobcat had been living exclusively on pack rats. Mixed in with the same, as testimony to his night of agony, were remains of sweet bay. Not only had he been biting these shrubs but chewing and swallowing bits of bark, leaves, and twigs. Thus the stomach told two stories: one, that for at least a day or two before being caught he had been going up and down the Refuge doing good; and, two, the story of the creature's rage, pain, and futile struggles before being mercifully released with a pistol shot. Of course, the contents of other bobcats' stomachs show that individuals vary their menu quite frequently from pack rats and other pests.

The raccoon—— But this species has such curious reactions to traps, and behaves so entertainingly in other human contacts, that I give over a chapter to him and to him alone.

4 DUST

I took a couple of weeks' vacation from the coast to follow up the windings of the Colorado River to its bitter end; that is, to dry arroyos of the Low Plains. Pushing on northwest a little further, we camped among mesquite in an area in which no drainage channels of any kind were visible. Water falling here doesn't run off but sinks into the sand; or, during excessive downpours, gradually seeks its level in low places to form "wet-weather" lakes. There is here no water erosion to speak of. Wind erosion, however, is another matter and a serious one.

This flat, sandy, mesquite country was being literally torn to pieces, as if the owners were determined to see just how much of it would blow away. I was particularly struck with the devastating capabilities of an ugly, enormous mechanism called the "bulldozer." It is a huge hog of a machine. To make way for highways among the limestone hills of west central Texas, thousand-year-old live oaks topple over, uprooted at the mere touch of its steel snout.

The mesquite in which I saw this raging mechanical boar at work was simply child's play for it. Whereas, only a few years before on a visit to this same section of the country, I had seen an army of Mexican laborers at the same work with shovel and grubbing hoe, now none were to be seen; only one man with his hands on the controls of this monster was creating more havoc than a whole army.

There is good geological evidence that, here in this region during the dry years of a weather cycle occurring long ago, an area as large as that now blocked off on the map as comprising fourteen counties had been an utter desert of drifting sand without one sprig of vegetation per square mile. But the "encompassing" cycle of time is so great that it is now impossible to tell whether the ancient dust-bowl is again on the march, or whether, perhaps, the ravage of desiccation and of furious winds is now in way of being healed. Surely, in the cases before my eyes, of the machines among the mesquite, old wounds were being reopened.

Normally and in course of nature, this mesquite has no business here. Its presence as well as its present eradication is man's work. This hardy shrub has invaded country north of the Rio Grande only during the last two or three hundred years. Formerly, during the Indian and buffalo period, it could make little progress, for the land was covered with a mat of grass; and mesquite beans, falling on this covering, could not reach the soil and therefore had no chance to germinate.[1] But the white man with his herds soon made holes in Nature's carpet, and in these exposed places, especially during wet weather, the mesquite beans, dropped from the hoofs of animals or the bills of birds, found anchorage, germinated, grew into scrubby trees, bore more beans, which spread on and on as overgrazing made places for them to take root. Not only the noxious mesquite, but

[1]In 1870 the U.S. Department of Agriculture yearbook, speaking of range opportunities in the Southwest, said: "Farmers upon land [in other areas] costing $20 to $200 an acre, in climate requiring four or five months of winter feeding, cannot compete with stock raisers operating under a sky that demands no shelter and upon a soil yielding perennial supplies of green food where land is so cheap that a single stock farm includes a whole county."

many other invaders encroached on the grasslands during this period and for identically the same reason. This is a twice- or thrice-told tale. Government bulletins tell it laboriously in scientific language and in great detail, but it needs to be told until people listen—or, better, *smell* (as I did on this trip) the very odor of destruction. The nose is, after all, the most convincing of our five senses.

Here see—and this is no fanciful suggestion—the last gasp of Nature in an effort to hold this precious topsoil in place. Since man with his greedy overgrazing was destroying the natural cover which kept the wind from blowing the soil away and, in other places, the raindrops from punishing the surface and starting the erosion gullies, Nature said, "Well and good, we shall do the next best thing to give it cover and support from wind and water. We shall introduce thorned shrubs which stock cannot eat, with tenacious root systems which will clutch and hold what remains, and whose tough body and branches will collect around themselves the blowing soil and keep it from being whisked off a hundred miles away." To this end mesquite and other drought-resistant, tough, thorny, bitter shrubs come in to do their bit when the natural covering has been removed.

I am not unaware of the counsel now being given to landowners, urging them to fight these intruders with might and main, uproot the mesquite, burn off the cedar, destroy (with chemicals, if necessary) the huisache, obliterate the cactus; and no doubt this advice is sound for given localities where the lay of the land is right, remedial treatment practicable, soil conditions propitious, and wherever the subsequent use of the land will aid in the further reclamation of it. But there are vast areas in which this is the counsel of ignorance, and unless it is applied with discrimination to particular locations, it will, if followed, simply complete the work of destruction already begun.

If one will abandon the present Russian predilection and listen to Pure as well as to Applied Science, he will often be confused by finding the two at variance; and I think it is never amiss to observe a little on one's own account, and apply common sense to a given situation, no matter what Science, pure or applied, may say. Every wood wanderer is occasionally driven by a sudden downpour of rain to take quickly to whatever cover is handy, skimpy as it may be, and he finds wild and domestic animals doing exactly the same. A naturalist tells me that he was once driven to shelter under one of the most cursed of all the wild shrubs and trees which now cover thousands of square miles of the semiarid Southwest, the so-called mountain cedar, *Juniperus mexicana.* It was a driving, pelting precipitation of oversized raindrops. The half-bared roots of the tree under which he was sitting ran along a ledge, forming a little terrace which had caught and detained leaves and other vegetable debris in the course of being washed down the slope—a considerable accumulation. The roots of that tree were penetrating the seams and interstices of the rocks, cracking, pulverizing, and mixing the ingredients which go into the making of soil. This, of course, is a slow, century-long process, but it was easy to see what would have happened to this slope long ago but for the cedar break; for there was an open, exposed area between this tree and the next. This open space had been swept clean as a floor and the solid, unseamed limestone was laid bare in exactly the condition to which the whole slope would have been reduced years ago but for the intercession of the despised cedar. "Be content," advised a pioneer ranchman, speaking to his eldest son, "to take little toll from these cedar slopes. Cut a few posts, graze them lightly. They are holding what soil there is and building more. Maybe your son, or son's son, will find a better way to hold this land, but, for the present, let the cedar stand." This son, now an old man, tells me he is letting the cedar stand, content with his toll of posts, and is advising his son to do the same.

Why did a horse take refuge beneath the next cedar, and why was a flock of field sparrows hopping happily about under another nearby cedar, fluffing up their feathers and shaking themselves but otherwise unconcerned with the rainstorm? Neither my naturalist friend, nor the horse, nor the sparrows like the pelting of big, driving raindrops. They didn't so much mind the rain after the cedar had intervened. The upright leaves of this tree, like a multitude of tiny spears pointing toward the sky, were breaking the drops to pieces, fragmentizing these plunging, liquid bullets from the heavens, *mist-ti-fying* them; that is, literally converting them into a mist and spreading the moisture upon the litter of leaves below as softly as a mother lays down a coverlet upon the body of a cradled baby. To paraphrase Kilmer, "How intimately shrubs live with rain!" The soil does not like pelting any more than animals do. It likes it so little that it runs away. And, if the area is so flat that the water can't run off, it simply seals up the soil, which then hardens in the sun, gets another sealing in the next rain, hardens, and so on until it is impenetrable by roots and impervious to moisture.

I visited this very cedar slope a few years later. The owner had taken the advice of experts and had apparently realized some ready money from the sale of posts. He had piled the trimmings helter-skelter over the entire area. When the slashings dried, the whole acreage had been burned off, leaving a ghastly sight. *All* the soil was gone, and huge, half-burnt stumps stood up as if on stilts, since the humus had been washed out from around and between the roots, ends of which, still anchored in crevices and seams of the rock, held up blackened remains as if in a conscious attempt to advertise this hideous devastation.

This is an exceptional case, but exceptional only in degree. The mesquite, for instance, or the retama, doesn't atomize raindrops, but both minimize their destructive pelting and certainly diminish run-off, as well as splatter erosion.

But there was another revenge in store for much of the mesquite country. It is so flat it can't wash away. Here Nature's problem was not water erosion but wind erosion, and she adopts another tactic and uses a different instrument—the mesquite. In this section to which I had just moved my camp, the mesquite grows nine tenths underground. Only scraggly shreds of vegetation show above the surface, but look beneath! Here see immense, octopus-like stems with solid bodies often as big as hogsheads, from which spread in all directions—ten, twenty, sometimes thirty feet—tentacles which search the soil for moisture and nourishment, accumulating, holding, pre-empting a hillock or mound, built of particles of soil and sand which have been snatched by the upper branches of the shrub from the passing winds. Marvelous ingenuity! One part of this plant grabs the soil out of thin air; the other part holds on for dear life to whatever portion is delivered to it.

Too often man's answer to this attempt to retain the soil in place is the Machine, the monster "bulldozer." The huge bulbs, which are really modified trunks, are rooted out as a hog would turn up an onion, along with their tough soil-grasping tentacles; and the hummocks they have spent years in building about themselves are smoothed down hopefully for the plow, but in reality to give the next wind a free sweep. In short, man's Machine here joins forces with the Devil, and Nature is again frustrated. It is quite true, as Oscar L. Chapman, Secretary of the Interior, points out, that these shrubs consume large quantities of much-needed water, but until a better means of reclaiming and using this soil moisture is discovered and made of practicable application, it would seem wiser to let it support these sturdy defenders of the soil.

It was as if this trip had been planned for me that I might see an actual demonstration in devastation; first, the silt-burdened waters of the Colorado River up which stream we had traveled for two days, camping on its shore by night; and, next, the cancellation of Nature's repair work in the northwestern plains. The afternoon of our arrival we camped right in the midst of mesquite. My companion had already gone to bed, and I was just about ready to "turn in" when a sharp crack of thunder directed my attention to the northwestern sky. We looked at it, and my friend dragged out a tarpaulin to keep himself dry during the approaching storm. But in the vivid flashes of lightning my more practiced eye saw that there was no rain at all in that solid bank of cloud.

"It is dust," I said. "Nothing but dust. In all probability it will sand us in tonight. In two or three hours the wheels of our car will be hub-deep or deeper. I think we had better get out."

Hastily we broke camp, donning slickers over our pajamas, and made for the nearest village twenty miles away. The dust was driving in full force by the time we reached harborage. Cars were having difficulty in the streets. Pebbles the size of small peas blistered our cheeks as we ran across the square to the little hotel.

For three days this dust storm raged. Tons of dust eddied about the buildings as drifting snow will bank up in places; and much shoveling was necessary to keep the strategic ways cleared. For three days the Powers of Evil, in league with man and his bulldozer, enjoyed a holiday. The fourth day the wind laid and Nature seemed to have recovered her good humor. The landscape smiled again, and we drove about a bit to see what the storm had done. There were some fields that had lost *all* their loose soil, and the scorings of the plow point were plainly visible in the clay subsoil, from which the brooms of the wind had swept every particle recently stirred by the plow. Some fields, curiously enough, had received more than they had lost, and some were unaffected, one way or another. We stopped for a drink of water at a rude farmhouse, hardly more than a "shack." Man and wife were at work shoveling up the dirt from their living-room floor and trucking it out in a wheelbarrow. The "windy season" was hardly half over. The farmer told us, with a sad shake of his head, that he would have to "plant all over again as the storm had blowed everything out."

But the demonstration was not complete. Two weeks later I was again on the Texas coast five hundred miles from where I had seen the bulldozer at work. The dust of the northwest was out of my nostrils and I could breathe again and feel the grateful cooling air in my upper nasal passages. I began to smell things—the fresh clean air from salt waters, or, when the wind changed to landward at night-fall, the odorous breath of marsh and meadows, of sweet bay, and of live-oak mottes.

It was then that I decided to give my nose a real rest. I selected a favorable campsite near Mustang Bay on the Aransas National Wildlife Refuge. Many native species—birds, mammals, reptiles, and amphibians—crowd into this protected acreage, as a relief from the mechanized barbarism which fills the world with stench and dust and raucous sounds, pump guns and human and animal misery. Anyway, I was there among animals which had little fear of man,

61

among wind-sculptured oak mottes, and dunes which, although practically soilless, Nature had managed to clothe with various stunted growth, principally oak and sweet bay, whose roots held much of whatever the winds brought within their grasp.

Wind and waves play fantastic tricks with dune sand on the Texas coast. The waters of the bays receive vast accumulations of silt (partly sand) from the discharge of swollen rivers. The winds whip up the waves, and the waves drive silt and sand up the beach, where it is churned and the silt leached out by the repeated action of wind, waves, and tide until little is left except the pure blowing sand. Then, as the beach dries in the sun and the wind comes off the water, the sand is blown landward. Eager vegetation, pressing down toward the shore, catches some of it and dunes arise. Then the wind turns and much of it is blown back into the water to be again ejected by the waves, dried and blown back onto the land. Endlessly and forever this driving of the sand back and forth goes on, with always a little adhering in the dunes, halted by the sturdy vegetation. Every few years the big, lawless disturbances called "hurricanes" occur, and the patient work of quieter weather is undone; the coast is disfigured but not demolished. Gently, as if there were no such thing as time, the massaging begins again, and so on, and so on. This is a part of the process of building the coastal prairie which has been advancing for geologic ages from the limestone hills two hundred miles northwest toward the final jumping-off place, called the "continental shelf," now only thirty to a hundred and thirty miles from the present shoreline.

Here is the kind of place to enjoy your nose. The sweet salt air "clears up the pipes," and dustless, moist sea breezes come freighted with a dozen different odors which, although you may not identify, you can enjoy.

When I arrived from the wind and dust of the plains here in this dustless haven, I felt, with the animals, that I had been driven to the very edge, and that one more nudge of the Machine and we would all be ousted helter-skelter into the Gulf of Mexico. I had a feeling at least of temporary security, and I am sure the animals around me felt the same: hunted, driven, shot, slaughtered as they had been until this narrow and precarious refuge by the water's edge was provided.

Our camp was sheltered in a cove of live oaks between Wild Hog and Mustang lakes near an old camp site of the Karánkaways, which at the time was being excavated by a party of archeologists. My first afternoon at Wild Hog Lake was rather fruitless on account of a pair of black-necked stilts which kept flying over me uttering their piercing, far-reaching cries and warning practically all the wild life in the area of my approach. I edged about here and there seeking a favorable nook from which I might observe the life of the lake, but these skinny sentinels sought me out, screamed, quarreled, hovered wherever I went, and frightened other birds away. The alarm note of these skeletons in feathers is among the most spiteful sounds in nature. It is cracked, querulous, high-pitched, and vindictive. Their tiny little skulls seem almost to burst with indignation as they call shrill and futile curses down upon you. I finally gave up and let them have their little lake in peace, but not before I had selected a clump of rattlebush in which to hide. So next morning at dawn, neatly secluded, I enjoyed a petty triumph over my two spies of the afternoon before as I watched them feeding not fifty yards away, unaware that their privacy had been invaded.

Thus, with the fast-reddening east to my back and well covered in a clump of rattlebush, which, by the way, stinks like sour sweat, I focused my glasses on a show which seemed to have been designed and directed especially for me. There were several patches of reeds scattered here and there over the swamp and around its edges, thick enough to please a rail. A windowlike opening in the rattlebush gave me a view of a stretch of water lying between two areas of tule. As the parade of animals got under way, up and down the swamp, they came from behind one patch of tule or the other into the field of my vision without ever suspecting that they were being observed.

Dawn drew the curtain and the show was on. Twenty-six different species appeared during the three-hour performance, not counting a brilliant cardinal which fluttered in from the denser brush and ate mustang grapes almost within my reach; and not counting, either, a turkey hen who was startled out of a nearby thicket, and came *putt-putting* in great alarm. Her curiosity at seeing a human figure crouched within a few feet of her, still as a statue, soon overcame the fright she had had in the bushes, and her prolonged *putt-putting* dwindled down to mere interrogatory *putt-putts* accompanied by a stretching of the neck and sidewise inclination of the head. Had she been one of Nature's odor-wise creatures, she would have taken flight immediately, but being guided by vision only, she couldn't quite make out whether I was alive or not: hence her cautious steps in retreat; hence that inquisitorial stretching and half twisting of the long, lithe neck—a twist to the right as she put down her left foot and a twist to the left as she put down her right—to turn full upon me first one lustrous eye and then the other, uttering her *putts* now *sotto voce*, almost within an arm's length. I felt that I was being rigorously cross-questioned, but chose to be an obstinate witness, and didn't twitch a muscle throughout about five minutes of grilling. Presently she chose to walk sedately away.

This hen and I had played out one of those games of chance and skill by means of which the fitness of feral creatures is tested a dozen or a hundred times a day, each species, in the course of its evolution and by virtue of the evolutionary process, having been equipped physically and mentally for these competitions with an amazing assortment of devices. Attack and counter; ambush and caution; mutual aid *vs.* individual prowess; pounce and dodge; camouflage and detection; tricks, guile, stratagems—with the individuals of many species changing roles from offense to defense and back again a dozen times in the course of an hour, day in and day out; it is thus that Nature keeps her instruments in tune.

The race goes not always to the strong, nor invariably to the cleverest; but, statistically, and in the long result of time, the issue tends always toward a more various as well as a more abundant life. New contrivances, known as "mutations," are tried, accepted, or thrown into the discard; and, on the emotional side, wild animals, forever living dangerously, seem to escape much of the boredom domestication exacts as the price of security.

I was completely absorbed for the moment in deceiving this wild bird, while she showed the same intensity of interest in unraveling my disguise; i.e., in being able to pronounce decisive judgment as to whether I was friend or enemy, neutral or none of these—perhaps merely a misshapen stump with no life in it at all. When she ventured nearest, I gauged the distance, muscles tensing, like a cat's. Had I the "spring" in me I once had, I could have caught her by the leg, and felt an impulse to try it anyway. I even sniffed gently to get a whiff of her odor, but perhaps she had clamped her feathers and seal~d her body odor away from the wind, as some birds of her family are said to have the power of doing.

These games between predator and prey are not always played out according to Hoyle. Startling innovations occur. For instance, we have all seen the "crippled wing" trick so often that we hardly notice it: the mourning dove leaving her nest in signal distress, the "crazy quail" in hysterics fluttering away from her hidden young, or the black-necked stilt sprawling and wailing to distract the intruder from a nest that is sticking up in the marsh, obvious as a sore thumb. But of all the birds I know, the killdeer relies most resolutely upon this transparent device. What was my surprise, then, to see this timid marsh bird stand above her eggs and fight like a tigress.

My friend Colbath called me from the porch of a ranch house to see this remarkable battle. The leader of a herd of thirty goats, grazing his way along, finally stuck his nibbling muzzle right into the bunch of grass which housed the brooding killdeer. Did she fly off as usual trailing a wing and uttering her shrill complaint? By no means: she stood her ground like a soldier, jabbing her bill repeatedly into the animal's nose while flapping her wings defiantly. She made herself so unpleasant that this particular goat turned aside. But the battle continued as one after another of the goats undertook to take a bite out of this brooding creature's bunch of grass. A second goat was turned away—a third, a fourth, a fifth. The whole herd went by while she stood on tiptoe, fighting like a game-cock, turning one goat off to the right, another to the left, splitting the herd, for a matter of fifteen minutes, until the tail end had passed. Then she settled down quietly on her nest.

To be sure that this bird was not merely a freak of nature, being for some reason exceptionally belligerent, I waited until the goats were gone and approached the nest myself. Immediately she resorted to her "crippled wing" trick, fluttering off, uttering cries of protest and despair. Later in the day, when a dog ranged near her nest, she behaved exactly as she had when I disturbed her. Colbath told me that he had seen a nesting killdeer fight a grazing steer just as she fought the goats. Thus, this bird changed her tactics to cope with the particular species which threatened her.

Therefore, paraphrasing Darwin's language, used in another connection, from these several facts we may conclude—first, that the defense of the killdeer against dog, man, or other predator is a particular instinct directed against *them* and not dependent on any general degree of caution arising from other sources of danger; and, secondly, that the killdeer's defense against grazing animals is a particular instinct directed against *them*, each defense an appropriate one: in the first instance, the threat of being intentionally eaten, and, in the other, the danger of having her eggs or young accidentally trampled upon by a big, blundering, but not malicious, beast.

Most obvious and certainly most plentiful among the birds were the egrets (American and snowy) and roseate spoonbills, with white and white-faced glossy ibises. There were many, many mottled ducks, shallow feeders, "ooching" themselves along in the thin slush, stretching their necks forward, immersing their heads for a spell and then sitting up to preen themselves. Several times I caught sight of their legs, which were a burning red.

There are no other shore birds, except a few of the small sandpipers, which feed as continuously and industriously, putting their whole souls into it, as the white ibises. The herons are leisurely— they relax their alert posture, stand awhile, take things easy—but the ibises seem driven under the lash of a terrific appetite. Here they plunged their long curved bills into the ooze fiercely, often clear up to the eyes, and so far as I could see, they captured a sizable morsel only at rare intervals.

And here I got the best view I ever had of the spoonbill's curious way of feeding. The bill is given, simultaneously, two sidewise motions while it is submerged, one by the twisting of the head and the other by the long, sidewise swing of the whole neck from side to side. It's as if you extended your arm at full length and swung it from side to side and at the same time kept twisting your hand on your wrist. You don't notice these two motions until one of the birds comes directly toward you, feeding at fairly close quarters.

A wood duck kept continuously in the range of my binoculars, rarely going behind the reeds, back and forth in my "window," as if jealous of the attention I was paying to the other birds and conscious that his "pattern" is something rivaling, in its intricacy and beauty, anything that can be found in either the flower or insect world. But I refused to be diverted. There were humbler creatures present that were to me just as interesting.

The glum, sour-dispositioned, weird, funereal black-crowned night herons were much in evidence, but not feeding. They stood aloof, humped up at the edge of the water, maybe jealous of the length and grace of the necks of the other herons, their cousins, and of those of the gracious egrets. They evidently had their young back in the bushes, for every now and then one, two, or half a dozen would fly over me, quawking their guttural and ghostly "quawks," as if all life were as dismal as theirs.

I recalled that a game warden, Tom Waddell, at Eagle Lake, had told me a story of these birds which I hope is a slander. He said he saw "with his own eyes" a night heron take a young snowy egret from its nest, deliberately hold it under the water until it drowned, and then eat it. Had a less credible witness told me this, or had it been told me even by Mr. Waddell "on information and belief," I would have put it out of my mind at once, knowing that an invidious folklore would naturally grow up about this species that has secret, night-prowling habits, utters strange sounds in the deepening twilight, generally holds itself aloof, and always appears cynical and disgusted with life. But Mr. Waddell told me that he saw this "with his own eyes"; and that, moreover, he had published the observation and had received letters from other observers who declared that they had seen this bird do exactly the same thing.

Deer, grazing along the far edge of the lake, lifted their keen noses toward me now and then; they were perhaps the only creatures there that knew a human being was about. But they were not frightened, merely a little suspicious. Three javelinas, on good terms with the ducks, were feeding in the same little stretch of water. One of the sows had two pigs following her, about the size of adult guinea pigs but of course with longer legs. These little fellows rooted around the submerged belly of the mother, throwing up their little snouts now and then in apparent bewilderment that they could find no place to nurse. But they kept on, snouts pressed against the mother's sides, occasionally lifting their heads, dumfounded that their dinner had in some way escaped.

By this time, about nine o'clock, I felt a little irritation in my nose and suddenly became aware of a haziness in the atmosphere. Gone was the crystal clarity of the early morning, and odors of marsh and woodland were dulled. Soon I realized that the air was filled with a fine dust. It was not mist, not fog, but dust—dust from five hundred, maybe a thousand, miles away, the tail end of such a storm as I had witnessed a week or two before; not silt, which is soil traveling by water, but dust, which is soil traveling by air. Two days later I was talking with a ship captain in Galveston who told me that he had met this dust storm two hundred miles out in the Gulf of Mexico. Thus ended with pedagogical emphasis the lesson and demonstration in dust begun a week or two before amid the mesquite hummocks of the plains.

A newspaper headline caught my eye—"South Plains Blanketed by Swirling Dust"—and I read the following Associated Press dispatch:

"Winds of more than 50 miles an hour scoured up topsoil to blanket the Texas South Plains with its worst sand and dust storm of the year Wednesday. Before the end of the day the winds had driven dust swirling into East Texas, dropping a haze over such big cities as Dallas and Fort Worth. Soil-filled winds darkened the South Plains sky shortly after dawn. Driving was hazardous. Chartered airlines bypassed Lubbock.

"About 4 P.M. skies began to clear as winds lessened and shifted from north-northwest to northwest. The Lubbock Weather Bureau predicted decreasing winds for Thursday with only occasional blowing dust. Large areas suffered considerable loss of topsoil. Heavy damage to wheat, already hard hit by greenbugs, was expected.

"The heaviest blowing was between Levelland, 30 miles west of Lubbock, through Whiteface and Morton to the New Mexico line. Loose sand land west and northwest of Morton was scooped up to pile a veil of soil over Cochran county seat and bring an artificial twilight from about 10:30 A.M. until late in the afternoon. In central Hale County the wind piled sand into dunes on county roads and in fence corners," et cetera.

5

COON CHARACTER

A week later I returned to my rattlebush blind on the border of Wild Hog Lake to see what changes, if any, had occurred in the wild life feeding there. On my previous visit I had made a list, and I now called the roll. Except for the wood duck, the javelinas and deer, things were going on much the same. Aside from a small rattler who uncoiled himself nearby and slid away, the only genuine surprise of the morning was the sight of six coons emerging from behind the tule, one after the other, feeding in water belly-deep right alongside the birds, and staying on especially familiar terms with the ducks.

I think these mottled ducks were stirring up from the bottom, and out of hiding, morsels of aquatic life which the coons themselves were not so well equipped to rout out—frogs, perhaps. I was reminded of the way cowbirds or Brewer's blackbirds, rusty blackbirds or even redwings cluster about the muzzle of a cow feeding in a grassy meadow in order to catch insects off guard as they are frightened out of seclusion by the grazing animal. Anyway, the coons stayed in among the feeding ducks, and neither the ducks nor the coons showed the slightest interest in each other. It was not a social gathering: they were together merely because they were interested in the same prey. I was all the more surprised to see this mutual tolerance, since I remembered how, in my youth, coons were always playing havoc in the hen house, chewing the heads off half a dozen chickens in one raid. I have never seen a pet coon, however, show any disposition to attack domestic fowl. One owner records that his coon picked up a downy chick one morning, sniffed it, and carefully put it down again.

Presently one of the coons tired of feeding. It was bedtime, and he slowly turned his curiously masked face toward the brush. His course lay within six feet of where I was seated in my clump of rattlebush, and I was interested to see if he would take alarm at my odor. He did not. He passed on by without a sniff in my direction and entered the brush to my rear. In about ten minutes another left the swamp and took identically the same route. Since there was no visible path, I decided that the coon's topography was perhaps nasal rather than visual. I watched the next one and made note of several of the weeds he brushed, now one on his right and then one on his left, and so on into the bushes. After a short interval another came out, took the same course and brushed the same weeds. One by one, spaced at about equal intervals of time, the whole coon family passed by me, brushing, so far as I could tell, the same weeds, right and left, and entering the thicket at exactly the same place.

On my way back to camp I found a coon in a trap. He was lying very still and at first I thought he was dead. But as I knelt down to get a better look at him, he rose and sniffed through the wire meshing, and turned his vicious eyes warily and wearily upon me. I later found that the Texas Game, Fish, & Oyster Commission was shipping five hundred of these animals to the West Virginia Coon Hunters' Association, Huntington, West Virginia, to be released on the range there and hunted for sport.

At first blush it seems a cruelty, if not the repudiation of an obligation, to tear these creatures from their "refuge" and throw them out to the hounds, so to speak; but what if the coon population of this Refuge were left to take its natural course? Relieved of natural enemies, the coon population would rise sharply in this land of marsh, brush, and good coon food. Some idea of how the coon will "take the country" may be gained from pioneer accounts of their dominance in certain favorable areas before the country was settled. It is recorded that Henry Andrix, a coon hunter, killed, during the fall and winter of 1876–77, around two hundred coons in Henry County, Ohio. If, as some contend, Nature should here be permitted to "take her course," there would soon be hardly a happy coon throughout the whole extent of this 47,000 acres; and the great majority of them would be sick and starving. Once man enters, there is no such thing as letting "Nature take her course." Effective protection of any one or more species immediately raises the problem of overpopulation. Perhaps the most humane way to handle this problem is to do as the Wildlife Service is doing; that is, give the animal "a chance" by restocking a range for hunters who are willing to pay for the "displaced" animals at so much per head.

I found the reactions of the raccoon to the trap extremely interesting. I am not surprised that some coon trappers and coon hunters always refer to him with great respect as *Mister* Coon. Certainly any such familiarity as the common "Br'er Rabbit" would be out of place. Trapped, his glassy eyes show no fear; only hatred and disdain. He stands ever on his dignity, if not upon an unconquerable contempt. And keep your hands away from him or he will snap off a finger. One trapper left just the end of his forefinger exposed while lifting a coon trap and suddenly felt a sharp pain. He found that the fingernail had been excised as neatly as a surgeon could have done it.

"One sunny day," says a famous naturalist, "I came upon a raccoon fast asleep in the low fork of a cypress tree. He made no objection to my lifting him from his bed, seeming not to mind so long as he could have his sleep out, and curled up in the hollow of my arm like a drowsy child."

I have tried to figure this remarkable coon out, and have come to the conclusion that he was hibernating, but curiously exposed in a low fork on a sunny morning; or he was a pet coon who had wandered off into the woods, as often happens; or he was in some way abnormal, maybe drunk from lapping about among the leavings of some moonshiner's still. Certainly he was not a Texas coon. Certainly he was unlike any wild, normal coon I have ever seen, for if there is anything that a coon in feral state resents it is familiarity, or a careless or undignified approach to his person. I have never known a naturalist, trapper, hunter, or anyone else of field experience with adult wild coons who would dare lay hand on one he found sleeping.

The coontrap used on the Refuge is simply a ·frame of two-by-fours covered with heavy wire netting. A wooden door in one end slides down its upright grooves as the coon steps on the trigger set in the floor.

The strength and adaptability of the coon's "hands" (i.e., the forefeet), driven by an intense, unrelenting purpose, account for his reputation among trappers as a "jail breaker." He is persistent rather than clever. A man in the predicament of a trapped coon, would, of course, explore every mesh in the wire and try every joint and intersection of the trap to find a weakness. He would be particularly interested in the door and try his wit and strength against it. Failing to find any encouragement, he would give up. A coon in the wild may be presumed to know nothing of traps or trap construction, but experience with him shows that he makes up for this lack of knowledge with an undaunted will to freedom, exceeding strength and endurance and inexhaustible energy. Trapped, he works as a particularly vigorous man in his plight would work who, knowing nothing of the construction of traps, fights the mechanism to the bitter end, sustained by a never flagging hope of escape. This blind kicking against the pricks sometimes gives the coon a victory. Trappers say he hasn't sense enough to quit. Certainly he never lies down short of absolute physical exhaustion.

Adversity tests character: a trapped animal quickly and clearly reveals his. One morning we found a coontrap with a neat little trench dug along three sides, about an inch and a half deep. The distance from the lowest round of meshes in the wire netting to the bottom of the trench was the exact measure of the distance from a ringed raw place on the animal's forelegs to the tip of his longest claw. With first one "hand" and then the other (he is ambidextrous) he had thrust, twisted, and squeezed these members, forcing them through each successive mesh to give his "hands" the feel of the good earth, and also to quiet his frenzied emotions with the illusion that he was indeed scratching his way to freedom. This minute moat around the wired portion of the trap made me feel a painful sympathy for the frustrated determination and futile heroism of this dumb beast's night-long efforts to get out.

Another trapped coon a few rods away had managed to enlarge a weakened mesh to accommodate his whole foreleg. Thus encouraged, he had devoted all his time to this one aperture and scratched away every bit of dirt within his reach. The dimensions, therefore, of the oval-shaped hole were set by the utmost stretch of the foreleg; and the length of the leg was the radius of the hemispherical excavation. This excavation was the physical evidence of the captive creature's night of labor and agony, struggling to be free. His legs were raw, his muzzle bloody, and, although he was limping, he was still alert and full of fight.

The coon perseveres, using tooth and claw and power of "arm" and leg, exerting every ounce of the strength in his twenty-pound body against every part of the trap that holds him, from the time the door falls until his betrayer appears; and then, my trapper friend says, if he sees you first, he feigns indifference or sleep.

On this trap line we found a steel trap (set for bobcats or wolves) sprung by a coon. The tracks showed that he had scratched under the spread jaws and set off the trigger without getting caught. It took either great intelligence to do this, or it was one chance in a thousand. I must believe that it was chance, although the trapper said this "stunt" was not unusual.

A coon caught in a steel trap occasionally twists or gnaws off a part of his leg to make his escape. More often, however, the coon works with his sharp teeth upon that portion of the leg below the point at which the steel trap has closed upon it, stripping off skin and flesh down to the very bone itself. Then the desperate creature pulls the mutilated member out by "main strength and awkwardness," as one of the trappers expressed it, scraping the big bones and detaching one or more of the digits in the process.

In the marshes one day I ran across the famous woman trapper, Mrs. Jack McCarley, who was running a trap line of fifty-seven "getters," that is, "coyote getters," that is (again), "cyanide guns"— certainly the most deadly gin so far devised by the ingenuity of man. This contraption, like all works of genuine mechanical art, is as simple as it is efficient. An iron stake, threaded to receive the "gun," is driven into the ground. The bait, "stunk up" after the manner realistically described in Chapter VI of Dobie's *Voice of the Coyote*,[1] is wound tightly around a pin or cylinder which is then screwed into the stake. The whole thing, viewed from the surface, looks like a harmless little nub of dead vegetation, perhaps the stump of a weed or shrub, about twice the size of a man's thumb.

This lady was trapping for red wolves, and we shall imagine one at a distance of half a mile catching a whiff of the intoxicating odor. Sniffing amorously along down the wind, the animal eventually approaches the perfumed snare, mouth watering and already steamed up into a reckless mood. After carefully smelling around and about, and going through those naïve, doglike preliminaries with which we are all familiar, he takes the bait in his front teeth and tugs at it. The cap, firing, sets off a charge of gunpowder, blowing a gust of cyanide gas right into the animal's mouth, down his throat, and into his lungs. Thereupon he rears on his hind legs, paws fiercely at cheek and frothing mouth, staggers, falls, flounces, grovels, dies, drooling a yellowish fluid between his unclenched teeth. On the loose dirt if it is dry, or on mud if it is wet, the stricken wolf inscribes the record of his agony in hieroglyphics as plain as print to the trapper's eye, step by step and stage by stage, all the way from courting antics and shot of cyanide to the final gasp and spasm of fire-withered lungs for air.

[1]Little, Brown and Company. Boston, 1949.

Trappers contend that this device is really more humane than the steel trap, since the period of suffering is shorter.

Occasionally, a red wolf gets a few hundred yards away before death overtakes him. Mrs. McCarley told me that, in all her long experience in trapping, only one wolf got as far as half a mile away from the "gun." It seems that this particular animal's tongue at the instant of the explosion happened to be in such position that it protected the lungs to some extent, as was evidenced by the hole blown through the center of it.

I asked her about coons. She said they fooled with the traps a good deal, were a great nuisance, but rarely got killed for their curiosity. She finds the bait cylinder loosened, sometimes completely unscrewed and lying near the stake. Such tampering, she said, is always accompanied by coon tracks. Sometimes a gun is set off without taking effect, and she explains this by the handlike grasp of the coon who, she says, standing with his face away from the bait, is able to exert an upward pull of sufficient tension to set off the exploding mechanism. The morning of our conversation, however, she had found a coon dead by an exploded gun.

But, to return to live traps; that is, to the traps which capture the animal without doing him any bodily injury: One day a trapper and I found a hole gnawed in the door with coon hair around its edges showing that the animal had squeezed himself through. It must have been a tight fit, for, although there was no skin or blood, there was plenty of hair. The trapper remembered an auger hole in this door only an inch in diameter which had served the coon as a starter. Even a nail hole, the trapper said, would sometimes inspire the coon to gnaw away the whole night long, littering the floor with little splinters, or, when the wood wouldn't splinter, with little "crumbs" of wood.

Occasionally a coon gets caught in a deertrap. This is easy: he digs out and goes on about his business. Trappers first thought to outwit the next coon so entrapped by setting the entrance of a coontrap right in the hole, hoping that the animal would walk out of one and into the other. This was man's thought, not the coon's. The next coon so imprisoned simply enlarged the hole and made his exit right alongside the open door so accommodatingly placed there to receive him. Records show, however, that there were several stupid (or lazy?) coons who walked from the big trap right into the little one.

My trapper friend devised a tilting-board trap for catching coons. The animal was supposed to explore the board, which was so adjusted that, as he passed its central balance rod, his weight would tilt the board steeply and slide him into the box below. He began catching opossums with this contrivance right off, but no coons. Still, the trapping trade doesn't consider the coon a hard animal to catch. It requires nothing like the strategy to take a coon that it does to capture a coyote. But this seems to be due not so much to lack of coon intelligence as to an excess of coon curiosity.

Against natural enemies, however, he is extremely cautious. Descending a tree, the coon nears the ground in a suspicious mood. He pauses and sniffs in this direction and that before trusting himself to the ground. He acts as if he expected some enemy to be hiding behind the tree. Holding himself upside down on a tree trunk at ground level, he is in position neither to fight nor to retreat, and he seems to know it. He can't climb the tree backward, and he is not in a posture to rear and snap. In short, he is so placed that an animal enemy would certainly win the first round, if not finish him off. So before putting himself in such a precarious position, he gives the air round about a good sniffing. This caution indicates imagination; or, if there is objection to the use of a term we should employ to explain similar precautions by a man, we may fall back on a word which does such large service in accounting for animal behavior, and call it "instinct."

I have found trapped coons usually quiet, morose, and contemptuous. They assume a stoic indifference to the calamity which has befallen them; and, unless punched through the bars, teased or otherwise molested, they raise no voice in protest or in anger.

The coon is generally a silent animal. Their vocal organs are undeveloped compared with those, say, of the coyote or of the panther.

Writers about the coon use "chirr," or "churr," to name the sound the coon makes in gentle or genial mood. This term is, of course, of imitative origin and is more generally applied to the noises made by insects.

There's no doubt about his "snorting" when in joyous or hilarious mood. The pet coon greets his master with a snort as he rushes into his embrace. Neglected, coon babies whimper, wild or tame.

"While watching for a fox squirrel one morning in a heavily timbered bottom," says Vernon Bailey, "I heard a scratching sound from an old cypress in the edge of the swamp nearby, followed by a loud splash. A young coon less than half grown had fallen from the tree into the water. At the sound the old coon and two more young ones came out of a hollow some thirty feet up in the trunk and climbed down to near the bottom of the tree. They came down the tree slowly but steadily, head first. . . . When the old coon saw the young one climb out of the water upon the tree trunk, she turned about and ascended, followed by the three young. The one that had fallen, besides being very wet, was slightly hurt, and climbed with difficulty. When halfway up he stopped on a limb to rest and began whimpering and crying. The mother had already reached the hole, but on hearing his cries turned about and climbed down to him. Taking a good hold of the back of his neck and placing him between her forelegs so that he, too, could climb, she marched him up the tree and into the hollow."[2]

The animal is said to squall if really surprised, but I have not been able to elicit this sound from any of the trapped animals with which I have experimented. But he "growls" a warning, which breaks into a vicious snarl on nearer approach of the disturbing factor.

I asked the boss trapper about noises the coon makes and he replied as follows: "The coon when in trouble, caught by the dogs or in a steel trap, for instance, makes a sound very much like the mating squeal of the red squirrel. Around the young they make a grunting noise—sorta *kunk, kunk*. I have heard them bark while in live traps with a bark somewhat like the unfinished bark of a red squirrel. As for the mating call, if they have one, I've never heard it." Other observers describe the mating call as a "long-drawn quavering

[2]North American Fauna No. 25, Biological Survey of Texas, by Vernon Bailey, Department of Agriculture, 1905, p. 194.

squall." Rowland Robinson says he has heard it "like a wild, tremulous whinny, shivering through the gloom." And again, as "a quavering cry" often mistaken for that of the screech owl. Others call it a "whicker."

What the coon can do with his forefeet, equipped as they are with mobile fingers and slightly retractile claws, is remarkable enough. He catches insects in flight; holds and nurses a bottle like a baby; acquires greater dexterity with one hand than with the other, i.e., becomes with training either right- or left-handed; can move one hand independently of the other; climbs a bare steampipe, using his tail, as a woodpecker does his, to steady the body; descends a tree headfirst, as a squirrel, reversing the hind feet; walks a rope without a balancing pole; unfastens the simpler latches to get at food; quickly learns that the hasp area is strategic and wastes no time fooling with other parts of his food box; turns over stones to grab hiding prey; searches pockets for food, or for whatever he can find, like a bold and inquisitive child; sits with back supported, holding a piece of food between his hind feet while picking morsels from it and "handing" them to his mouth; often rises on his hind legs to explore some object, but rarely stands upright merely to sniff the wind as an armadillo does; loose in a pantry, lifts covers from jars of sweets and even uncorks bottles with his facile fingers; and so on.

This pocket searching[3] comes, of course, from his method of gathering food in feral state. Watch a coon feeding at night, and you will see that he is constantly sticking his hand into holes or crevices or other hiding places under leaves or among roots to catch the creeping, crawling, or swimming things upon which he feeds. He sticks his hand in and pulls out whatever living thing he can get hold of. Every dark little cubbyhole he finds in his nightly meanderings is a grab bag, and he is a natural-born gambler. His favorite food is crayfish, and what more logical than that Nature should set a prober to catch a digger. The white ibis probes the crayfish hole with his long decurved bill; the coon, with his legs and "fingers."

[3] A pet coon will sometimes make the rifling of your pockets a more ridiculous spectacle by looking you steadily in the eye while he is doing it.

Fishing in shallow water, his method is to corner a minnow, or frog, under a stone or in the hollow of a submerged rock, thrust in his hand and pull the wriggling, squirming morsel out. He must have a firm grip to do this, for his prey, besides being lively, is slick and slimy.

If it's a dry hole, he will usually stick his nose in first. The pet coon that scared the wits out of a sleeping pup by sniffing deeply into his ear was not guilty of a practical joke, as the observer believed, but was simply yielding to a racial habit of sniffing deeply into hollows of convenient size to see if the odor therefrom justified exploration with the hand.

Alfred Henry Lewis's story of the pet coon's grasping a piece of food in a small-necked bottle and then dying of hunger because he could not pull the fistful of food out is true only up to a certain point. Like the tale of the donkey which died of hunger between two stacks of equally desirable hay, it sacrifices natural history to moral instruction: in the donkey's case, the evil of indecision; in the coon's, the penalty for greed. I have no doubt that the Lewis coon thrust his hand into the bottle; I am equally sure that he took a firm grip upon the food. I am positive that he dropped the food when he found he couldn't pull it out. My friend's pet coon amuses himself for a whole afternoon with a marble in a jug. He takes hold of it, tries to pull it out, but finding that the hand enclosing the prize is too large to be withdrawn, drops it, pulls his hand out, looks it over, thrusts it in again, tries again to extract the marble, drops it, tries again, and so on until he tires himself out. He never thinks, however, of turning the jug upside down and letting the marble roll out. That would be the solution a baby still in his crib would arrive at in a few minutes.

Give your pet coon a hollow stick or short piece of light pipe, and he will likely thrust a hand into one end and shortly stick the other hand into the other end, trying to make his fingers meet. He knows that he hasn't completely explored the hollow until one hand touches the other. He will "wear" this hollow object, as a lady wears her muff. A story is told, perhaps apocryphal, of the antics of a pet coon when he was given a pipe with a mouse in it. The piece of pipe was just a bit too long to permit his touching his hands together inside; and in the space between his hands the mouse took refuge. This tantalizing situation finally infuriated him as much as it must have frightened the mouse. He worried with the problem a long time, the story goes, but solved it at last by putting the pipe down, inserting his nose in one end while holding a hand over the other, snuffing vigorously, meantime, until the frantic mouse took refuge in his hand.

His habit of washing food gives the Latin name to the species, *lotor*, "the washer." Audubon says he never saw his pet coon wash his food, but the great naturalist was nodding or had charge of an abnormal animal. I have found only one other owner of a coon who says his pet didn't wash his food. Both laboratory experimenters and naturalists generally agree that it is an almost universal habit of coons to wash their food if water is available; and, if not, to give it a token washing by rubbing it over in their hands. The coon's common name in German is "Wash Bear"; and a Spanish local name for him in Venezuela means "Fox, Wash Thy Hand."

There are various speculations regarding the origin of this habit. Ernest Thompson Seton suggests that he washes his food because it is dirty. I think it is not unusual for any land animal capturing muddy prey to wash it if water is handy, much as a dog shakes dirt off his meat, or as a grackle soaks a crust of bread he finds too hard to swallow. This bird will fly a hundred yards or so to water with a piece of hard toast, dip it in the water until it is softened, and then swallow it. I myself saw a whooping crane take a dirty piece of bread from the edge of a pool of muddy water, walk several feet to a pool of clear water and swing the morsel back and forth therein several times before gulping it down. It is worth noting that no one has ever reported seeing a coon wash a bird before eating it.

Nearly all the coon's names come from some use he makes of his hands, which goes to prove that this member has most impressed his human observers. Our name for him, "raccoon," is of Algonquian origin in eastern Virginia, spelled "ara'kun" from "arakunem" meaning, "he scratches with his hands." John Smith, reporting from Virginia, spelled it "aroghcun." The Indians of New England called the

81

coon a "scratcher" and an "oyster eater"; and Indian folklore contains many tales of the animal's cleverness with his hands.

"The little wailing lemur," with which Tennyson starts to trace the ascent of man, also has hands made up of efficient fingers and opposable thumbs. A fanciful person might amuse himself in an idle moment by predicting a similar evolution based on the coon's *four* hands, and by trying to support his phony hypothesis with specious analogies. Pursuing his speculation, he would stumble hardest against the barrier of speech, which has played so important a role in human evolution that behaviorists often contend seriously that we think not with the brain but with the vocal organs. Here certainly our evolving coon meets a roadblock, for he doesn't chatter and grimace and gesture as the humblest monkey does. Fancy's self cannot trace a pattern in the coon's grunts, growls, snorts, squalls, and whickers bearing the slightest resemblance to the primate's flood of patter of almost human syllables.

The next roadblock nearly as difficult to negotiate is the unfortunate disposition of the weight of the coon's body, which compels him to remain four-footed. And is it not difficult to admit (even for the sake of argument) that so delicate an instrument as the human hand can ever develop so long as it has to serve the crass purposes of transportation?

Ho-hum! I fear the coon will continue to look down instead of up, remain quadruped instead of biped, a grunter not a talker, on and on to the last syllable of recorded time, or such a matter.

The coon is a terrific fighter. John Burroughs says that he is probably the most courageous creature among our familiar wild animals, and will always whip a dog of his own size and weight. This is a conservative statement. I have seen a coon whip three dogs at once, each of which was heavier than he. "Twenty-five pounds of coon," an old coon hunter told me, "will whip a hundred pounds of dog." Somewhere between Burroughs's estimate and that of the coon hunter, the coon and dog will generally strike a balance. There are, of course, individual coons and individual dogs which upset any generalization concerning the relative fighting ability of the two species.

And much depends upon whether the fight is a land or water engagement. The coon, able to submerge longer, occasionally drowns a dog twice his weight. The coon-dog fight was a favorite pioneer spectacle, and is still a rustic sport of great popularity, as is evidenced by the numerous coon hunters' associations scattered throughout the entire range of country inhabited by this animal. The coon's courage (or lack of judgment, or ungovernable temper) occasionally plunges him into a struggle against larger animals, including man. There is a case on record in which a coon scored a victory over an able-bodied man, not only once, but twice in a fair fight.

In the small town of Morden, Manitoba, a man purchased a young coon as a pet for his son, and brought him to the hotel where he lived. It was a friendly animal and became a favorite with the hotel guests and with townspeople. However, one man, a porter named Hewitt, started a feud with this coon by beating him with a broomstick while he was chained. Ever afterward the animal plainly showed resentment whenever the odor of Hewitt greeted his nostrils—growling, showing his teeth, and otherwise giving evidence of a vengeful memory of that beating administered at a time when he could not defend himself. He apparently realized that the man had taken an unfair advantage of him. Hewitt resented the growling and the mutual antagonism gradually became deadly.

One day the coon got loose, rambled over the village, greeting his friends and visiting about, eventually ambling back to the hotel, where he was admitted by a guest to the barroom. The record states that he went around sniffing legs and making "coony" investigations of dark corners for some little time. Finally he jumped up on a chair, looked out the window, "and," the court record says, "otherwise conducted itself in a becoming manner."

Fate decreed that just as the creature coiled himself up, carefully laying his tail over his eyes to darken the room, as is the coon custom in napping, who should enter the barroom but his enemy, Hewitt,

the porter. One sniff of the polluted air was enough for him to identify its source, "and," as the bartender on the witness stand expressed
it, "the coon seemed to think that it was a good time to get even and
he made for Hewitt." As the animal approached, teeth bared, snarl-
ing, and each particular hair standing on end, Hewitt kicked, the
coon dodged, and the man fell flat on his back, as the kicking come-
dian in a slapstick movie falls from the very violence of the action.
Sinking his teeth into the fleshy part of the man's leg, the coon held
on like a bulldog. Hewitt wound his legs about his assailant, and
called loudly for someone to come quick and kill the coon with an
ax, "but," says the restrained legal account of the affray, "those present hesitated to inflict the extreme penalty." Instead, an onlooker
produced a poker, inserted it under the coon's collar and, twisting,
gradually choked the enraged animal loose. Meantime, Hewitt had
received another painful bite on top of one of his fingers.

The coon was "dumped outdoors," and everyone thought the incident closed, especially as he had been choked to insensibility. Later
investigation showed that he shortly recovered consciousness,
skirted the building, and entered the yard adjacent to his master's
quarters. It happened that the back door of Hewitt's shop opened
into this enclosure where the coon was now nursing his wrath to
keep it warm. Hewitt, meantime, had returned through the lobby to
his shop, and was treating his wounds when he heard a noise at his
back door. He opened it and in walked the still-belligerent coon. In
pulling his legs back out of reach of the growling animal, Hewitt fell
heavily against the door, slamming it to, so that the small shop now
became the arena for a finish fight. Hewitt first grabbed his assailant
with both hands, by the hair and skin of his cheeks, held his head to
the floor, attempting to crush the skull with his knee; but the coon
managed, after fifteen or twenty minutes of hard fighting, to get the
man's thumb between his teeth and crush it to a pulp. Again Hewitt
yelled for the help of his own species. This time a guest in the hotel
called a butcher, who killed the coon with his meat ax.

Dr. Parr treated the survivor, who, "for a period of about three
months was unable to do any work in connection with his business."
The thumb was saved, but the "first joint practically disappeared,"

and the injury was considered a "permanent disability" by the court, which assessed damages against the coon's master in the sum of five hundred dollars and costs (Andrew v. Kilgour, *Manitoba Law Review*, 19: 550).[4]

It is another proof (if one were needed) of the anthropocentrism of our legal system that no issue is made of whether or not the coon's actions might not have justification, which, in turn, should influence the amount of damages assessed against the defendant. The legal assumption seems to be that the coon had no right to attack the man, no matter what the man had done to the coon. Hewitt had beaten this animal unmercifully with a broomstick while he was chained. At first opportunity the coon evened the score, attacking, at peril to his life, a physically superior animal six or seven times his own weight.

[4]This case is digested humorously in *American Law Review*, 44:756–58, S. 1910, under title "Raccoon a Ferocious Animal—a Manitoba Roughhouse."

The plaintiff tried to blacken the character of this particular coon by digging up the fact that he bit a man when he was first captured. The defense was able to show that the handler was at the moment pulling the coon's tail. Plaintiff next tried to establish viciousness by testimony showing that the coon had bitten his master. The defense in rebuttal proved that the bites were in play, even affectionate, and that the pressure which brought blood a time or two was accidental. The plaintiff was thus attempting to show *scienter*, i.e., knowledge on the part of the master that he owned a dangerous pet. The court, in ruling out this plea, cleared the character of the coon from aspersions thus cast upon it.

It seems that in cases of this kind, the law recognizes two distinct classes of animals: (1) lions, tigers, bears, etc.; and (2) sheep, horses, oxen, dogs, etc. The court ruled the coon a small carnivore belonging to that section of animals of the order which contains bears, weasels, badgers, etc., citing the *Encyclopaedia Britannica* as its authority. [Burroughs called the coon "that brief summary of a bear."] Sir Matthew Hale is quoted: "Although he [the master] have no particular notice that he did any such thing before, yet if it be a beast that is *ferae naturae*, as a lion, a bear, a wolf, yea an ape or monkey, if he get loose and do harm to any person, the owner is liable to an action for damages, and so I knew it adjudged in Andrew Baker's case, whose child was bit by a monkey, that broke his chain and got loose." (*Hale's Pleas to the Crown*, Vol. I, p. 430.)

Also, if a domestic animal, known to be vicious (*scienter*), injures someone, the owner is liable.

In the case of Hewitt and the coon, Judge Metcalfe indulges in this bit of sound natural history: "A wild animal may become tame and kind. Its nature may sleep for a time, but it may also wake up and, if the animal has lost its fear of mankind, it is undoubtedly more dangerous. There is no doubt that this raccoon was capable of causing damage. The results speak eloquently as to that."

Call revenge a low motive if you will; it is one highly respected among men. Warriors enter battle with vengeful cries on their lips, and, dying, win monuments of brass and the impassioned encomiums of orators and poets. Military leaders on eve of battle rehearse to their men the outrages committed upon "our peace-loving people" by the enemy. Between halves in the mimic war of football, the coach in the locker room incites the heroes to revenge. Of course, there is another type of human hero, but no claim is made for the coon to any of the higher martyrdoms.

Still, I hear the oral pleas of defense attorneys insinuating this very issue into the case; and judge or jury, if human, could not but be influenced by the heroism of the little animal and by the manifest justice of his cause. It is certainly not in contempt of court to suggest that the comparatively small sum assessed as damages is perhaps due to the fact that the judge felt in his heart that really Hewitt "got what was coming to him."

Trapped coons are held day after day on the Refuge until a sufficient number have been accumulated to justify shipment—say, fifteen or twenty. They are placed in a large, cagelike affair with meshed wire sides and top, set up on a solid wooden floor. Misery loves company and comparatively few fights occur among the prisoners. They drowse away the hours. I wanted to find out what fate probably had in store for these victims, so I directed an inquiry to Mr. Hays Honaker, Route ⚹2, Huntington, West Virginia, Secretary of the Federated Coon Clubs of West Virginia, to whom shipment of the animals was then being made. He sent along with an informative reply a copy of the Federation's *Field Trial Hand Book and Directory*. From this pamphlet I learned that the organization is made up of sixteen different coon hunters' associations, the majority of them formed on a county basis. Each club has a President, Secretary, Treasurer, and an "F C C Director," and the proem reads:

The better than three thousand members of this
Federation, composed of the following sixteen
clubs, wish the field trial men and women larger,
cleaner and better field trials.

Then follow thirty-eight rules by which field trials held under the auspices of the Federation shall be conducted. The first rule gave me a sympathetic shiver for the extradited Texas coon: "The drag shall be composed of live-coon or coon-grease scent." If you know that the length of a "drag" is a couple of miles or so over rough country, you can imagine the shreds and tatters of a coon which would reach the end of the trail. A sack filled with litter from a coon kennel serves the purpose very well, is more humane, and is ordinarily used in the eastern states. Rule nine provides that a coon, other than the coon used in laying trails, will be placed high up in the judge tree, etc. This animal is caged and "shall be concealed as much as possible with natural foliage." The whole intent of the rules is, as it should be, to give each dog entered an equal opportunity to demonstrate the superiority of his nose by trailing the animal over the course, which at its close passes "through a line of flags," and indicating to the satisfaction of the judges that he knows that the coon is actually in the tree.

Many of the rules have to do with emergencies which may arise in connection with the dogs themselves. For instance, what shall be done in case of a fight, the barring of dogs known to be unduly quarrelsome, the banishing from the grounds of females in season, so that all entries may give undivided attention to the coon, ruling out shouts of encouragement to any dog, and, finally, that all dogs "must be hauled to the starting post by conveyance furnished by the management."

The fact that the phrase "judges decision shall be final" occurs several times, and is finally printed as rule thirty-six in capital letters, implies that disputes occur among the human beings as well as among the dogs.

I found Mr. Honaker a genial, pleasant correspondent, with a flair for picturesque phrases. It seems that the reason for forming coon clubs is that "the western part of the state [West Virginia] is rolling hills, mostly thickly settled, and the raccoons have been so depleted as to be a rarity in large sections. . . . The coon hunters got tired of this and banded together and formed their own organization to fight for their rights. The organization is recognized by our game commission as the strongest and best organized club in the state. . . . The fox hunters are with us; in fact we have no opposition to date, and can cope with it if it comes. . . . Farmers are cooperative and the majority will protect our coon, and are continually asking us to release them on their farms. . . . I have known them [i.e., the farmers] to carry coons' corn to the den as well as a chicken now and then."

It was quite a satisfaction, as I saw the trucks loaded with Texas coons, to know that a genuine West Virginia hospitality awaited them at the end of their long journey.

Mr. Honaker tells me that his club alone has released four hundred coons (as of May 23, 1949), and that neighboring clubs have released hundreds more. "In fact, we are now in the market for one to two thousand coons a year."

It will please the professional Texan to be told that "Texas coon differ from our native coon by being longer nosed and longer legged. Our native coon have a stumpy face and short legs, consequently they don't give us the long chase we require. Texas coon have been known to run if necessary several hours, and to be very tricky in eluding the dogs. They seem to adapt themselves here easily. . . . We receive them poor as fence rails; but, after being released several months, they are very fat and saucy, and give a good account of themselves in a fight. They also take to water more than our coon." So, even in the production of a sharp-nosed, long-legged, long-winded, tough-fighting, and aquatic coon, Texas seems to lead the nation.

I was further pleased to note that the coons with which I had become personally acquainted were not released immediately in their weakened condition to become the sport of West Virginia dogs. On the contrary, Mr. Honaker assures me that they are not released until they are fattened on corn and the coon-hunting season has closed. Thus the Texas coon is given six to nine months with which to familiarize himself with the new terrain, devise escape strategy, "select his home, raise a family, and know his way around before the hunting season"; and, adds Mr. Honaker thriftily, "that way we get three or four coon for each one we invest in." It will further satisfy the "Texas spirit" to know that a Texas coast coon has no difficulty in ousting a West Virginia fox from his den and appropriating the same to his own use and behoof.

It is evidence of the true sportsmanship spirit infusing the FCC that a "workshop" educational course is provided the newcomers before subjecting them to the grisly business of staying out of reach of the fangs of trained West Virginia coon dogs.

Mr. Honaker states, rather apologetically, that a few coon must be killed in old-fashioned coon hunts in order that the dogs not lose interest in the field trials. I have participated in coon hunts and also observed field trials. I know very well that the dogs know the field trial is a faked-up affair and simulate interest in it just to please their masters, as we feign interest in a child's game that the child may get more pleasure from it. Really, a coon dog who couldn't tell the difference between a coon trail and the trail of a man dragging a live coon or a bag of coon litter or coon grease should be relegated to chasing rabbits or nosing about trashpiles for opossums. So, to maintain dog interest, the FCC permits hunting, but has established a limit of ten coons per man per season.

"Before the season opens," says Mr. Honaker, "we chase them and tree them to educate them, sometimes even shaking them out for another chase [holding the dogs until the coon has a good start]. This makes the coon wiser and when the season opens he stays pretty close to home."

This business of educating a game species to make the taking of it more difficult is good not only for the animal but for the sport. It is the humane reverse of the practice of taming deer to make them easy for the decadent sportsman. Fox hunters with whom I have associated classify foxes as "ten-minute," "half-hour," "hour-and-a-half" foxes—meaning that a "ten-minute" fox will run only ten minutes before he takes to a tree. The "hour" fox runs sixty minutes, and so on. They tell me that a fox's classification may be changed by giving him the "toothless dog treatment." The short-term fox is shaken out of the tree into the gums of a toothless old hound who wools him about, the other dogs being tied while the lesson is in progress. This treatment, so fox hunters tell me, often converts a "ten-minute" fox into one that does not take to a tree so readily.

The transfer of the Texas boar coon to a brand-new habitat in West Virginia does not interfere with his family life to any great extent. He maintains his polygamic habits, traveling from female to female on a wide round. "I have found out," says Mr. Honaker, "that a mature male coon travels a circuit maybe fifteen or more miles long. He knows where every female shacks up on his circuit, and it may take him a week or ten days to complete his milk route. . . . A yearling female may or may not breed her first year. If she does, it is only one or two and they may not survive. The male is not capable of reproduction until he is past three years old."

Although the Texas coon is of a different race than the West Virginia coon,[5] there are no race conflicts occasioned by this intrusion. The two races get along. No segregation occurs. All seems to be harmony and good will except, of course, for those individual differences over one thing or another which bring on a few snarls of displeasure and even fights common to all the animal world. There is no human attempt at exterminating each other or endeavor on the part of one to enslave the other, or even to reduce to milder forms of subservience. The adjustment which ensues is more in accord with what we know of protoanthropoid communities before we became human—all too human.

Mr. Honaker ends on an optimistic note: "After we get a reserve built up and all the terrain stocked, we expect to let nature take a hand and harvest only the surplus. We will then build a club house and set down to really enjoy life."

[5]Specimens of raccoons from as far down the Texas coast as the Aransas Wildlife Refuge differ from the typical *lotor* of northeast United States, according to Mr. Vernon Bailey. "The slightly larger size, wider muzzle and usually heavier dentition show a tendency toward *mexicanus* into which it grades to the west."

6 CAMP IN THE BRUSH

On this trip to the coast I left the plains, coming down off the cap rock into the limestone country of wide valleys and scattered buttes; then to thicker greener hills and across a brief prairie, at lower and lower levels, onto the edge of the Karánkaway Country near where these stalwart savages went yearly to their "feast of the tunas," as the doughty and rarely discouraged traveler, Cabeza de Vaca, called it. Yearly, patiently, in his capacity as Medicine Man Extraordinary, he plodded along with his savage captors from the vicinity of a bay now called Matagorda, to or near the present site of Alice, Texas, for their annual gorging on prickly pear apples. He records that it was on the seventh annual festival-excursion that he managed his escape and began his triumphal trek clear across the continent to the Gulf of Lower California in the Year of Our Lord 1534.

I camped in a far corner of the R. J. Dobie Ranch some twenty-five miles north of Alice, Texas, in the heart of the "Brush Country."[1] The "brush" is scrubby, rarely more than fifteen feet high, thorny, skinny-leaved, as semiarid plants must become in the intense sunlight of long days. Old-timers tell me that this country was practically all prairie when their fathers and fathers' fathers occupied the land.

It was during the early seventies of the last century that G. C. Duncan, pioneer cattleman, drove many herds of mules in from Mexico for the Texas market. His course lay from Wharton to Kingsville and from there straight on across the Rio Grande, returning by the same route. His son, I. V. Duncan of Eagle Lake, tells me that his father declared there was not at that time a bush between Wharton and the Mexican border. In the early seventies it was all grassland; now it is the brushiest of the Brush Country. The plains between the Nueces River and the Rio Grande were once known as "Wild Horse Desert," indicating an absence of brush.

W. L. Bray, in the *Botanical Gazette*, August 1901,[2] says the outlines of the Gulf Strip are approximately indicated in Texas by the range of the *Vachellia* (*Acacia*) *farnesiana* (huisache) and *Parkinsonia aculeata* (retama); and Bailey adds *Daubentonia longifolia*

[1] A large section of southwest Texas appears on the physiographer's map as "the Rio Grande Plain or Embayment," and that part of it most densely covered with shrubs, small trees, tangled vines, cactus, and other thorny growths has come in the last fifty years to be called the "Brush Country." Only remnants of the vast prairies described by early explorers remain. Spotted here and there in the brush, one finds now and then open spaces where bull nettles, thistles, and other weeds betray the site of an old homestead or a worn-out field, long since abandoned. Little cultivation persists. The Brush Country is given over largely to ranching interests.

But not altogether. Let no one suppose that the "Brush Country" is all brush. Maqui, or chaparral, is merely its predominating feature. There are oases of cultivation, about seven hundred farms, aggregating 72,000 acres in Live Oak County in which I was camped, including 3,000 acres under irrigation. There are areas of black land—black, waxy, and gray sandy soils under plow which, taken along with the stock-raising industry, support a vigorous population of about nine to the square mile, with average annual income of around five million dollars. Other counties in the "brush" of the Rio Grande Plain are not all brush, either.

[2] Quoted by Vernon Bailey, North American Fauna No. 25, Biological Survey of Texas, U.S. Department of Agriculture, Washington, D.C., 1905.

and *Lantana camara.* All of these plants have penetrated far into central Texas since the Bray-Bailey time, that is, within the past fifty years.

Indeed, the brush delayed its invasion until long after the aborigines were dispossessed and the white man and his multiplying herds had skinned the prairies of their native grasses.

Here thrives the huisache (pronounced wee-satch). The first record of this invader lives in an anecdote of the Dougherty family of Beeville, whose forebears were pioneering folk of the last century. About seventy years ago Jim Dougherty's father came to his home at San Patricio, on the Nueces River, about dinnertime one day, with an account of "the most beautiful blooming shrub I have ever seen." That afternoon he hitched up his buggy and took Mrs. Dougherty and the children ten miles up the river to see it.

The newcomer, *Acacia farnesiana* (herald of a terrible horde at its heels), was in full bloom, thus entering Texas history in the gorgeous panoply of early spring. However, Albert S. Gatschet[3] says the blankets of the Karánkaways were fastened with "guisache" thorns. If the identification was correct, there was at least an advance guard of this invader already in the Karánkaway Country by 1840; or maybe the thorn was imported as an article of commerce with more southerly tribes.

It is a shrub or small tree distinguished among its companions of the brush for its symmetrical crown and its dark-green, delicate ferny foliage, but most of all for its feathery clusters of odorous, globular blossoms, golden as good Jersey butter. The spherical bloom is really compacted of many tubular flowers whose pale, protruding stamens, seen closely in a good light, produce a fuzzy effect, but, in semidarkness, give an illusion of glow, or aura, as in medieval paintings of the head of Jesus, as if these tender filaments were truly and in fact radiating beams of light. Literally thousands of these fuzzy globules occur on a single tree spaced so evenly throughout its whole extent as to suggest, in twilight, Christmas dec-

[3] Archaeological and Ethnological Papers, Peabody Museum, Harvard University, Vol. I, No. 2. Cambridge, Mass., 1891, p. 61.

orations. I have found this remarkable vegetable effulgence in the seclusion of dense and tangled chaparral, surprising it, so to speak, in its finest hour; and it is all the more memorable as a momentary apparition: sudden, evanescent, a brief candle enjoying its little period of unchallenged triumph over the slumlike darkness and degradation of the brush-covered hillside.

It is occasionally a winter bloomer (December to February), and so beekeepers do not share the ranchman's detestation of it, for the honey made from its nectar, available in early spring, is famed throughout the country. On a warm, bee-enticing day of February, I have seen these tender balls of bloom bent down on their flexible peduncles and trembling under the rude, six-legged embrace of the ravaging and voluptuous bee, avid, after winter's dearth, for the first nectar of the season, while the leaves of the shrub still remained sealed in their cautious buds.

Rare seventy years ago, it is now one of the commonest shrubs of the region, a great nuisance and marked for slaughter, unless, indeed, one is willing to put up with 358 days of annoyance for the sake of one week of glory. To tolerate it on that account is a luxury only beekeepers and the cultured opulent can afford.

No animal will eat it except some gaunt herbivore. In early youth, for fear a hungry browser may be tempted to take a bite of its bitter foliage, it arms itself with the most terrific thorns of the desert, bristling savagely like an enraged porcupine. Only a few of the more devilish species of cactus can produce anything as ominous. Conspicuous against the leaves, these bright gray thorns of the young huisache, thick and threatening on branch and twig, extend their needle points to cover practically every angle of approach. Leathery the lip of the browser who braves this hedgehog defense to nibble at a bitter leaf. As the plant grows up, the thorns become fewer, greener, and better concealed, since the leaves themselves, now toughened and increased in pungency, offer a sufficient defense; but even then it is ready and vicious as a viper to punish the too nosy animal for any undue familiarity. Nature chooses here a curious economy, fortifying the leaf with a new defense as she diminishes the number and threatening character of the thorns.

Upward and onward from Mexico across the Rio Grande and north far into the interior of Texas, the Queen of the Brush Country continues its march, held in check only by occasional freezes. The severe winter of 1948–49, for instance, killed huisache all the way from central Texas (its present northern limit) to the Texas coast south, and on down the coast almost to the mouth of the Rio Grande.

But the roots of the frozen huisache, like those of the retama, send up sprouts. An old schoolteacher named Sutherland, who lived at Bluntzer in Nueces County, said to a friend of mine: "I have seen the huisache combat the mesquite and take its land, and I have seen the retama make the huisache retreat."

As a lawn tree or as highway decoration it offers, sometime in late winter or early spring, its globes of golden bloom, and for one supreme moment in the year eclipses all other vegetation in sheer beauty, as a goddess touching earth for just a little while, but keeping her effulgent wings outspread to take off at once, lighting only momentarily with her presence the gloom of her mortal associates. Ranchmen, being rather of this world, if not, indeed, entirely materialistic, abominate it. The nature lover grows tender, remembering its one week of ecstasy, as a lover remembers a mistress far too difficult to endure except in one of her rare floral moods.

I was camped solo, bedded down between two live oaks whose top branches touched and tangled; and, as I stretched out that night, fitting my back, as best I could, to the hollows and protuberances of the ground, I looked upward at "a starred and leafy sky." The lazy creaking of a nearby windmill and the parauque's *ker-whee-you* out in the bushes soon put me to sleep. The bird was still going on when I awoke near daylight, but politely ceased as a cardinal began. Then a mourning dove chimed in with a series of "coos" which an ancient Persian poet interprets as "Where? Where? Where?"—onomatopoetic in Persian, but not in English.

Our own Spanish-Americans of the Southwest have contributed the quaintest version of what the turtledove is really trying to make clear. The Texas-Mexican cowboy says that the mourning dove was anciently a little Indian girl who fell in love with a shepherd, but the ungrateful fellow deserted her to follow his herds and soon found another sweetheart. The little Indian girl grew very sad and wept many months for her faithless lover until the Great Spirit, taking pity on her, changed her into a dove. The memory of her "pastor" still troubles her heart; so, says Mrs. Jovita Gonzáles de Mireles,[4] her lament is easily understood by anyone who lends an attentive and sympathetic ear:

Cu-cu cu-cu [Coo-coo coo-coo].
¿Qué quieres, pastor [What do you want, shepherd lad]?
Comer comas, comer comas [I want to eat comas, eat comas].
Adiós, pastor. Adiós, pastor [Good-by, shepherd lad. Good-by, shepherd lad].

("Comas" is a small berry growing on a shrublike tree.) Spanish on the tongue of a native lends itself to the mood of melancholy; and Mrs. Gonzáles's little fable enriches for me the plaint of this most musical of mourners.

I lay there, as Hudson said he did many a time and oft, content "to contemplate the sky and the earth wet with dew," tasting the air to which aromatic shrubs in the moist darkness had imparted (oh, so faintly!) their delicious body odors, breathing by long-drawn, deep inhalations, "like the aspiration for eternal life."

I did not anywhere near equal Roger Tory Peterson's lying abed record of distinguishing the songs and calls of forty-two different species of birds, but I heard a good many. Now the master melodist finds his voice. Beginning in a low, almost apologetic strain, he becomes presently vociferous, irritated by hearing certain ineffectual chirpings in the brush. His mood changes, and in a tone of angry protest I heard him make this plain announcement:

"Ladies and gentlemen, there has been so much sentimental nonsense repeated by people who should know better to the effect that I take, steal, confiscate, and appropriate to my own use the compositions of other birds, even to the screaming of the raucous and abominable blue jay—there has been so much of this twaddle, and from

---

[4]*Folk-Lore of the Texas-Mexican Vaquero,* Publications of the Texas Folk-Lore Society, Number VI, 1927, p. 8.

responsible sources, it seems to me necessary to announce concerning this morning's program that any resemblance you fancy you hear in any part of it to the twitters, squawks, squeaks, trills, pipings or other vocal efforts of any alleged songster, living or dead, is purely coincidental."

With this declaration the mocker shed his ill humor and resumed the prelude, soft and tentative. Soon a wild turkey began gobbling, but not for long. As the world was assured of a clear sunrise, the mockingbird, like the imperious sun itself driving the stars from the sky, took over in this world of Brush Country melody. One mocker after another entered the lists, until the brush thrilled with their morning raptures. I lay there longer than I should have, listening, for there are other things to experience in this jungle solitude besides the competitions of these Meistersinger.

The sun also brought the "crow" of the rain crow; not the slow, subdued utterance said to be a sure prediction of bad weather, but his long series of "clucks" ending in a reduced tempo, *keow, keow, keow*, or the Virginia pronunciation of cow, i.e., *kyow*. It's a call not so nightlike as that of the parauque, nor nearly so much as the call of any owl, and still there is nothing of the joy of morning in it. There's a mixture of night and day, or, rather, a transition of night to day in the yellow-billed cuckoo's "song," as some of the bird listeners flatter him by calling it.

The earliest pipe of half-awakened birds in a new location always gives me a thrill. After a few mornings you begin to make a mental list of them in the order of their occurrence, and unless you are a late sleeper, you soon learn to expect *the* early bird, not the one in the proverb with the still earlier worm in his bill, but the singer who yields first to the inspiration of the new day.

The listing of bird songs in the order they occur from dawn to daylight and from daylight to sunrise is one of the best—that is, one of the most conscience-satisfying—excuses I have ever found for delaying that dingiest period in every camper's day which, you remember, is the interval sandwiched in between the moment when you kick off the covers and that in which you seat your-

97

self on a smooth log with a steaming cup of coffee in your hand.

My ancestry is of the Old South, and the one tradition of that culture which has survived in me the slings and arrows of outrageous fortune concerns the serving of morning coffee. I like my coffee in bed. I never get it there except while camping out, and then but rarely, for I hardly ever include a thermos bottle in my camping kit. I am against these newfangled gadgets on principle, and my courage is high during the packing to be off, so even when I think of it, I scornfully refuse it a place, only to repent this hasty heroism in the drowsy leisure of the early morning hours.

It is surprising how changes in the weather may affect the order of bird songs. One July I made this entry: "Summer showers always render the screech owl vocal. He will precede the redbird, with the mocker third. But is it fair to enter a night bird in this competition? I think not." So I scratched the little owl off my list. For the same reason I dismissed the chuck-will's-widow, and even considered excluding the mockingbird, who is as apt to greet the sinking moon as the rising sun. But in the dark of the moon he rarely sings at night, and because he has always had preferential treatment—any time, anywhere—I left him on. At home I listed martins, but the fact that the martin sings in his sleep caused me to put a large question mark beside his name. Austin, Texas, is an unsatisfactory place anyway for this idle enterprise, because the tower lights diffuse a glow over the city that any light-sleeping bird, or one shifting position and half awake, might mistake for the break of day. Florence Page Jaques[5] says that the violet-green swallow "is the only bird I ever heard of to serenade its beloved by late starlight." Mockers are thus romantic.

The weather, however, is a constantly unconstant factor. Another entry in my notebook says: "In the long hot spell [drouthy, too] of the fall of 1947, there was a drop of about five or six degrees in temperature on the night of October 18, and at 6 A.M. on the nineteenth, the thermometer stood at 70. Until this date, since September 15, the only early morning singer was the mocker, who began about daybreak. This morning, however [Oct. 19], the Carolina wren began

[5]*Canadian Spring*, Harper & Brothers, New York and London, 1947, p. 101.

at seven o'clock and sang continuously. At first he was a bit husky, so much so that my wife mistook him for another bird; but after an hour's vocal exercise, the ring in his voice returned, and his song was unmistakable." Again at the end of the droughty summer of 1948 (not even a shower for months), I noted in October that the mocker was the only bird singing in the early morning, that is, by daylight.

Maxim Gorky was addicted to this early morning diversion. "Robin redbreast now wakes up," he notes. "He stands shaking on his thin legs and also sings a song of quiet joy. Birds know better than humans how nice it is to be alive on earth. And the robin is always the first bird to greet the sun. In far away cold Russia the robin is called the dawn-bird, because the colors on his breast have the color of dawn."

Crows caw and ravens croak. Both are early risers, but I refuse to enter them in my competition.

I am indebted to my friend J. Frank Dobie, himself addicted to this lying-abed diversion, for the following note on the early morning activities of crows in New Jersey by Samuel N. Rhoads, entitled "Crow Roosts and Roosting Crows," published (1886) in the *American Naturalist:*

The programme of dispersion from the roost in the morning to their feeding grounds is as follows:
After an hour's babel (for such verily is the seeming confusion of tongues) a few Crows essay to take leave, but as soon as this folly is observed it literally "brings down the house," and when one imagines the simultaneous shout of 20 acres of Crows, one may not wonder that "the house" is fully able to bring down the Crows. The few [uprisen] Crows resume their perches and comparative quiet is restored.
Numerous attempts are thus made with a like result until nearly sunrise, when detachments of 500 to 1000 successively take wing amid the wildest enthusiasm, . . . in many lines of flight. . . .
Ere the sun looks out upon the scene a silence almost oppressive broods over field and woodland, and to one who so recently beheld this departure, a scattered remnant of the mighty host only serves to heighten the feeling of contrasted desolation."[6]

[6]Quoted in *The Common Crow of the United States,* by Walter B. Barrows and E. A. Schwarz, Bulletin No. 6, U.S. Department of Agriculture, Washington, D.C., 1895, pp. 16–17.

"The hillside's dew-pearled." Most flowers come out of the darkness rested and freshened by a bath in the spring night's distillations. All of them around my camp were awake long before I got up, even the late-rising evening primroses and Lesquerella—all except the "sleepy daisy," which was still twisted up in a profound slumber. Another folk name for this "Margarita" of the Mexicans (*Aphanostephus skirrobasis*) is "Lazy Daisy," which I like better than the name "Sleepy Daisy," for the drowsy jingle, and because it imputes justly a little blame to the slugabed who rarely comes alive before noon, and never opens its eyes throughout a rainy day. Really, the until-noon sleeper is not merely sleepy, but lazy; and "Lazy Daisy" is my name for her, although she is as lovely as a miniature Shasta when fully awake.

A steer grazing nearby introduced a sour note into my early morning symphony by stepping into a bunch of lantana, and immediately my nose was affronted with its indignant protest. Although one of the more decorative shrubs hereabouts, it has that curious defense: a bad breath. Armed with no thorns, as many of its associates are, it effuses into the nostrils of the threatening browser an odor which generally turns him away in disgust. Step on it and its fumes repel you. If a fore wheel crushes a clump, your car is filled with a stinking remonstrance. I know of no speedier natural odor, except the skunk's, which outruns any breeze.

I watched the splendid shafts from the rising sun find their way through the heavy foliage of undergrowths encircling my bed. A leaf in shadow would suddenly glow, another darken, as a ray from afar found its mark, or was shut off by some obstruction. Occasionally the wind stirred, favoring a new group of night-hungry leaves with a taste of sunlight; and, steadily as the rolling eastward of the happy earth altered their angle of incidence, there was a more general sharing in the photosynthesis, source of all life as we know it. As these searching rays found new apertures and neglected leaf surfaces to bless, I kept thinking of them as "filtering through the leaves," a literary cliché I have picked up from too much reading of second-rate writers or careless first-rate ones. It is a false figure of speech. What is it you filter, anyway? Always a dirty liquid from which you wish to remove impurities, or some laboratory concoction, or cultures containing germs which are to be "filtered" out. It is through a filter that you strain fresh milk. Rainwater reaches your cistern through a filter set there to catch bird droppings and dust. Suggesting the sieve or the strainer, the word "filter" is always used when an undesirable element is to be taken out of some contaminated medium.

How can any poet (and many have) employ a figure with such connotation to describe sunlight passing through an earthly medium?—sunlight, which is another name for purity itself! Does this celestial radiation reach you in a purer state by coming to you through the leaves?—this light that darts ninety million miles through temperatures that would instantly congeal any known liquid, having emanated only a few minutes ago from the heat of a thousand atomic explosions.

Lately, I understand, students of the stratosphere have discovered another antiseptic bath which seems to make assurance doubly sure that our little ball of dirt and salty water shall receive no contamination from the sun. Once within 15,000 miles of earth, these rays, now showering on my camp, encounter heat again, 4,000 degrees Fahrenheit, persisting through a stratum more than 14,000 miles thick, out of which they emerge during the early part of the present second into cold again, fifty degrees below zero. And poets talk of filtering them!

Thus, idly speculating, flattened out on the good earth, I had no urge to think, and certainly felt no faint flicker of a moral impulse to be up and doing. With will pleasantly benumbed, I yielded myself up to the raw sensuous delights of nose, ears, and eyes. My head was on a level with low reeds and grasses from leaf and blade of which dew dangled, sparkled, and fell off, offering the convenience of a shower bath, which a pair of titmice presently accepted. This particular species, the black-crested, is one of the cleanest, trimmest birds I know, and a skillful acrobat, although his cousin, the chickadee, outdoes him as a mere stuntist. He is the only small bird in this brush that wears a crest, which gives him an air of jaunty confidence and self-satisfaction. I noted that these bathers took an oc-

101

casional sip of their bath water, getting at it from the underside. As one stretched his neck to touch the tip of his bill to a drop glistening in the sun, the gem appeared to dissolve and trickle down his throat. Thus bathing, as folklore fairies, in dew; rubbing feathers against wet leaves, shaking, shivering, as if in ecstasy; twittering and chirping—all this business made them seem far daintier than they are, for I have observed on occasion that this little bird is a hog for fat, fuzzy caterpillars, which he pounds against a limb, dissects, and gobbles, pausing only now and then to wipe the messy fragments from his bill.

I have run across tiny birds in desert bushes—the verdin, for instance—miles away from any water, much farther than they can fly for a daily drink and bath, and wondered about it, not thinking of how generous, in the early morning, desert plants are with their dew. In this case, however, there was plenty of water in a dirt tank at the windmill fifty yards away, but my titmice preferred something more poetic.

Presently, in a lull of mockingbird competitions, I became aware of a tinkling chorus, as of tiny streams deep in an underground cavity coursing over small stones well worn by ages of liquid friction which had gradually purged the water's voice of any "dash" or "slosh," until it came to the listening ear clear as a sheep's bell, albeit thin and wiry. So, I was eavesdropping on a group of contented cowbirds. It was not one voice but the mingling of many that made this liquid melody; and I was startled as the genial chorus began to be punctuated now and then by a mouselike squeak of a jesting male with cracked and cracking voice, as of an aged roué cackling over dirty jokes or indulging in ill-timed, fleering banter. I managed to screw around in bed and get a look at this individual through binoculars just as he was uttering his most odious notes, and he certainly followed Hamlet's advice to the players, suiting "the action to the word, the word to the action," for at each cachinnation he spread his wings and tail, ruffed up the feathers of his neck and brought his head down, gaping, until the tip of lower mandible touched the breast, apparently gagged at the thought. "You scalawag," I muttered, "you literally *vomit* your notes."

I wonder if this aging male did not recall, cackling, the Greek tradition of those two famous brothers, one a king and the other a king of kings, each one, however, so unfortunate in love that every time he displayed his scepter in public the people saw an insolent cuckoo perched upon it. The big burly jackdaw, *Cassidex mexicanus*, of these parts, distant cousin of the cowbird, makes a similar display, fluffing up his feathers and spreading his wings; but at the conclusion, instead of looking down he looks up, instead of directing his utterances toward the earth, he launches them toward the sky with bill pointed exactly toward the zenith; and, far from gagging, he barely opens the tip of his bill, emitting a long, far-carrying, penetrating, and not unmusical whistle, startling one unaccustomed to it with its definite human quality, as of a small boy signaling his pal across a block of city residences.

The subdued, insistent, sociable chatter continued uninfluenced by this jester's occasional interruptions. So sing, in the seclusion of the deep brush, these thieves of love, the male to the female, who answers in kind, enjoying a community of nefarious confessions, plotting their cruel practical jokes upon the thoughtless blue gray gnatcatcher, the earnest little vireo, and even upon the cheerful, trusting lark sparrow, handsomest and most melodious of all the sparrow tribe resident in this Brush Country. There are satiric quips and gibes, nudges and winks, half suppressed titters and giggles in the cowbird's tinkling chatter (patent to the initiate), such as sometimes characterize the confidential gab of sophisticated folk, gathered for social diversion, who find gossip of small marital jealousies quite savory, while sly references to the more serious derelictions of "dear" and *absent* friends are tremendously amusing. Indulgence without assumption of parental responsibilities seems funny to these cowbirds, also; and my high-perched scoffer nearly cracks his throat. The recounting of adventures in cuckoldry is really so excruciating!

It so happened (Nature is not without her gentle ironies) that this group of gossiping cowbirds was holding its party fairly well concealed in the brushy top of a cockspur hawthorn, radiant with clusters of freshly opened flowers, whose wide-expanded petals of

103

snowy white persuade the poet to adopt it as a symbol of rustic innocence.

And every shepherd tells his tale
Under the hawthorn in the dale.

But Nature's ways are not man's ways. Each species is endowed with its own nontransferable morality by which it must live if it live at all, since morality may be defined as honoring those rules of conduct by which a given species maintains itself in health; and all this interpretation of conduct across species can only be for the amusement of the moment. Cowbirds have their code and are not only healthy but exuberant in the observance of it. The female mantis who, simulating acquiescence, turns and casually bites off the head of an amorous suitor, satisfies a yearning but not for love; and her action receives in the tolerant eye of Nature an unconditional sanction. Does she choke as she quietly masticates the body of her too-ardent-and-incautious mate? Not at all. She thrives upon it. Mantis morality is duly approved, the same as mine. The crisscrossing of moralities creates conflicts and confusions in thinking, and is responsible for much of the green sentimentalism we encounter in nature writing.

Dan O'Brien, "King of the Hoboes," more than twenty years ago wrote that the sentencing of a hawk to death for the murder of a pigeon in Chicago proved that "we have not advanced much in common sense. In 1314," he recalled, "a bull which had fatally gored a man in Europe had been sentenced to death after a trial."

7

STILL IN THE BRUSH

This country was originally prairie with gentle swells of sandy land (subdued sand dunes, one might call them), not rolling, as in the north, but merely swelling here and there. From time immemorial their summits have been crowned with live-oak mottes, and many of the early pioneers, of course, chose these shaded, picturesque knolls for their residences, at present mostly deserted, as many ranchmen have moved to town. Now among the oaks you find often only ruins of dwellings, or mere bunk shacks for ranch Mexicans to occupy now and then. Meantime came the brush, marching over hill and dale, swamping the remnants of grass and even invading the sacred precincts of the great oaks themselves. I found a number of knolls so invaded, with the ancient defenders holding their upper branches aloft as if for air, as fish almost suffocated with silt stick their heads above the muddy surface of a

105

stream. How these grand, thousand-year-old trees, often with a spread of a hundred feet or more, noble patriarchs of the vegetable world, must scorn this invasion of proletarian brush—it being literally, from their standpoint, the "scum of the earth," and that from a foreign country! Is it not too much?

But in spite of how the live oaks may feel about it, the march of lesser breeds comes in accordance with a wise provision of Nature. This was ancient grassland—buffalo pasture and Indian country. So thick was the covering of grass that a seed of huisache, huajilla (pronounced wah-hee-yah), *Acacia greggii,* bean of the mesquite, or wind-blown or bird-borne germ of any other species fell on a deep cushion and perished.

Darwin remarks concerning the pampas that "few countries have undergone more remarkable changes, since the year 1535, when the first colonist of the La Plata landed with seventy-two horses. The countless herds of horses, cattle, and sheep, not only have altered the whole aspect of vegetation, but have almost banished the guanaco, deer, and ostrich."

So, also, to our own Rio Grande Embayment came the mustang and the longhorn, both exotic species, and the rangemen who protected them. They spread and multiplied like the rabbits in Australia introduced into a habitat with none of their hereditary enemies to serve mercifully as a population check and keep the bursting fecundity of Nature within manageable bounds. The old Indian-buffalo balance was upset and no new longhorn-mustang-white-man equilibrium established. The beating rains swept down from the North and the tails of Gulf hurricanes, lashing the gentle slopes, churned up and dislodged the soil, sweeping it away with rushing fury. The creeks were choked with silt and sand. I tramped up and down Ramireño Creek (anciently a clear running stream) for two days without finding a vestige of water save one little puddle of dirty slime a dozen feet across, and this in the middle of the wettest spring in years! The streams are buried under yards of silt, and the hillsides which furnished it are gashed and gullied, and the banks of long ago are tumbled in.

But Nature is forgiving. On ground thus bared the seeds of shrubs and vines fell and were tramped and tamped into the bare soil to germinate and produce the most formidable covering of matted underbrush to be found this side the tropics.[1] It is an heroic remedy, as if Nature, finally aroused with long abuse and terrified at the prospect of utter, irremediable damage, declared, "You cannot do this," and drew over the bleached and bleeding soil of those far-flung gently undulating prairies a mantle so thick, tangled, thorny, tough, and virile that even the brush-reared cattle, moving from their grazing areas to water and from water back, have to keep to their narrow trails. "So," Nature continues, "I am holding this heritage for a generation that, living on the land, will learn how to use it."

However much stockmen of the region deplore the brush, it is only this extension of subtropical jungle plants which has saved thousands of erodible hillsides from complete wreck after their denudation by ravaging pioneers under an illusion that there were no metes or bounds to cheap land on the North American continent.

The next chapter is now being written. There has been devised a machine which cuts swaths through brush like a mowing machine harvesting hay in a grassy meadow. Under the advice of optimistic range-management men they will likely cut this country clear; and, unless measures are taken which are really revolutionary, clearing and "reclaiming" will be but the prelude to a final catastrophe. I am quite aware of "discoveries" of certain foreign grasses as reclaiming agents, drought-resistant, and all that, but no experiment of sufficient time-space amplitude has yet been recorded to justify *wholesale* clearing. And even if all the facilities were present, it is doubtful if they could be applied, cursed as much of this area is with "lease-rob contracts" under which absentee landlords let their holdings to lessees, often town dwellers themselves, who, in turn, dele-

[1]Several good authorities (John Muir included) attribute the protection of grasslands from encroachment of brush to the prepioneer burning off of the prairies by the Indians in fall and winter. The fire certainly helped, since it destroyed the seeds of brush entangled in grass. But when the prairies were overgrazed, seeds of noxious brush were no longer held aloft for the flames, but were tramped into the soil and were therefore not destroyed by the far weaker fires then occurring on the depleted range.

gate the actual work of ranching to hired hands. The whole economic urge of such tenure is summed up in the phrase, "Get yours while the gettin's good." Absentee ownership does not provide the one thing that counts more than all else in conservation, that is, love of the land right down in the heart of the individual human being who has the immediate daily supervision of it. As in human relationships, so in man's relationship to Mother Earth, the magic properties of love provide a solvent for difficulties where Science fails: "love is the fulfilling of the law." Though they have the gift of prophecy and understand all the mysteries, if they have no love of the land they become as sounding brass and tinkling cymbal, and "whether there be prophecies, they shall fail; whether there be tongues, they shall cease; whether there be knowledge, it shall vanish away."

Some of the wealthier owners, it is true, and especially corporations, hire well-trained managers who actually live on the land and personally direct the workers. This arrangement is much better than "lease-rob," since many of these men, besides having professional pride, come, by constant association with it, to treat the land affectionately. But even this is not a marriage of love but of convenience. The system now under trial in Russia has been driven to awarding little parcels of land to individual farmers as their own, in an attempt, I conjecture, to supply this missing element of love which cannot be infused into the grandiose communist kolkhoz. A similar device developed in the hacienda system of land tenure in Mexico and in other Latin-American countries, whereby the peon was given his own vegetable plot of ground. The traveler is impressed with these tiny miracle patches blooming in the midst of dilapidated plantations. Traveler, *it is love*. Look no further for an explanation.

And so here in the Brush Country or on the high plains when I hear landlord and lease holder discussing brush clearance and quoting the learned bulletins of agricultural experimental stations, and when I see them readying the terrific machines for action, I can imagine the debouchment areas of the Nueces and of other Texas rivers yawning for the gargantuan mouthfuls of soil which have been detained in their place for the best part of a century by invasion of the despised brush.

Any kind of tree or shrub holds an umbrella (a leaky one, it is true) over its little domain which breaks the force of the pelting drops, while at the same time clutching with its tough root fingers—each equipped with a hundred stringy rootlets—any truant bit of humus which shows a tendency to slip away. I have been cited statistics which estimate the tons, pounds, and ounces of moisture the tree or shrub consumes; but I have seen with my own eyes cleared areas washed or blown away down to the rock or sterile subsoil so that it makes little difference, so far as man's welfare is concerned, whether or not any moisture ever falls on it again. Not only mechanical laws are here involved, but man-made laws as well, human relationships and political systems, and especially how a given piece of land proposed for clearance is to be administered and the length of time such administration is to endure. Until this is settled, nothing is settled, and the mere agronomist might as well keep his mouth shut.

Earnest, competently trained range-management men have been at work on this problem of brush for many years and in many different parts of the world. They have studied geography and history, and know that it is a problem handed down from the time when man first began living by grazing herds of domesticated animals. The introduction of agriculture and settled populations aggravated it.

They realize that the crux of the problem lies in what will happen after wholesale clearing has been accomplished. Anyone can see that they have the best of the argument for complete clearance if one grants them their "if," but that "if" in historical perspective happens to be as big as a house. If the cleared area can be sodded at once or otherwise protected from erosive action of wind and water; and *if* the area, after it has been duly protected, remains in the hands of owners who will not again overgraze or otherwise abuse it; and *if* the new forage is maintained in health and vigor—then the arguments for clearance are conclusive. No one can reasonably oppose such a program.

But our range authorities are tender on this very point. They say much "education" will be necessary. Education takes time. They say scientific study, investigation, and experiment in "succession of plants" and "care of forage grasses" following clearance will have to be done. "Landowners," they say, "must be urged" to do thus and so. Some believe they must be *paid* to do right by their cleared ranges, after the clearing itself has been duly subsidized, and so on.

It will be noted that these injunctions verge into a field outside the metes and bounds of strict range management. We begin to deal with people, with ignorance, with prejudice, with superstitions, with the general "cussedness" of man, with greed for quick profits—indeed, we find ourselves drawn against our will into the field of social and political science, and first thing we know we are milling around in the old vexed field of land-tenure systems, et cetera. These considerations would seem to constitute the "horse" of the old proverb, while "brush clearance" is the cart; and cart and horse, according to ancient wisdom, should be arranged in proper sequence.

Ignorance of the conservative function of brush has hung like a pall of smoke over popular thinking since remotest antiquity. Land stripped of forest or of grass seems to know that nakedness is sin. It hastily grabs up anything within reach with which to cover its shame. A deserted field becomes matted with weeds, recently deforested areas with densely foliated sprouts, or, as the soil is further impoverished, with maqui or chaparral; while overgrazed grasslands welcome hardy weeds, invading shrubs, vines—in short, anything offering cover. Nature abhors an organic vacuum as much as she does an inorganic one.

Some idea of the long way education has yet to go in establishing any kind of land ethic, or any feeling of citizen responsibility in land use, may be gained from the following incident, which is typical.

In a hilly, timbered area a few years ago I became acquainted with an intelligent farm woman who was endeavoring to bring life back to half a dozen of her ruined hillsides. What a struggle she was having, not only against the forces of erosion, but against the blind ignorance of man!

On these once forested slopes Nature was seeking to cover her nakedness with the most luxurious sprouts I have ever seen any-where. Sprout leaves are normally much larger than leaves of the adult tree, but here their abundance and size seemed to show that the forces of life were conscious of an unusual emergency. I meas-ured the leaves of a sycamore sprout one morning and found that they averaged 11 × 12 inches. Leaves of sprouts from stumps of other species were magnified in proportion, and vines of various sorts coursed over intervening bare places. It seemed that Nature in a panic was using almost anything to protect the disrobed slopes from pelting and washing rains now overdue. Her desperation was so obvious, her signs so clear, and the road back to a stabilized situation so plain that stupidity itself could not err therein. But, verily, "Though thou shouldest bray a fool in a mortar among wheat with a pestle, yet will not his foolishness depart from him," as shall shortly appear.

We were talking over a rail fence on a windy afternoon when suddenly this woman sniffed, looked to windward, and rushed off to the telephone, exclaiming, "Fire!"

Flames were sweeping into an acreage which she had been nurs-ing tenderly for several years. An efficient fire-protection crew were soon on the scene and they extinguished this fire before it did a great deal of damage. The vicious lick of its flames, however, gave me a better idea than I had ever had before of what it might have done.

I wrote her a letter some months later asking how she was get-ting on with her fires and her pyromaniacs. Here are a few pertinent excerpts from her reply:

"One year a neighbor of mine came running down the road with bucket and sack to fight a fire that had gotten off his place onto mine. I thought he was certainly a swell neighbor. After a while I thought of his wife and three babies alone in his house. I told him he had better go back and see about them. He said, 'No, I have already fire-guarded it.' This is circumstantial evidence, item No. 1. Later he said, 'Well, there's one thing—it will sure make fine pas-ture,' item No. 2. I asked him how it caught fire. He said, 'I don't know—it came over to me from the Walker place.' This is a place

111

I own. Well, I had stock over there, so next morning I walked over to see my dead stock, and not a leaf on the place had burned, nor had there been any fire south of him. Plenty of evidence, but all circumstantial. This was one of the windiest March days I ever saw, and it swept over my pasture like it was burning oil. By lots of hot work he and the man on the place saved the barn, but much fencing was burned, a pile of lumber stored for another building went up in smoke, to say nothing of humus and damage to timber. The regular state firefighters were too busy to come until it had done its worst.

"At the time I didn't suspect him of starting the fire on purpose, so I had one satisfaction. I went into some elaborate speech about what I thought of anyone who would start a fire on such a windy day. These natives claim the fires keep down the ticks and help the pasture. The literature I got last spring from the State Forestry stated that it does not help the tick situation, and, of course, any fool knows that mowing is much better for pasture, since it saves all the stuff they burn up for fertilizer.

"While some claim a cigarette thrown carelessly down will start such fires, and the Forestry warns against it, and it will [start fires] in *grass;* but they tell me it is practically impossible to start *leaves* that way. Many of our fires here are started intentionally by misguided people who think they do the pasture good."

If the antiquity of a custom sanctifies it, we shall have to tell such complainants as my correspondent that these things have been, time out of mind, are now, and will ever be, and therefore they will just have to be tolerated until the earth is so impoverished that it will not sprout anything with sufficient substance in it to burn. Ages ago the Mediterranean basin was devastated in much the same way. "The long dry summers," says Ellen Churchill Semple,[2] "and resinous character of the Mediterranean *maqui* shrubs made forest fires frequent and disastrous, while the high winds of the hot season fanned

[2]*The Geography of the Mediterranean Region; Its Relation to Ancient History,* by Ellen Churchill Semple. Constable & Co., Ltd. Henry Holt & Co., 1932, pp. 290–91.

the flames. Such fires were commonplace in ancient Palestine. Isaiah describes one . . . 'It shall devour the briers and thorns, and shall kindle in the thickets of the forest, and they shall mount up like the lifting of smoke.' [How well I know!] Homer, also, knows the brush fire well, . . . 'Through deep glens rageth fierce fire on some parched mountain side and the deep forest beneath, and the wind, driving it, whirleth everywhere the flame.'

"Fires were often started," Semple continues, "intentionally or accidentally, by the herdsmen who ranged the mountain forests with their sheep or goats in the dry season. Burning improved the pasturage, because the ashes *temporarily* enriched the soil, and the abundant shoots from the old roots furnished better fodder. The forests once destroyed were hard to restore. Goats clipped the young growth from the hillsides as with shears. Trees which depended on deep root systems for their moisture could not survive the summer drouth; saplings with shallow roots could not get a start. Moreover, there was *no shade* to help conserve the moisture in soil and root, at a season when the dry atmosphere was especially pervious to the sun's light and heat." (Italics supplied.)

As one travels over the once forested hills, grassy ranges and maqui of our own Southwest and sees the havoc wrought by the lumberman, grazier, and farmer, it is evident that little has been learned about land use in five thousand years. It is the old, old story of civilized man bludgeoning his natural environment instead of conciliating and living on peaceful terms with it.

The embers of last night's fire of good seasoned oak wood were still awake as I began stirring about to prepare my breakfast. Every time I camp and have to handle burning wood there is a simple lesson to be painfully relearned, and this time was no exception. A piece of burning wood, if left to itself overnight, invariably burns further back on the underside than it does on top, so that it presents a deceptive appearance. You sleepily grasp your stick at an apparently safe distance from the burnt end, only to find with highly sensitized finger tips that coals are very much alive on the under-

113

side. And then, of course, comes the inconvenience of blisters on the "picking-up-surfaces" of your hand for a day or two.

I found two weeks later that I had committed that morning another indictable offense against good camping practice: I scorched the sole of my right boot so that it crumbled to pieces in the center. That's what comes of indulging in heavy reflections on the state of the nation while standing too close to a campfire. I am proud of these boots. They are new, easy on the feet, and so constructed as to afford excellent protection against rattlesnakes.

Only early education really counts in camping-out behavior. I was not reared near a campfire. In my youth, the stove and fireplace had already brought the element of fire into human habitations under severely controlled conditions. As I grew older, I handled heat by means of gas and electric gadgets, and so have to relearn fire's treacherous ways whenever we regain together the freedom of the woods. Any properly reared youngster should acquire this simple technique so early and so well that the whole intellectual content of the operation is reduced to the lower centers of the brain, which are all the more dependable since they are operative without conscious thought at all. I have often envied trappers, cowboys, and other out-of-doors men their knack of campfire manipulation and especially their facility in handling burning wood without ever scorching their skin, lighting a pipe with a burning coal, or nesting a stewpan in a nook of embers just hot enough.

But even had I the means, I would not take a cheap advantage by hiring a camp cook and cleaner-up, as I have seen some pale, tender-skinned grubs out of the cocoons of civilization do. I insist on performing the really educative work myself. I do not want to descend to the European level where people no longer hunt but merely picnic. "Europeans do not camp, cook, or do their own work in the woods if they can avoid doing so," says Aldo Leopold. "Work chores are delegated to beaters and servants, and a hunt carries the atmosphere of a picnic, rather than of pioneering. The test of skill is confined largely to the actual taking of game or fish."

I was impressed with J. M. Barrie's *The Admirable Crichton*. It is a book every ambitious camper should read.

Disposal of camp waste always constitutes a problem. In rocky areas around campsites where the soil is difficult digging, some campers burn everything in order to avoid attracting flies, ants, and other insect pests, and are criticized for thus denying birds and small mammals succulent and sometimes much-needed food. If any such feeding is done, however, it should be carried on not less than a hundred yards from the camp. I have had some satisfaction from "baiting" a place with camp scraps within view of my binoculars and observing the competition that often ensues. Even this, however, draws flies within range. It is best under such circumstances to burn or bury. Dishwater is a prime offender, since grease and small particles of food in it bring in hordes of ants and flies. Even those campers careful with disposal of solid material are often careless with liquid waste. I heard an old roustabout camper sharply rebuke a dignitary, quite distinguished in this world's affairs, for tossing into the grass a half cup of creamed and sweetened coffee.

In this sandy, brushy country, however, camp sanitation is simplified. Besides general sandiness, always a convenience and one of Nature's finest filters, countless gopher mounds increase facilities for the disposal of waste. With the toe of your sturdy boot simply kick out a cavity of suitable size in one of these mounds, deposit residue therein, and remold to as near its original contour as you can, this time using the side of your boot.

Waste is no longer "waste" as it joins the current of all natural things, entering upon that joyous alchemic process by which natural forces transmute your most scorned offscourings into the gold of new life. Shallow internment in the sand is far better than burning and better than burying so deep as to be out of immediate reach of those agencies which are busy with the important work of manufacturing humus. Also, the beneficent worms rejoice; and remember that in each consecrated spot which receives your refuse, next spring's vegetation will look up with a greener, healthier visage. "I sometimes think that never blows so red the rose," et cetera.

You may say that your camp castings are but mites lost in an infinitude of sterility. But not so fast. Darwin himself computed the castings of earthworms at six hundred pounds per acre, and so why

115

scorn one's own contribution, certainly mammoth by individual comparison. Besides, this procedure may be tested and approved by Kant's famous principle, which is made by him the very bedrock foundation of morality: *Act only on that maxim whereby thou canst at the same time will that it should become a universal law.*

We look with unjustified scorn upon the use of "night soil" by "inferior peoples" in their fields and gardens, but ignore the pollution to no purpose of our own rivers with millions upon millions of tons of sewage, and smell without any conviction of sin the city incinerator doing its deadly work. "How canst thou say, Brother, let me pull out the mote that is in thine eye, when thou thyself beholdest not the beam that is in thine own eye?" Every citizen knowing the polluting destiny of city sewage and its general annihilation as fertilizer should have a feeling of guilt that the monstrous system is perpetuated without his own loud and insistent protest.

All this, of course, is for the consumption of the camper during his catechumenate. These are camping procedures stressed by any efficient scout leader as he begins instructing his raw recruits in the conventions of natural living. These simple lessons may never be learned on a "dude ranch," or in those elaborate summer resorts "with all modern conveniences," miscalled "camps," and patronized by opulent parents under the illusion that their pampered offspring are gaining "camp experience."

8 SKY

Our people came to this sunny Southwest
from the fogs, drizzles, rain, storms, and meteorological violences of
central and northern Europe, by way of a few generations of inclemencies just as bad in the northern part of this country, where
one must have a roof over his head at least six months in the
year and be ready any time, like a chipmunk or prairie dog, to
duck into his burrow at the first sign of celestial disturbances. It's
too bad, because we brought the dismal dwellings of the North and
East with us. We are not original enough to abandon them, as the
Indians I speak of in another connection who retain their tepees
in the lee of an enormous European house used principally for
storage. Our residential architecture is not what the profession calls
functional, but is constantly quarreling with its environment. I
happen to have lived most of my life on the edge of the Spanish or

117

Moorish architectural domain—where there is just a trace of it which strengthens as one goes south.

In fact, I live in a downstairs apartment with a good deal of human nature going on unintermittently between me and the glorious heaven of sun and stars. This divorcement is doubtless partly responsible for my passion for camping out. Had I a housetop, such as the common sense of peoples living in other semiarid sections of the world provide themselves with, many a camping trip of the last forty years would have been deferred and eventually forgotten; and, if this house with a living area on the roof were set looking out over one of the coastal bays, or, better still, on a coastal island with its utmost stretch of sky, I might have become actually sedentary. Like any other diurnal, burrowing animal, I have spent too many of my nights shut away from the sky. For the peace of my soul, I should have been sleeping all these years, as a bird sleeps, lifting a drowsy eyelid now and then for a reassuring peep at the starry heavens, so to dissolve those smothering, burrowing, underground dreams which linger in the recesses and cubbyholes of the brain, stored there during the dark, shut-in, endless centuries during which our forebears dwelt in caves. I call them my caveman nightmares.

Our dress, as well as our architecture, needs reformation. Just why should I be loaded during warm winter days with coat and vest designed for those who live where blizzards drive and drift the snow, crust it over and keep it frozen for weeks at a time? I can't see any reason for this nor can anyone else. It's just another proof that the herding instinct in man predominates over rational considerations, from which we may derive whatever of cheer there is in the thought that when our leaders finally "run violently down a steep place into the sea," we shall all follow and, swinelike, have the gregarious satisfaction of perishing together.

The walls and ceiling—that is, those parts of the closed and shuttered room in which so many human beings spend most of their time—are its most obvious and certainly its most oppressive features. That's why interior decoration is such a profession, and why we spend so much thought, time, and money adorning and disguising our walls, oftenest with landscapes, sea scapes, vistas, and other views from the outside—sun or moon in the act of rising or setting, mountain peaks, gorges, and the like. We try thus expensively to ameliorate our imprisonment. I know of a millionaire, fond of his bed, who has had constructed at great expense a system of mirrors in the ceiling of his bedroom by means of which he may, while reclining, get glimpses of the out of doors without so much as twisting his sacred head one way or the other. "I never pray in a room," says a famous French philosopher; "it has always seemed to me as if the walls and all the petty handiwork of man interfered between myself and God."

"Kenneth Grahame was not at home beneath a roof," says Clayton Hamilton. "Indoors he would lapse into a silence that might endure for an hour, for—as I observed with gratitude—he felt no social compulsion whatsoever to keep talking in the presence of a visitor; but as soon as we started out on a ramble across country, he would break into an easy current of cheery conversation." I have had many companions similarly affected by the out of doors.

Cavemen a hundred thousand or so years ago decorated the walls of their dingy and smoke-begrimed interiors with reminiscences of the chase and of other activities out in the open air. The cave was merely a cover or retreat to be driven into on occasion and from which escape on any kind of pretext was a welcome relief. Even when the larder was well supplied with meats, nuts, and fruits, still the males of the group managed excuses, as they do to this day, for getting out and away, while their women were tied to the children and to tasks necessary to keep the emergency resort habitable.

In spite of its dangers, war with another tribe came as a relief from the humdrum dinginess of cave dwelling. There is to this day a kind of "indoors" urge toward war. It is rebellion against a walled-up routine, even if war involves entanglement in another routine which eventually becomes more irksome. "Off to the wars," is an electrifying phrase. The romantic youth with an eight-to-five indoor routine may be pardoned for dreaming (and dream he does!) of free winds and open skies. The designers of publicity for the armed forces are certainly not blind to the lure which a roofless existence holds for the adolescent, as the phrases and pictures on the billboards in federal buildings attest. I have yet to look at one of these pictures, or read one of the legends, suggesting barracks, dugouts, or interiors of any kind. No, these handsome young men are always out in the open, with wind-blown hair, on mountain lookouts or on decks of vessels cleaving boldly forward through the open sea.

Once, while crossing the old Indian Territory (now Oklahoma), I remember seeing Indian families living out in the yard around a campfire near their mansions built with an excess of oil-lease money. These common-sense savages wanted a house like the whites had, but not to live in. They dwelt within the unencumbered view of the heavens as their fathers had before them. The house was only a more elaborate tepee, a convenience for storing goods, wares, and merchandise, which, of course, the faithful squaws kept in good order.

The overwhelming difference between indoors and outdoors is the sky. Once escaped from cave or other dwelling, it is the most obvious as well as the most exhilarating thing to be seen—not only for human beings but also, I think, for birds.

As a boy I trapped quail successfully by building upon the principle that the bird never looks down except for food. A baited trench running under the wall of a trap—nothing but a frame covered with chicken wire—did the trick. The birds "ate" themselves into the cage, cleaning up the grain as they went; and, once inside with full crops, they looked up—and only up—for escape until I arrived and wrung their silly necks. I have been told that wild turkeys are betrayed by the same device.

Nonclimbing animals with less flexible necks than the two species just mentioned seem to be mainly concerned with the floors of their traps or cages; and, it will be noted, such animals, free and out in the open, are quite unconscious of the sky. The javelina, the armadillo, the domestic hog, badgers, rooters or diggers, lift their gaze to a plane level with their eyes only with effort, and maintain it there in evident strain. A hog can look you in the face only for a short interval; and the same may be said, with certain qualifications, of all knee-high animals, or lower, whose dominant sense is that of smell. The upward looking and the light is for those animals in which vision is highly developed. It is doubtful if these rooting, sniffing creatures are sky conscious at all. Their spiritual uplift, if any, must come from odors.

What does the fish or any other denizen of the vasty deep see in his watery sky? Nothing. He has no sky. An ancient Icelandic poet, Thorhall, exclaimed: "Let us make a bird skillful to fly through the heaven of sand," meaning, Thoreau interprets, "Let us make a boat which can sail over the sea, arched over its sandy bottom like a heaven." The poet takes his position on the sand at the bottom of the ocean and sees the boat sailing through its sky, as we now see a B-36. But this attempt to give the ocean creatures a sky like ours does more credit to Thorhall's kindness of heart than to his knowledge of optics. The air of which our sky is made is something else than sea water. A perch in the pellucid pond is extremely sensitive to a shadow falling upon the water, but it is very likely unconscious of the sun, which casts the terrifying image. His perspective is limited to the earthen tub which holds his little dab of water. Death looks *down* upon him, even as death looks *up* from the water's depth to the air-breathing animal above. What a suggestive division of life have we here! And yet from the humblest marine worm to the philosopher in his study stretches a "life"-line with no break in it. Gradations infinitely minute join one to the other in almost imperceptible succession.

The more imaginative a human being is the more he is concerned with the sky. The poet spends half his time with his head in the clouds, not, I think, with "clouds in his head," as a cynic suggests. "I would attempt," says one poet, "to wake the thoughts that lie slumbering on golden ridges in the evening clouds." Wordsworth made his only genuine and undiluted villain impervious to skyey influences, as much as to say that, had the scoundrel permitted it, the sky would have formed him differently:

At noon when, by the forest's edge
He lay beneath the branches high,
    The soft blue sky did never melt
    Into his heart; he never felt
The witchery of the soft blue sky.

121

Camped out on the flattest of flat plains one night, I happened to awaken just as the nearly full moon was touching the rim of the western horizon, appearing distorted by some unusual layers of air through which I was seeing it. I thought it looked like a mountain of gold, broad-based and curiously constricted toward the summit. I lay there and looked at it in amazement, thinking that perhaps my powers of observation had been thrown out of gear by recent dreams, or that the generally weird surroundings had gotten on my nerves. My companion was sound asleep as I could tell by his regular breathing. But I needed confirmation, so, at some risk, I shook his shoulder and told him to look at the moon. He was a matter-of-fact person, free of illusions of any kind—a star basketball forward in his college days—phlegmatic, and of infallible vision. He rubbed his eyes, lifted himself from a prone position onto his elbows, shook his head, and sniffed, "Well, I'll be damned."

"What does it look like?"

"Looks like a golden haystack," he grunted and let himself down, cheek plump into pillow.

I had made a mountain out of a haystack, and still a moon as big as a haystack is certainly something.

The other morning I heard a gentle rain pelting the canvas and pulled my tent flap back to take a peep at the bay in an early morning shower. Instantaneous as a flash on a motion-picture screen, a perpendicular rainbow appeared, upright as a post in the middle of the bay. I was breathless with wonder, standing transfixed, witnessing a miracle, forgetting for the moment the cause of a rainbow. Then in the tail of my eye I caught a yellow gleam on the grass and glanced eastward to see a rift between cloud and horizon, a clear sunrise in the rain! But only for a moment. Even as I turned again in its direction, a low-lying cloud swept over the sun and the colored apparition vanished. I tried to feel an emotion of sympathy for the poor indoors person who sleeps and probably snores through such astounding revelations.

Really, I owned this rainbow, in a manner of speaking, by right of discovery—had acquired property in it, that is, an "exclusive right to possess, enjoy and dispose of." Aye, there's the rub: "dispose of." The thing had unceremoniously departed without any exercise of volition on my part. Anyway, I argued, I retain the memory of it: it was now my memory if not my rainbow. But I was not ready to relinquish my claim. If mine were the only eyes that saw it, did I not myself create this rainbow? There are three necessary conditions for every reappearance of the divine remembrancer, or "token of the covenant": 1, rain; 2, sun; 3, eyes. Delete any one of them and no rainbow is possible.

Forgetting, however, the good Bishop Berkeley's argument, and matter-of-factly granting that the rainbow would have been there, eyes or no eyes, it was certainly by a special dispensation of some sort that mine were the eyes present with skin flaps open at the right moment to witness the celestial manifestation. This favor, or preferential treatment, bestowed with an air of secrecy, probably exclusive, is worthy the special acknowledgment I am at this moment trying to make. Such an experience sets one apart, at least for a moment in his secret, secret meditations, as a traveler returned assumes a superiority on account, merely, of having seen something you haven't seen.

The physicist disparages my revelation by pointing out that the perpendicularity of the rainbow was not miraculous or in violation of any of the well-known laws that govern rainbows, but was merely an illusion: the sun so low on the horizon built a rainbow arch of such magnitude that the segment of it within my view only *appeared* to be standing bolt upright. You see, there's nothing to it, after all—just a rainbow in the sky.

Moreover, the capricious and unusual sky is not what I set out to tell of anyway, but the sky in its everyday aspects, normal and recovered from occasional tantrums, or theatricality. Had I wanted to pursue such phantoms, I should have gone to memories of my years homesteading in an arid section of southern New Mexico, for it is in the desert that one finds a really deceitful sky. Overcasts are rare; clouds wandering about forming and re-forming are seldom seen; the sky is a deadly blue with bronzed edges on the horizon—the same shade of blue week after week for quite long stretches of weary time. Mirages and other illusions are introduced merely to break the monotony. With wind-blown particles of desert dust the sunset occasionally clothes a mountain in fire, or presents cliffs and promontories dripping with blood, or turns tumbled and jumbled boulders as big as skyscrapers into gold. I have seen forests arise in a desert sky, fronted with lakes, skirted with inverted cities; and I have read stories of this same sky holding out false promise of bubbling springs to men crawling on hands and knees or on their bellies like reptiles, wilted down and crazed for drink—a most cruel illusion, which is referred to in ancient oriental literature as "the thirst of the gazelle."

I avoid, also, an astronomical sky. The downfall of the Ptolemaic dictatorship in astronomy was a bitter disappointment to the popular mind, because our cozy pre-Copernican sky was transformed by the scientific imagination into a kind of ghostly abstraction. It was reduced to thin air, which became more and more diluted the deeper you went into it. Where were now those comforting and ancient "presences of Nature in the sky" to which the poet often addressed his appeals?

Until the sixteenth century the sky, including the heavenly bodies, was thought to govern the larger affairs of men. Astrology was the "science" which explained the sky's participation in mundane matters and foretold in detail its impingement upon the individual lives of lords, rulers of the earth, their important kith and kin, as well as upon the lives of parvenus. Astrologers were not greatly concerned with the sky's influence in the individual affairs of the Common Man; nor had these worthy practitioners the ingenuity to promote an Organized Charity for the purpose of paying the astrological fees of the indigent. Subsequent history shows that they were overlooking a bet. And governments were not advanced sufficiently to provide Group Astrological Service.

But when, due to the researches of Copernicus, the earth itself was identified as a heavenly body, a writ of divorcement was granted, finally separating Astrology from Astronomy; and Omar's advice not to look to the sky for help, "for it as impotently moves as you or I," gained greater validity. So tenacious, however, is the pre-

Copernican faith that the so-called masses have not yet given up the belief in our firmament's functioning as a shaper of human destiny. A glance at the newsstands with their array of prosperous-looking and evidently popular astrological magazines puts Copernicus in his place. Indeed, if one cares to take the trouble to look about a bit, he may still find the solemn practitioner himself in some loft with ready access to the stars,

Where at his desk and book he sits,
Puzzling aloft his curious wits.

Astronomy, although the legitimate heir of astrology, is not nearly so careful as its parent was about rubbing human beings the right way, quieting their emotional upsets, and soothing their prejudices. On the contrary, it succeeds in giving us some of our ghastliest nightmares. The moon's sky is black; the day there lasts two weeks; the stars don't twinkle. Consider for a moment: a coal-black sky, punctured with pinpricks of fiercely burning stars that won't twinkle, but stare, like the lidless eyes of serpents—and a solid week of it, longer than you can possibly sleep. How gentle and loving seem the confidentially twinkling stars in our own heaven at night—dark, but darkness tempered with a memory of blue!

"An instinct," says Wordsworth, "teaches men to build their churches with spire steeples, which, as they cannot be referred to any other object, point as with silent finger to the sky and stars, and sometimes when they reflect the brazen light of a rich though rainy sunset, appear like a pyramid of flame burning heavenward." Much better this pleasing fancy, it seems to me, than disturbing your sky with astronomical speculations, as Richard Jeffries does, standing by the sea, sick and yearning for a better and a fuller life. "Looking straight out," he says, "is looking straight down; the eye-glance gradually departs from the sealevel, and, rising as that falls, enters the hollow of heaven. It is the edge of the abyss as much as if the earth were cut away in a sheer fall of eight thousand miles to the sky beneath, thence a hollow to the stars." I don't like this heroic mutilation. It destroys the domesticity of "that inverted bowl" whereunder, snugly cooped up, we are permitted to pass our mortal years. It distorts geography. It introduces alien elements into precincts long known and long loved for their burden of intimate associations and tender memories. You wander about, bemused, disinherited in ancestral halls—the strange and the familiar, each disguised and exchanging costumes, as in a dream.

The horizons of childhood give one throughout life his sense of direction. Are they undulating, straight line, cut by jagged mountain ranges, or traced with the mild curvature of the earth as you look out upon a sea? No matter. Here you get your definitions of east, west, south, and north. Without them these words are as empty of content as X plus Y equals Z. I refer to my memories automatically when points of the compass invade the conversation. Do you say such an object is south of another? Immediately I visualize south as toward the sheep pasture from our home, where, mounted on a swift pony, I chased jack rabbits behind the greyhounds. Do you say west? I see the sun setting across a gentle slope in the direction of the village cemetery. North? The village itself. East? I look away across a wide valley toward the rising sun. These are my definitions of east, west, south, and north, and every man has his own. Macaulay celebrates man dying in battle for the "ashes of his fathers and the temples of his gods," but I believe the hero dies as often thinking of the horizons of his childhood, that magic circle which holds forever in its heart his home.

Dear native Regions, wheresoe'er shall close
My mortal course, there will I think on you;
Dying, will cast on you a backward look; . . .

Another objection I have to the astronomer, as such, is that he talks airily—far too airily—of "holes in the sky," an unpleasant phrase which gives me a shiver, as if one were talking of holes in my roof. And I still harbor enough pre-Copernican superstition to resent the attempt of the popular lecturer on astronomy to reduce this earthly refuge of ours to as near nothing as possible by means of space comparisons. I once heard one map out a portion of the solar system on which, by the scale used, Texas could be fitted into a space the size of a man's thumbnail with still room around the edges. In these quite *un*popular lectures, so far as I am concerned, this globe, our only possible home in the cold vastness of starry space, becomes a mere mote in a sunbeam. I don't like it. I had much rather peep through the other end of the telescope and reduce someone else—or, better, look through a microscope to find out how big we are by comparisons just as valid.

Indeed, there is a certain dignity attaching to mere size. I dislike the view of earth from an airplane, although many people go into ecstasies over it. I don't like to see a great city reduced in appearance to a mold or scum along rivers, bay shores, or other wet places, as if due to the activities of microorganisms; nor is the view improved when, approaching nearer, you see a highway thronged with moving objects that look like beetles skittering here and there—long, straight strips working with energetic bugs.

I prefer experiences and conceptions which raise the stature of man and magnify his importance. I like Bishop Berkeley because he makes the very existence of the whole universe dependent upon man's perception of it. Wipe out man and you reduce this whole dream of appearances to the "exquisite tranquility of nothingness." His theory seems to say, "Yes, grant that we are a mote in a sunbeam, but we are a quite important mote at that. Destroy us, ye Powers, if ye dare, and everything else tumbles into ruins, vanishes, and is no more."

Mathematics and astronomy are for intellectual not emotional moods. The heavens declare the glory of God and the firmament showeth his handiwork. This is emotional appreciation. But the mind, not satisfied, studies adjustments of the celestial bodies and their manifold and co-operative motions, derives laws, abolishes chaos. The mind sees a mechanism, unbelievably intricate yet sublimely simple. The mathematician struggles to embrace the thing in all its compass and extent and eventually reduces his conceptions and explanations to curious-looking formulas, reminding the uninitiate of that hieratic writing by which the ancient priest befuddled into silence, if he could not convince, the people who supplied him with choice cuts from the sleek and fatted heifer. In another mood, however, this same mathematician, swept with emotion at the grandeur and mystery of the visible universe, forgets his runic writing and murmurs with the ancient poet, "The heavens declare," et cetera.

This is about all I remember of a bedtime story told me by an astronomer of some note as, cot by cot, we lay under our mosquito bars in the stillness of a windless night on the shore of Copano Bay with the yellow half-moon hanging large and low across the water. And the marvel is that, passing from emotion to intellect, from what the Karánkaway brave *felt* as, long ago, he looked out over this moonlit bay, to what my astronomer *thinks,* the enigma is not solved but intensified. One has to know a good deal to be overwhelmed with the mystery of what the sky conceals.

9

LIVING IN THE OPEN

I have been lured onto Galveston Island by the seductive press notices of the city's great "Oleander Festival," late in May. I want to witness "a huge parade climaxing the festival, including such pictures of the past as Col. M. B. Menard drawing up plans for the city back in 1836, when the island had just been taken over from cannibalistic Indians and the famed pirate, Jean Laffite, and the recapture of the island from the Yankees during the Civil War.

"The saga of over 50,000 days," continues the rhapsodist, "will also be told by means of the historical pageant . . . 750 will be in the huge musical extravaganza . . . rainbow hues of oleanders will be the color scheme . . . costumes will be authentic . . ." Who can resist such talk? I couldn't.

But first I revisit the West Beach, where long ago I experienced my first bodily contact with the sea. Now it is thronged with bathers, nearly nude. These bodies thirst for the sun's rays, greedily absorbing them along with the cool salt water in the brilliant air and under reaches of blue sky pasturing herds of clouds with gleaming white flanks and shaded centers. All these the normal human being loves unconsciously; his spirits rise in their influence. He shouts, races, splashes. The whole throng is swept with a contagious exhilaration.

I lounge and listen, participating in the communal merriment, apparently isolated, but conjoined as in an electric network, myself a knot in interlacing strands, receiving and transmitting joyous impulses. I glory in the browned, wet bodies rising sleek from snow-white breakers. I am reminded of Darwin's remark: "A white man bathing beside a Tahitian is like a plant bleached by the gardener's art, compared with a fine, dark, green one, growing vigorously in the open hills."

In each face, there is a kind of happiness shining through a crust. Some crusts are thin, almost transparent; some medium; some so thick that only a faint illumination shines through at all. I contrast these faces with the dismal procession they would make moving along the hot, hard pavement in the middle of a city. These are a different people, almost a new species, emitting a spiritual effulgence drawn out, uncovered, responding to the sun and sky. By contrast with my downcast street procession, these are sky worshipers, sun devotees, children of wind and rain—some of them, perhaps, Alumbrados, receiving an illumination directly communicated from a higher source.

One may envy the facility with which a bird looks at the sky. Human eyes are not set and the human neck is not equipped with a universal joint of sufficient swiveling range to permit us to take a casual bird's-eye view of the zenith. Tilting back the head is uncomfortable and especially difficult for the aged, who tend to reassume the primordial stoop. Our only recourse is to lie flat on our backs when we wish for any protracted period to look the sky frankly and fully in the face.

So, dismissing the bathers for the moment, I stretch out. Gently I am drawn away from earth. I am a veteran sky traveler, but rarely go by airplane, where one is housed up, sensing the enormous forces fighting gravity at every moment: the roar of propellers, engine-driven, or jet plane shrieking protest at such prodigious effort. Sky traveling, I lie on this sandy beach looking straight up at a mite of a swift fluttering in the vastness, or at a vulture soaring still higher on wings asleep. I become only distantly conscious of the shouts, laughter, and splashings of a hundred happy bathers—mere threads of sound they are, holding me with pleasing insistence to the reality of the warm earth to which I may, if I choose, instantly return. My air voyages are inexpensive, immensely profitable, quite without hazard —never a crash landing or a bailing out.

To get the greatest good, however, from these celestial contacts, one should vary the program to include an occasional wooing of them in private, withdrawn and solitary, where the vulture does not remain aloof but swoops low with head turned sidewise to assure himself of your availability as food. At your slightest movement he retreats into the depths of the sky with, perhaps, a guttural "not yet."

No other bird takes such intimate interest in the last illness of an individual of another species. The sick or otherwise incapacitated animal is almost assured that he will not come lonely to death's door. Silently, with muffled wings, they gather in a rough circle about the sufferer. Apparently bowed down with grief, but really couched in act to spring—the hypocrites—they patiently, like kinsfolk avid for unmerited bequests, await the end—still as statues, solemn and restrained, while life ebbs away. As long as life lingers, these feathered mourners maintain a respectful distance; but as the expiring creature's eyes close for the last time upon the earthly scene, an unseemly competition occurs for these very eyes and for other tender parts. Thus Nature, with ghastly humor, parodies a situation not unknown in the family relations of our own species.

Now you engage the curiosity of the shallowpated squirrel, but only momentarily, since everything is momentary with a squirrel; or maybe some nosy animal, whose world is nine tenths nasal, ambles near, gets a whiff of your dangerous odor, and makes off in a jiffy.

131

These, also, are enjoying clear sun and open sky; but not so hilariously as our bathers.

If one would know the *superlative* of softness, i.e., if one would become conscious of an integrated presentment of all the gentle, sweetly yielding, soothing, impressionable things in nature, let him lie upon his back and look steadily upward into the summer sky as a cloud dissolves, or, rather, scatters itself into frayed fragments of gossamer-like webs, indifferently woven, with tangles or knots here and there, soon becoming but the shadow of a wraith upon the blue, and then not at all. . . . There is at last a fugitive afterimage which you know is illusion, leaving again the blue vacancy as a patient backdrop awaiting another one of the sky's vagrants, drifting into dissolution. I name this act "The Death of Indolence."

Be not afraid of wasting time. Clouds are medicinal. One may become so fussed with hurry that he loses not only his pocket knife but his immortal soul. Besides, there is plenty of classical justification for this exalted idleness. Think of that orphan lad, Coleridge, at Christ's Hospital,

Who yet a liveried schoolboy, in the depths
Of that huge city, on the leaded roof
Of that wide edifice, thy school and home,
Wert used to lie and gaze upon the clouds
Moving in heaven . . .

"I shall never 'grow up' to the point," says one authority, "where I believe there are more important occupations for a man than lying on his back and looking at the sky." He may even lie under a green tree, as old Andrew Marvell suggests, immersed in vegetable life and be repaid, indulging reverie until "all that's made" becomes "a green thought in a green shade"; but, better still, in spiritually ambitious moments, face the unshielded sky, annihilating everything to blue.

So much for what the eye, with the skin flap open, sees as it lifts its gaze away from earth. We receive through the skin still another class of experience from the sky and skyey influences, if we may include in the term "skyey influences" the sun's rays, X rays, cosmic rays, and the many other yet unidentified forms of radiation—as well as wind, rain, storms, lightning, seasonal changes, temperatures, and so on.

Ideally, of course, as our Alumbrados will agree, the skin, weather permitting, should be bare, giving sun and wind free access to play with it, tease and tone it up—the breeze chilling, the sun warming; the sun heating, the wind cooling, by turns, in stimulating alternation, thus compelling the exercise of those important adjustments called by a great anatomist the "adaptive mechanisms," and promoting the healthy functioning of the skin as an organ. And what a marvelous organ it is!—this finely textured, minutely perforated, exquisitively sensitive, sufficiently elastic, delicate-but-tough, self-renewing,[1] perfectly fitting sack in which it has pleased Nature to sew us up with all-but-obliterated seams.

Physiology textbooks usually devote a paragraph or so to the skin as a cooling system. It sweats, they say. Sweat evaporates and, evaporating, cools. A trio of ethnologists[2] attribute to this cooling function of the skin certain changes in body form, producing the desert type—of course only after many generations of living in a desert environment. Heat with lack of moisture continually applied to human beings through a sufficient number of generations develops, according to these distinguished physical anthropologists, "the tall, lean, skinny men of the desert with long arms and legs, short shallow bodies and narrow hands and feet." That is to say, they are literally *skinny* in the sense that they have an unusual apportionment

[1] I use the term "self-renewing" literally and advisedly. A skin-grafting surgeon told me just the other day of a patient of his, a girl in her teens, with skin lovely as a rose, who suffered a terrible burn. Seventy per cent of the entire skin surface was badly injured, leaving only 10 per cent of good skin available for grafting. He used what he called a "thin, split-thickness graft" of postage-stamp size, planting "islands" of good skin over the burned surface. These islands grew and eventually coalesced, as did the "islands" from which the grafts were taken; and the patient was made whole again.

[2] *Races . . . A Study of the Problem of Race Formation in Man,* by Carleton S. Coon, Ph.D., Curator of Ethnology, University of Pennsylvania Museum, Philadelphia; Stanley M. Garn, Ph.D., Research Fellow in Anthropology, Forsyth Dental Infirmary for Children, Boston, Mass.; and Joseph B. Birdsell, Ph.D., Assistant Professor of Anthropology, University of California, Los Angeles. Charles C Thomas, Publisher. Springfield, Illinois, 1950, pp. 36–40.

133

of skin. "Their skin surface is great in proportion to their volume and weight." Their bodies thus "present the maximum skin surface area in proportion to mass and weight to the external environment . . . permitting a maximum cooling surface for evaporation. Now, fifty per cent., more or less, of the body's blood is inside the legs at any given time. A long, pipe-like leg is an excellent radiator; it exposes much more cooling surface per unit of weight and volume than the short, barrel-like one, which may be useful in other environments."

The authors hold up to our view some rather ghastly illustrations of this thesis. Skins of human beings—the long, skinny ones alongside the short, fat ones—appear flattened out on a wall (drawings, not photographs, of course), illustrating the fact that the 150-pound man with a volume of 75 quarts has a skin surface of 720 square inches; whereas the short tubby individual, of the same weight and content, has a skin area of only 464 square inches.

Types mentioned as exhibiting this desert skinniness include the Tuaregs of the Sahara, Somalis of the desert regions of the Horn of Africa, and the Australian aborigines—all long-time, desert-dwelling peoples.

So, in a not too farfetched sense, the skin, give it but time enough, actually remolds the body nearer to the heart's desire.

Many people, tutored, deceived, and nose-led by advertisements, act as if it were only those trifling bits of skin covering the face and the hands that require care, or only about one sixty-seventh of the surface of the organ we call the skin. The money and time lavished on these fragments would, if extended intelligently to the complete organ, greatly improve the general health of the nation. The skin is a unity and resents the favoritism of these piecemeal ministrations. And let us not be deterred or diverted by any "scientific" headline hunter. One specialist "discovers" the value of actinic rays upon the skin, and is awarded a headline. Soon another "discovers" that sun tan produces cancers, and makes another headline. In a year or two another specialist finds moderation in sunbathing good, and in immoderation bad, claiming another headline, although this last "discovery" is at least three thousand years old.

Our skin thrives best when it is set against, and in stimulating competition with, those natural forces from which it was originally designed to protect us; that is, against heat and cold, sun, wind, rain. Changes of weather, especially violent changes, tone up the organ. This thing of staying indoors in what we call "bad" weather, and keeping our children in, is one of the worst habits which we as a people have acquired. There should be dress and "undress" for all kinds of weather, and those who really want sky experience should be out in bad as well as in good, foul or fair, just the same. How can one expect to get and stay on familiar terms with the sky if he turns tail and scoots into his burrow every time she frowns or scowls a bit?

"Let the moon shine on thee in thy solitary walk and let the misty mountain wind be free to blow against thee." A little mist hurts no one. It is the kiss of a cloud and a kind of downward bending and salute of the sky itself, or, at least, the friendly touch of a duly accredited messenger.

When I was a boy living in an upstairs room which opened out through a window onto a slightly sloping roof, spring and summer showers in the darkness were my delight. My roommate and I took them as naked as we came into the world. A shower straight from heaven is bearer of electrifying communications which the skin understands; and I still permit my skin such indulgence, especially in camp where there are no near neighbors and no embarrassment at night from vivid flashes of lightning.

Observe the ecstasies of children whose mother is wise enough to let them take what they call "a bath in the rain," i.e., the original showerbath, which children, restored to it, recognize with rapture. The savage woman who pushes her protesting son out naked into a cold thundershower is responding to as sound an instinct as the parent bird which forcibly ejects a hesitant nestling when the nest-leaving moment finally arrives.

Skin is the mammal's most ambitious bid for a purely physical immortality. This paper-thin envelope, paling or flushing in response to physical condition or to emotional disturbances, bleeding at a

135

pinprick, shriveling if scorched—this filmy incasement would certainly seem to be the first part of the human body to wilt and dissolve at death. Far from it. It is the most permanent part of the habitation the Spirit of Life builds for the period of its tenancy here on earth, especially those adaptations of it for some specific purpose, as for scratching, hooding the head, mastication of food—in short, nails, hair, teeth. Skins of prehistoric Egyptian mummies are so perfectly preserved that in many of them evidence of the rite of circumcision is plainly visible.

Delicate but imperishable!—especially the teeth. The to-do we make over the successive emergence of baby's teeth is not mere sentimentality, but recognition of the fact that here is coming into being that modification of the skin which outlasts all else. The poet's "muddy vesture of decay" does not include the teeth. Housman's macabre poem, *The Man of Bone Remains,* is inspired by the thought of the persistence of the fleshless skeleton; but a poet is not always a scientist. This one was a mere classicist, and failed to rhyme in that part of the physical man which resists longer than any other the abrasive gnawing of the tooth of time. Long after the man of bone, the man of teeth remains. Teeth sound and whole are found in ancient sites nested in the dissolving dust of bones.

I talked of the dating of human remains with a paleontologist the other day. His eye lighted up and his voice thrilled with emotion as he told me of the longevity and radioactivity of teeth. He said that no other science is so concerned as paleontology is with dating as accurately as may be the leavings of life. Its chief contribution to human knowledge is the establishment of a chronology in the history of the earth. Geology has its clocks, but they have no hour hands or year hands, either. They tick only with the ages, and the term "age" itself is a variable and slippery conception.

Now the thing that was exciting my friend is that teeth as well as charcoal (often found with human remains) lose radium at a constant rate. He had just been advised that, in all probability, teeth are better than carbon, since loss of radiant energy in teeth is more easily measured. With this new key the paleontologist may soon be able to date with much greater accuracy the steps by which the Past became the Present—such steps, for instance, as the one which placed man on the American continents. For all of which we have to thank the enduring quality of skin. A birthday cake should be cut for every permanent tooth as it shows its pearly surface above Johnnie's gums, for it may be—or become—charged with a message to those of our kind now sleeping deep in the womb of time.

Skin, building teeth, captures from somewhere in earth or sky and imprisons a radioactivity with which to time our dissolution. By virtue of this process, the skin of those long dead shall give us a clue to their origin and to the chronology of their development; while we shall take with us into the dust similar tokens to be read by faroff, curious kin of ours eons hence. Distant generations shall be bound together by the skin of their teeth! Skin seems destined to be stretched from everlasting to everlasting.

If we are ever to get an introduction to the neglected pleasures of really living in the open, it is necessary to deal with certain physiological details not yet on the best of terms with good taste in popular writing. Sensuous pleasures are always suspect. Many of us have been reared in the belief that any really virtuous activity must be unpleasant. The practice of enjoying bodily sensations, that is, "pampering the carcass," as the Reverend Robert South puts it severely, was sin itself to the Puritan mind, irrespective of the results of such practice.

But we have come a long way from puritanical thinking in this matter. We now discriminate between the artificial and the natural, between exercise and a massage (rubbings given the lazy fat), between sucking chocolates and the satisfaction of legitimately earned hunger—in short, between bodily pleasures which result from robust health and the activities which produce it, on the one hand, and mere sensuality on the other. A habit that is hygienic is certainly not to be condemned merely because it is pleasurable. Plotinus is said to have remarked that he was ashamed to have a body. Ellen Terry said, "I love my body"; and I lean toward frank and beautiful Ellen Terry, instead of toward the Egyptian philosopher.

137

The experimenter who discovers and propagandizes an indulgence which in no way impairs health of mind or body is a benefit to society, even though the indulgence be entirely sensual. I heartily approve the Apostle Paul's "I buffet my body to bring it into bondage," but even this ultrapuritan resolution is not incompatible with bodily delights. The body is like a willful child. Occasionally buffeting does bring him into a proper bondage, but often one can do more with kindness. Indulgence in the kind of pleasures I am talking about is comparable to humoring the child a little bit as an aid in bringing a rebellious body into bondage.

Throughout nature we see animate life enjoying activities conducive to health and not out of harmony with their own respective ways of life. I have seen English sparrows trembling all over with the delights of a dust bath. I have seen them working like beavers to make themselves dust holes in fragilely crusted earth, and fighting like demons over a dust hole which one happened to get hollowed out first. Would the Puritan, or his intellectual or emotional descendant, condemn or even deprecate the dust-hole indulgence of the English sparrow or begrudge him his little shivers of delight, as the cool, smooth, cleansing dust touches the sensitized skin around the roots of the flushed-up feathers? All day his little body has been encased in a tight envelope so close fitting that it almost excludes the air and fends off any skin sensation whatever, except, indeed, that caused by the wicked crawling of mites, which the cooling dust chokes to death. Imagine the relief the soft-powdered earth brings to the body fully equipped with sensory apparatus but necessarily denied its exercise for long periods. The sparrow earns this pleasure by rigid self-denial—incubating eggs, building a nest, feeding the young, et cetera—and by the labor, often severe, of constructing his dust hole. In the language of the Puritan himself, "Does not God provide this reward?"

Young turkeys, Thoreau says, do not have sense enough to head into the wind, but turn tail and have their wings blown over their heads. I have observed this, but have attributed the action to a desire of the bird to experience the refreshing air under his feathers and feel the pleasing sensation of having the roots of the feathers worked back and forth, embedded as these roots are in a network of nerve endings, just as I experience a pleasurable sensation lying prone and feeling across my bare back the fingers of the wind tugging at body hairs whose roots have a similar emplacement. A hunter friend tells me that he has seen turkeys in winter roost with tails to a tugging norther. Well, maybe turkeys are just too stupid to turn around; but maybe they're just too plain lazy to turn round, as I have been many a night in camp, enduring the discomfort of a sudden norther rather than get up and rummage around in the dark for more cover. I have seen other domestic fowls—chickens, particularly—on a hot windy day turn tail apparently to enjoy the refreshing puffs from the rear.

Man has lost the power of ruffing up his body hairs as a turkey cock does his feathers or as a dog his bristles. Hence these atrophied muscles of horripilation with their long-unstimulated nerve endings which ages ago gave us the pleasurable sensation of bristling—these mechanisms, sick and slack for want of exercise, again like to function. But let us not get too deep into the physiology of atrophied organs or vestigial sensations. Physiology or no physiology, the movement which the wind gives the hairs on the sunbather's body is one of the exquisite, if incidental, pleasures of exposure to the elements.

"Give me the splendid silent sun!" Give me the fingers of the wind! Give me the sky! These are "primal sanities."

Reported practices of the nudist cult shock me as much as they do anyone. This matter is always argued, however, almost solely on prejudice. Science is taking an increasing interest in it, and well it may. Anthropology is surveying clothing needs and clothing tabus throughout the world. It has completely destroyed the long-held fiction that man has an innate sense of modesty, and that the custom of wearing clothes arose to satisfy it. The development was the other way around. Clothing was adopted for one reason or another and modesty arose as a result. Clothing has been used as a protection from the weather, from thorns, from insects and from a hundred other things. It has been used to indicate rank, as an ornament, and to increase the profits of the clothing industry. Its primary purpose should be to promote the health of the skin, and of the body generally. Skin comes first because it is the organ which was evolved to function as a first line of defense against inclemencies of weather or other hazards or harshnesses of a given environment, while at the same time making available for the better health of the whole organism all those benign ministrations which the environment offers. Unless clothes are used as a supplementary or emergency skin, strictly in behalf of skin functions and for no collateral service which in any way interferes with this, we are antagonizing Nature, not co-operating with her.

Anthropology is not the only science which is interesting itself in wholesome and decent clothing. The Physical Education texts in schools have for years included sound chapters on the functions of the skin and on the proper care of the same, along with contextual and intelligent discussions of clothing problems. Economists have analyzed statistically the nation's clothing bill and have found it inflated. Observe what has happened to bathing suits in the last quarter of a century, and to hats in the last decade, and to men's shirts—all in the direction of more air, more sun, less constrictions, greater simplicity.

What a solid phalanx of science is closing in upon dress! And its abuses are now being attacked from the rear, so to speak, inside their very citadel, loosening the icy chains of Custom, since people have taken to hopping about in airplanes from tropic jungle to arctic ice, from mountain fastnesses to ocean shores, where human life is largely amphibian. This free circulation of humanity at constantly accelerated pace confuses convention and benumbs prejudice.

More powerful, however, than any of these exterior forces or rational promptings is the inner urge, an emotional drive, an almost universal want-to. A desire has been created! The educated skin, having had a taste of what it means, now yearns like an immured outlaw for the zest of the out of doors.

IO BAY-SHORE RAMBLE

On a fresh March morning I had gotten out early, hoping to visit a small body of brackish water, supporting here and there patches of tule and margined with other aquatic growths, all hidden away deep among the dunes. Some call it Big Tree Lake, because of a monster live oak growing nearby. Another name is "Dike Lake," because it is the result of a low embankment thrown across a shallow depression which opens into San Antonio Bay.

I had just formed a pleasing image of myself in a ringside seat on the eastern shore of the lakelet, secluded in a natural blind with the light to my back, when I discovered Rex, the camp dog, sneaking along in the weeds, intending, like a stowaway, to announce himself only after we had gotten too far afield for me to scold him back. Dogs are given to these curiously human deceptions, and, when I

141

called out, letting him know that I was onto his tricks, his look of guilt was human too. As he came wagging out of the weeds, his expression was a compound, in about equal proportions, of humiliation at being discovered, guilt, apology, and hope.

"Rex," said I, "you are a thief; a thief of my time, a thief of my entire morning. You chase my birds away; you scare coons into hiding, deer, javelinas; you even worry the big female terrapin looking for a place to lay her eggs (a sight I have much wanted to see). You make a desert; your very odor announces to all wild life the presence of its arch-enemy, since your kind has done the dirty bidding of my own kind since the memory of man runneth not to the contrary."

Rex tried to wag all this away. I flourished my stick. Rex turned, tail down, ears wilted, holding me, however, in a sidelong glance so weighted with its burden of disappointment and injured innocence (the hypocrite!) that I weakened. He caught the signal either from my eye, or from some unconscious, relenting gesture, or from an odor of forgiveness given off from my body, and bounded to my side. After all, I murmured to myself, you can profitably devote this one morning to plants which "stay put," even if you do have a large, nosing and noisy dog along.

Much of the vegetation of the coast country seems to crouch down as if in fear of hurricanes. Even the oak, ancient symbol of sturdy self-reliance, stays close to the ground, presenting, especially along the edge of the bay shore, a streamlined crown toward the sea. Further inland, this same species adopts a communal defense against the violence of tempests by congregating in so-called "mottes," with the upper branches of individual trees bracing each other so as to give the whole structure remarkable stability. Indeed, the tops of such clusters are so interlaced and matted together as to form dense, fairly flat areas of considerable extent, which, incidentally, the great blue heron selects as a favorite site for its huge platform nests. This "roof" is supported by trunks, limbless to a height of six or eight feet, with ample passageways between, giving the whole "motte" an artificial appearance, as of an arbor, under which the larger mammals, both wild and domestic, seek refuge from pelting rains or heat of the midday sun.

A live oak living alone is either blown down or develops into a huge, squatty affair, as the one on Goose Island, said to be the largest live oak in Texas. Scarcely thirty-five feet tall, it has a spread of a hundred and fifty feet, with lower limbs larger than the average trunk of upland live oaks. One can imagine the vast root system in dune sand necessary to support the monster crown in winds which sometimes reach a velocity of one hundred miles an hour. Many of these noble trees have survived the worst the winds of ten centuries can do. Besides spreading their roots far and wide, they sometimes develop another precautionary defense by thrusting the tips of two or more of their limbs into the ground forty or fifty feet away from the trunk—getting down on their hands and knees, so to speak, to resist the tug, twist, and terrific rocking to which they are occasionally subjected.

As the tip of a lower limb touches ground, sand drifts over it, thus giving the impromptu prop firmer anchorage. Instead of rotting off under the damp soil, as one would expect, the ground-seeking limb now turns upward at about the slant at which it entered the ground. It is not unusual to find limbs six inches or more in diameter covered a couple of feet deep, while the end branches, fully leafed, are seeking the light ten or fifteen feet further out. Architecturally, this is better bracing than if the limb were thrust straight into the ground, since the angle, or "knee," yields a little under extreme pressure, cushioning the tree from the shocks of those sudden, violent gusts typical of hurricane winds. Thus we have a tree stalwart in storm, but in quiet weather, lazy-looking, lounging, and digging its elbows into the sand for apparently unneeded support.

Lesser vegetation, however, cannot afford such lordly defiance. Delicate flowers—phlox, puccoon, daisies, asters, and many others—grow, bloom and seed right down against the ground. Common spiderwort, a plant two or three feet tall in central Texas, here attains a height of only two or three inches, with flowers, however, as luxuriant as the species produces anywhere else. That morning I found scattered clumps of blue-eyed grass in hiding and faded to utter dinginess—not at all the hopeful, upward-looking little iris, common on northern prairies, bearing a rich blue-to-purple flower with golden center. Baby blue-eyes, which spreads luxuriantly in tangled masses over acres of northern bottom lands, is here, among the wind-swept dunes, a starved dwarf bearing pigmy flowers with their "eyes" dimmed out, leaving but a narrow rim of blue. The coast species of purple thistle, on the other hand, the so-called "bull thistle," becomes stout, with stem three to four inches in diameter, multiplying spines upon its fleshy blades, and presenting a formidable appearance, as its specific name, *horridulus*, suggests.

Since so many plants take to cover, it would seem natural that the ground-gripping, or creeping, members of grass families would monopolize this area of thin soil and high winds, driving out all others. But not so. Here many of the tall grasses thrive without losing stature. Streamlined and pliant blades present little resistance to the winds. The slender stems bend but do not break. They are tough, resilient, and straighten up as a gust of wind passes, giving root and rootlet the tension they require to take an ever firmer clutch on the inconstant soil. In many of the most exposed places, tall grasses predominate. Even out on coastal islands, which take the full fury of the winds and are the first barriers set up to break the rush of landward-driven waves, stand some of the more stately species. Here, for instance, thrives "wild oats" or beach grass (*Unicola paniculata*), arrow-straight and six to eight feet tall, erect, or, in windy weather, bowing low to the land today and, as the wind veers around, to the sea tomorrow, as a gymnast exercising for a trial of strength.

The dunes which line this quiet bay shore are beneficent ones. They bear the brunt of attack in hurricane days when, having o'erlept the island defenses, mounting sea waves, "thundering like ramping hosts of warrior horse," now threaten to override and ravage the hinterland. As in Holland and Denmark, dunes are here the best defense against the sea, although public appreciation of their function is certainly not so great as in those ancient, sea-besieged little countries whose people "deal as carefully with their dunes as if dealing with eggs, and talk of their fringe of sand hills as if it were a border set with pearls." I have actually seen the gigantic steam shovels of road-paving contractors tearing the crown off our precious coastal dunes to get at a stratum of oyster shell lying underneath! They are generally stabilized by natural growths, preventing those disastrous migrations which have occurred in other parts of the world, as on the Bay of Biscay, where dunes have marched from year to year, burying cultivated lands, farmsteads, villages, and even church spires in their relentless advance. "Practically all of the wide area lying between the coast range of the eastern Mediterranean and the Euphrates," says the late Howard Crosby Butler, of Princeton University, . . . "an area embracing more than twenty thousand square miles, was once more thickly populated than any area of similar dimensions in England or the United States is today if one excludes the immediate vicinity of the large modern cities." This vast territory now appears on maps as the Syrian Desert. "How far these settled regions extended in antiquity is still unknown," says Professor Crosby, "but the most distant explorations . . . have failed to reach the end of ruins and other signs of former occupation." Geologists estimate that shifting sands now cover many more thousands of square miles of towns and cities in central Asia—where "Sultan after Sultan with his pomp abode his destined hour and went his way."

Although I was chiefly occupied with trees, flowers, and grasses, Rex soon proved himself to be a nuisance. There were interesting wading birds along the shore which he kept driving further and further away; and once he dashed into the water to frighten a reddish egret while I was observing this bird's curious method of feeding. Then I had just gotten my glasses focused on three javelinas trailing along single file, unaware of my presence, when Rex, getting a whiff of their odor, bristled and plunged into the bushes after them. Why hasn't some kennel developed a naturalist's dog, trained to discover and indicate, but not to flush any form of wild life?

By this time we had reached a point where a trail led off from the bay to the little lake bordered by dense woods which was simply working (I knew) with wild fowl. I determined to get rid of Rex. Not having the candor or the courage to scold and stone him back to camp, I proceeded to trick him. I feigned interest in a fresh gopher digging, making out that it was a discovery of importance. He set to work with a will, excavating the caving sands, and soon, under my urging, had nearly buried himself.

Then I slipped away, and had gone about a mile in the woods when the whir of a hummingbird's wings brought me to a halt. Presently I discovered a pair hovering over a big bull nettle full of blooms. They darted off, but I knew that, having had a taste of the nectar of this plant, they would be tempted back, so I sat on a log only a few feet away. Soon the male bird returned.

This pair of midgets had chosen to live adventurously, for it was still early March and a spell of sudden cold, as often happens here during this windy month, would nip them to death as it does the early flowers which have enticed them northward. Audubon, during his visit to this coast in April 1837, records a week of bitter weather, "in which many ruby-throats were numbed with cold and many dead."

Maybe Aristotle was nodding when he announced that a minute creature cannot be beautiful, "for we can see the whole in a moment and [thus] lose the pleasure arising from a perception of order in the parts." This ancient Greek had never seen a rubythroat at close range feeding on the white tubular blossoms of the bull nettle (*Jatropha texana*), most ferocious of the weeds on the Texas coast. My bird probed a flower, backed away, and hungrily plunged his bill down the throat of another, and then another—intense, notionate, and jerky—until presently he came to rest in midair. Here, poised for a minute or more, so close to me that I forgot to breathe, was this tiniest of birds, really not much larger than a big moth.

I saw the "whole in a moment": iridescence, blur of buzzing wings, both chin and throat black and crimson by turns (fire and blackout), needle bill half as long as the bird's body—all this in one impression, as he paused irresolute above the shaggy nettle. Verily, astral wings held this darting sprite for a moment within six feet of my unbelieving eyes, in suspension motionless, except for slight bodily undulations and an almost imperceptible opening and closing, fanwise, of the forked tail. I noted the dullish parts, also; the

146

dirty white below and outer tail feathers sooty, with instantaneous successions of greenish shimmer in the space between them.

Suddenly he sat. A pair of miniature feet had materialized out of the lower feathers; and there he was, quiet as a mounted specimen in a museum but for the sidewise swing of the neck and that coincident twisting motion of the head which the neck bones are fashioned to accommodate. He rested upon a dead branch of this repulsive weed, amid the white fuzz of stinging hairs and clusters of dainty blossoms. He was unaware of my presence, perfectly posed, turning his head this way and that, seeming to pierce every angle of space with his sparkling little pinpoint eyes.

The hummer dies daily. Liveliest of creatures in warming sunlight, in darkness he sleeps literally the sleep of the dead. His torpor at nightfall becomes so profound that "he loses all power of movement or feeling," according to Dr. Oliver P. Pearson, of the Museum of Vertebrate Zoology, University of California. Dr. Pearson's clever metabolism tests tend to confirm the opinion of those who contend that a hummer cannot possibly fly five hundred miles across the Gulf of Mexico, as required by the migration route usually attributed to him. "The radius of flight was calculated from metabolic rate, average speed in flight [50 miles per hour], and the amount of fuel they carry [one gram] of fat." Dr. Pearson's computations from these data would limit the bird's cruising radius to about 385 miles.

The fact that rubythroats are found far out in the Gulf is not, of course, proof that they make it across. They may have erred, or may have been driven from a shorter to a longer route by storm and wind. Mrs. Houstoun[1] mentions "an immense flight of humming birds" alighting "in a small garden in the middle of town [Galveston]"; and then takes occasion to remark: "It is strange at what great distance from the land these little creatures are occasionally seen; when more than two hundred miles out to sea, between Texas and Havana, a hummer settled on the rigging of the Dolphin."

Aristotle, who unfortunately cannot reply to my assault upon his theory, would say that I am fudging, that I am seeing much more

[1]Mrs. Matilda Charlotte (Jesse) Fraser Houstoun, *Texas and the Gulf of Mexico; or, Yachting in the New World*. London: T. Murray, 1844.

than a simple hummingbird, since I talk of a bull nettle associated with the hummer, of light bouncing off the bird's back to give the exciting illusion of iridescence, and that sheer accident produced a contrast in placing this daintiest of birds against this most uncouth of plants. In short, he would say that the nature observer is constantly seeing things in a frame and must so see them because the natural object *in situ* is always framed, and that museum artists recognize this principle in constructing their clever dioramas simulating the environment in which bird or beast occurs typically in nature.

"What you are trying to describe, sir, is a picture of many related parts. Your professed subject is merely spotlighted; and the only pleasure you can hope to arouse in your reader will come from the skill with which you construct your wordy diorama. You are not seeking to isolate the bird in vacancy, but to relate him to the significant elements in his momentary environment."

I yield on at least one point: the contrast must have had something to do with the extreme brilliance of this particular apparition. I have seen hundreds of hummers at one time or another plunging their bills into nursery plants on city lawns, honeysuckle, wisteria, and the like, but never one as beautiful as this one was, dipping into the throats of bull-nettle blossoms, suspended over that ugly, dangerous weed with its background of grotesque folklore planted in my mind long ago. I had seen a fairy, utterly spiritual, hovering over this earthy vegetable; and his sudden eclipse heightened the illusion.

I awoke from my trance to find that mosquitoes had not failed to take advantage of it. I hadn't moved a muscle during the visitation.

Aristotle pushes his theory a little farther by saying that a creature of vast dimensions could not be beautiful to us, "one a thousand miles long," since "the eye could not take in all the object at once." That depends upon whose eye is doing the looking. An anatomist might sense at once in such a monster's foot or toe an adaptation to function, and relate this member to leg, and leg to backbone, and so proceed, perceiving in "the order of its parts" a beauty to which a less learned observer would be blind. Astronomers profess to see great beauty in the (to me) inconceivable thing they call "the universe." Nor do I get the austere beauty of pure mathematical conceptions; but I doubt not the sincerity of the mathematician who is stirred to rhapsody over the transcendental beauty of "an invariant reality, immutable in substance, unalterable in time."

Anyway, I delight especially in a natural stage, one that is not so large as to confuse the interest by dissipating the attention, nor so small as unduly to limit the action; for that which at any given moment an intelligent, sympathetic, and sensitive observer sees in nature is not a single aspect; not an analysis but a synthesis; not a fraction of something, but a stage set and the drama in progress.

Rousseau's criticism of Linnaeus is sound: ". . . he has studied too much from gardens and collections of dried plants, and too little from nature herself." The best one can say of a garden is that it may be the best that can be done under the circumstances; and of an herbarium, that it is indispensable to the taxonomist. There are natural scientists as well as many ordinary observers whom skeletons do not satisfy; to whom the husks and leavings of life are interesting but not sufficient; and who, feeling with Blake that a "robin redbreast in a cage sets all heaven in a rage," visits zoos only as a last resort. There are those who hold the book, the zoo, the mounted specimen and drawers of bird skins valuable chiefly for verification —as a note made in the margin of a difficult text—and who take their pleasure more as the poet does, in excursions afield, where each natural object may be experienced in its natural setting, since it can be only truly—that is, completely—revealed by its congenial associations. The difference between a Linnaeus and a Sir Patrick Geddes is the difference between the letter and the spirit, between a scholiast and an interpreter.

It was probably the arrival of Rex which had dissolved my hummingbird into thin air, for he had caught up with me and was digging in a gopher hole nearby when I recovered from the surprise of noting that the bird was no longer there.

Mosquitoes, members of a particularly vicious species, had congregated during my late séance; and recruits kept arriving in a hurry to snatch a little nourishment before the choice locations were all occupied. A leisure-class mosquito of the Texas uplands rides the wind, hunts, hums, and bites only at night. The species with which I was now beset, however, makes no claim to respectability. It is empty and active right around the clock.

For a few minutes, while Rex was still deeply concerned with his phantom gopher, I gave these pests my undivided attention. They repaid the compliment with interest. Their investigation proved me to be a thin-textured sack of warm blood—a huge, ill-defended, liquid bonanza, while I found them to be burly insects, individually sluggish, moving in undisciplined hordes, like queenless bees, or like an army without leadership degenerated into mobs of marauding rabble. I had on two shirts. To protect the back of my neck I clamped the edge of a large silk bandanna under my hat rim, permitting the remainder of this flowered garment to fall sheetwise on my shoulders. My legs were encased in knee-high boots and heavy navy trousers. Thus armed cap-a-pie, and with two kinds of repellent (with lying labels on the bottles), I felt sufficiently fortified to give these creatures, thirsting though they were for my blood, a period of unprejudiced consideration.

In sitting posture my trousers wrinkled; and I soon noticed that individuals alighting on the ridges thereof were dissatisfied, shifting uneasily from one place to another, since they were striking "dry holes," as the oil prospector says. The more fortunate ones, wildcatting in the furrows of the wrinkles, "struck oil," and plenty of it. By enduring some discomfort, I found their favorite facial locations to be the temples and a small space under each ear. In these tender areas a puncture produces a welt about the size of a small bean, which itches for a while but disappears overnight. In a way, this lumbersome species is harmless and unable, even though maliciously disposed, to inoculate its hosts with malaria or other disease. Undisturbed in a favorable location, this mosquito gorges until its narrow, fragile wings can scarcely support its cargo of human blood. I watched one after another take off clumsily, like overloaded aircraft, and fall into the grass a few feet away. On the back of my hand I mashed one loaded to capacity, and it made a red splash about the size of a dollar.

A puff of tobacco smoke causes the feeding mosquito severe annoyance. Your victim wriggles, twists, buzzes, tugging to get away, but can't withdraw its proboscis, and remains tethered in your flesh. The smoke is so offensive that its backs away abruptly, shifting its foothold, and so must pull at an angle instead of withdrawing the instrument by vertical lift. I have seen this pastime amuse a group of campers sitting around a fire after supper, but I am unsympathetic. To drug your opponent is to degrade a sport to the insect level, mimicking warfare of wasp and spider, which should be beneath the dignity of any mammal.

The Gulf exposure of Texas coastal islands, being clear of vegetation, is generally free from mosquitoes, while the weeds and scrubby vegetation on the bay side, only a few hundred yards away, swarm with them. Especially is this true in a Gulf breeze. The mosquito rides the wind for miles, but he can't stand up against it for a minute. Occasionally outdoor work on the mainland has to be suspended, and workers screen themselves in. Atop sand dunes in the wind there are none to be found, while a hundred yards away in the lowlands, and especially in the lee of brush or building, the hungry hordes swarm upon you. You rush indoors, flapping everything "flappable" about you; and, once in, slam the door in their greedy faces, as if you were pursued by furies. They get in your mouth, nose, eyes, and cover any exposed portion of your skin in a moment. I have mashed a dozen with one slap on cheek or hand. They bite through trousers of ordinary thickness, while a summer shirt increases their effectiveness by giving them the kind of foothold they like. At one time I found even the trappers "holed up," as they expressed it, since baiting traps, all located in lowlands, and generally out of the wind, was impossible. Lotions help for a few minutes, but no longer. The smoke of a campfire is of little assistance.

One or another of the oil companies makes a spray, however, which will clear a screened room in a moment or a closed automobile; and there is an "insect bomb" on the market, said to be effective, which I have never tried. During these plagues even the wild turkeys sleep with head under wing.

There is another species of mosquito on this coast about one tenth the size of the monster just described, and quite ten times as hard to deal with. She—I say "she," because among mosquitoes also "the female is deadlier than the male"—she rides blithely in on seaward breezes from inland marshes—an athletic, silent, bite-and-scoot pest, capable of squeezing through the meshes of any ordinary netting. This is doubtless the species William Kennedy entertained while traveling along this part of the Texas coast in the thirties of the last century, which he characterized as "minute and malignant." I would add "multitudinous" also. The sting of one of these little blood-suckers is much like the bite of a small ant, also common on the coast; and on one occasion a few years ago my failure to discriminate these bites, one from the other, murdered my sleep, as well as that of a companion, for a whole night. We had made camp after dark, and were hardly asleep before the mass assault began. We twisted, slapped, kicked, spoke evil, rubbed, scratched, retucked our netting and threshed about with pillow slips, but finally gave up, believing that we were beset by that species against which a bar is no bar. Although the night was hot and humid, I pulled the sheet over my head, determined to sweat it out. It was all to no avail; they bit through the sheet.

Needless to say, we were out of bed before daylight the next morning, fumbling about and grumbling at the inaccessibility of cooking utensils, at the heat, at the wind and wet wood, and at other inconveniences; both of us in that evil humor with which loss of sleep tarnishes the sunniest disposition. Coffee (the second cup) set us to discussing the night's adventure and to recounting previous experiences with the "little stinker." We knew her well. She could ease herself through a germ filter. She never gives a warning hum, but sets immediately about her business and makes off, like a thief in the night. And they always attack in hordes, we agreed, just as last night. My companion remembered even the scientific name. Packing up in the sober light of day, however, we found our sheets covered with pismires. In the darkness we had set our cots in a veritable town of ant hills, the occupants of which had swarmed up to make infuriated defense of their peaceful community.

Annals of this stretch of Texas coast abound in references to the perniciousness of its mosquitoes. Cabeza de Vaca found them here four hundred years ago. "When the time came," he says,[2] "and we went to eat tunas, there were a great many mosquitoes of three kinds, all very bad and troublesome, which during most of the summer persecuted us. In order to protect ourselves we built, all around our camps, big fires of damp and rotten wood, that gave no flame but much smoke, and this was the cause of further trouble to us, for the whole night we did not do anything but weep from the smoke that went to our eyes, and the heat from the fire was so insufferable that we would go to the shore for rest. And when, sometimes, we were able to sleep, the Indians aroused us again with blows to go and kindle the fires.

"Those from further inland have another remedy, just as bad and even worse, which is to go about with a firebrand, setting fire to the plains and timber so as to drive off the mosquitoes, and also to get lizards and similar things which they eat, to come out of the soil."

Some two hundred and fifty years later (circa 1795) "mosquitoes killed the mission, La Bahia, after a year and it was deserted." The padres, so the quaint record continues, still "hankering after the souls of the Karánkaways" traveled "some ten leagues southward and set up again on the present site of Refugio."

The morning was now far spent. I had finished with the mosquitoes, although they had not yet had enough of me. The lake, which had been my early objective, seemed now less attractive; and I was anxious to get out of the woods and on back to the camp. Answering my whistle, Rex came up out of his cavernous excavation, eyes blinking under heavily sanded eyebrows, bedraggled and panting, almost gasping, for breath. His whole deportment confessed defeat.

[2]The Journey of Alvar Nuñez Cabeza de Vaca and His Companions from Florida to the Pacific, 1528–1536, Allerton Book Co., New York, 1922, pp. 92–93.

As a matter of fact his life had been one defeat after another, an unbroken succession of disappointments, which had left their marks upon him.

When I first came to the Refuge, this disconsolate German shepherd stalked about the camp supporting the double dignity of age and size. I was at once favorably disposed toward him, not only on account of a natural sympathy for an aristocrat in reduced circumstances, but because the breed itself comes to us with fewer perverted instincts and with less repulsive physical deformities than is usual in strains whose somatic characters have been so long subjected to the whims of man. Rex knew the futility of effort and only rarely betrayed an enthusiastic interest in anything. Ennui is not unusual in man, especially in elderly individuals, but it seemed out of character in this dog; for Rex, although old, was by no means feeble.

When a trapper's truck drove up loaded with the night's catch, reeking with the odors of the dog's hereditary enemies and of his hereditary prey, I expected a show of normal canine emotions. No such thing: Rex took it all as a matter of course. He sniffed casually around the cages, and carried himself with the bored air of one no longer a victim of the illusions of hope.

The place abounded in pocket gophers. Burrowings with fresh earth showing at entrances were everywhere; and the early morning air must have been laden with gopher odor. Rex showed little interest. Occasionally he strode out a rod or two from camp and did a little "token" digging, putting down one huge paw after the other with slow precision. Digging was plainly not a diversion but a duty. He had no thought or hope of unearthing a gopher. People seemed to expect dogs to dig in gopher holes, so he acted in character—that was all.

When I tried to make friends with him, he neither encouraged nor repulsed my attentions, but was exactly neutral: "Man bores me—I merely put up with him." Presently I began to learn a little of the history of this great dog. I found that his life had been one frustration right after another, and that he had probably never experienced the pains and pleasures of normal dog life.

In a camp such as this, trappers come and trappers go. It is a shifting population; and Rex had no sooner become attached to some likely master than he found himself deserted. Then he would try to be faithful to someone else, with a like result. The whole world of man, upon which his species has learned to depend, was fickle and inconstant. The nasal memories of many masters, refusing logical assortment, bedeviled his thinking. There was no security. His dog nature, suspended in a vacuum, had neither earth below nor heaven above. He was not permitted to exercise and develop his affection for man, his hatred of wolves, his gust for the chase, or the satisfaction of enduring pain and inflicting injury in breast-to-breast and tush-to-tush combat with an individual of his own species worthy of such attentions. And there were no females about.

When I first knew him, Rex was still down-in-the-mouth over the loss of his latest master. I was told that he had showed greater fondness for this young man than for any other person to whom he had endeavored to attach himself since the days of his happy puppyhood. And his love was reciprocated. He was permitted to sleep near the young man's bunk, receive his table scraps, and accompany him here and there about the camp, nose at heels. This intimacy lasted for six or eight months; and Rex was beginning to smell the world through new nostrils. Then all at once the blow fell: no master! The young man had been given another assignment.

Nor was he permitted to "run the trap lines." Morning after morning as the men drove away, he would sit for a long time in the middle of the road gazing after them, until finally, hope deferred, he would turn back and flop in the shade of a shack to doze out the day, hunting in dreams.

I was told that formerly he met the returning trucks with enthusiasm, bouncing about, barking his delight. They were loaded with coons, wildcat, deer, wolves—all securely caged, but burdening the air with their exciting odors. Rex was challenged by growls and snarls, which at first he answered in kind, but his surging emotions were given no vent in action. He rarely got his teeth into live fur, although occasionally a warm skin was tossed to him, which he would wool savagely about, much to the amusement of the men.

155

The confounding of the pompous is legitimate humor—basis of much slapstick—whereas defeat of the modest individual, absorbed in an enterprise which seems to him important, is not humor at all but pathos, proper to melodrama; and laughter here becomes one of the spurns which patient merit of the unworthy takes. When the animals had been disposed of, Rex was left with the lean satisfaction of prowling, growling, and bristling about empty cages. Finally, odors came to have no meaning, and he sank gradually into a conviction of defeat.

I gave him a condoling pat now and then, but when he attempted to follow me into the woods, I scolded him back. A dog is bad company for the bird or animal watcher. Under my threatening tones, and stone or stick hurled his way, he would stand awhile, sniffing the wind, after which gesture of longing, he would turn slowly about and retrace his steps.

Nevertheless, he began eventually to attach himself to me, showing now and then a faint animation when I appeared; and, occasionally, I relented and permitted him to follow me. But even then our association lacked much of being footed on a warm, man-and-dog basis. It was encumbered in a two-way distrust: I was ever fearful of his disturbing my quarry, while he felt that it was his first duty to do so. Then, too, man with camera or binoculars cuts a sad figure compared to man with gun or steel trap. I felt that I was a makeshift to be discarded with contempt in favor of the first superman who came along redolent of animal odors and with a congenial lust for killing.

Really, John Muir's little dog, Stickeen, is the only one I ever heard of who, in the open and equal competition of the camp, preferred the naturalist to the hunter. "When the Indians went into the woods for deer," he says, "Stickeen was sure to be at their heels, provided I had not yet left the camp. For though I never carried a gun, he always followed me, forsaking the hunting Indians, and even his own master, to share my wanderings." Now there was a dog after my own heart, but Stickeen died without issue many years ago.

Generally speaking, this is a false weight in the canine scale of values. Except in a primitive environment, dog as dog makes no distinction between predatory and nonpredatory man. He loves the humblest or the most august human being with the same devotion, demanding only in return affection and constancy. But with Rex it was different. His whole life had been spent in camp; and, through daily association with trappers, he had come to consider them and only them as genuinely human, and the rest of us a degenerate species. I felt keenly this invidious distinction. There is a similar invidiousness (in human opinion) in the degradation of the dog from the hunting dog to the dog as beast of burden.

Friendship cannot be built upon mutual distrust, nor with one party to it feeling that the other harbors condescension secretly in his heart of hearts. Read Emerson on this point. So we didn't get on very well. I had no dog; he had no man; so we tried to put up with each other. At least, I was not whisked away from him every morning in a truck as the trappers were.

There are propitious moments for advancing a friendship. Mood matches mood, be it sad or merry: mutual tolerance, forgive-and-forget, pardon's the word for all. It was in some such coincidence of humor that Rex and I had set off together that morning down the bay shore. I suppose I was acting more like a human being, and I know that he was more like a dog. He frisked about, raced ahead, and presently fell to digging with animation in a gopher hole. With my encouragement he pawed away vigorously, flinging back the caving sand, ramming his head deep into the hole now and again for profound inhalations, withdrawing it, and then applying his paws with renewed energy. Of course, if the gopher felt any uneasiness at all, he was making his way through the soft, moist soil at about double the speed of his pursuer. But Rex didn't realize this. My one word of sympathetic urging had electrified his aging frame. At which juncture I left him to his Sisyphean labor and sneaked off, as previously reported.

He had fallen in close behind as we returned along the bay shore, each of us absorbed in his own thoughts, when a large duck, a female shoveler, fluttered out of the weeds and into the shallow water barely five feet ahead. Rex plunged forward, and was almost upon

157

her—indeed, his great mouth had opened to take her in when, by a clever dodge, she evaded him. Then the chase began in water not more than a foot deep.

I first thought she was wounded, but soon discovered that she had gotten herself dabbled in oil, which is a mounting menace not only to ducks but to all other water birds, as oil exploitation in this area proceeds with increasing tempo. Around and around in the shallow water Rex chased this oiled duck, as if inspired.

Ordinarily, my sympathies would have been with the duck, but knowing that, caught or uncaught, her death was imminent, I wanted Rex finally to have the satisfaction of catching wild quarry out in the open. Time and again she must have felt his breath hot upon her, and she would take a short dive and escape. Rex used good strategy in herding her toward the shore, but her instinct, just as true, told her that it was either death or deep water. Her ability to dive gave her a great advantage which she utilized to keep edging farther and farther away from the land. There was a sand bar about fifty yards out in the bay and here I thought surely Rex would triumph. But the duck was not unaware of this danger, and instead of permitting herself to be driven gradually over the bar in two or three inches of water, she trusted her oil-bedabbled wings and feet tipping the surface to carry her over, taking off while the dog was still belly-deep. Rex realized that it was now or never and made heroic plunges, which grew longer and longer as the depth of the water decreased, with such success that he had his nose in the duck's tail as she got over the bar; and, even after she had reached deeper water, he managed to plunge astride her, striking at her with his huge paws. Again she dived, and was soon leading him on the surface by a nose, and a short nose at that, heading for still deeper water.

When I saw the dog had gotten out over his head, I knew that further pursuit was futile; but Rex didn't think so. Ignoring my calls, he kept after the duck, swimming as vigorously as he could, while she, now in her element, stayed a safe but tantalizing distance in the lead. Back and forth, around and about, she finally drowned his determination.

The incident seemed to epitomize this dog's life—heroic, but hopeless, striving for an impossible reward. He came out with his long hair plastered to his body, showing, as I had never seen it before, the bony skeleton, especially the great hip bones and ribs. With sand still clinging wet in his eyebrows, he gave me one sorrowful look and made off in the direction of the camp. He was there lying in the shade when I returned.

There is surely a last frustration which breaks the heart—man's or dog's—as there is a last straw that breaks the camel's back, and a last experience which fills to overflowing the cup of bitterness. Curiously enough, Rex never followed me again. Not long after that disastrous morning, I whistled to him as I was leaving camp for a tramp in the woods. Chin on paws, he was cooling his belly under a tree in a bed he had pawed out in the loose sand. He lifted his head, looked hard at me, while his ears wilted and his tail did a little token wagging: that was all. It was a snub more in sorrow than in anger, and much harder to forgive, since one knows that such a snub is considered, unimpulsive, final.

II COCKS OF THE BOOMING GROUNDS

"The prairie chickens are booming—'courting,' you call it. Try to come down right away and we'll go out and watch them. Tom Waddell, the game warden, says he will locate the courting grounds for us."

This invitation was from my old friend, I. V. Duncan, whose ranches in Colorado and Wharton counties touch the upper edge of the Karánkaway Country, perhaps as far from salt water as those savages ever went in search of prairie chicken eggs or flesh of the birds themselves.

In the "good old days" this delightful grouse, about the size of a small guinea hen, a subspecies of New England's heath hen now extinct, flourished throughout the coastal prairies of Texas. They numbered during peak years more than a million. Now only a few scattered islands of them remain in their ancient range—perhaps less than ten thousand birds in all. They are on their way out.

When I arrived in Eagle Lake one Saturday afternoon late in March, my friend happened to be out of town, so I called at once on Tom Waddell. We arranged for an excursion to the booming grounds the following morning.

At the tourist court where I spent that night, I engaged the proprietor, an elderly gentleman, in conversation about prairie chickens. He remembered vividly the great hunts of thirty or forty years ago. Not only were these birds killed to eat, but killed for sport by the enthusiastic hunters—much as wolves, having gorged on sheep meat, then range through the frantic herd, killing for the pure joy of it. Other preying animals besides wolves and men seem to enjoy a refreshing blood bath after eating their fill of fresh meat, but it is far from a general practice among predators. The great majority of them are content to kill only what they can use.

"Hunters from Brenham," he recalled, "used to have 'killing contests,' lasting several days, with prizes going to the hunter who killed the most birds." They gathered, he said, on the Bernard prairie, about ten miles north of Eagle Lake, camped under some trees at the confluence of Coushatte Creek and Bernard River, and shot "chickens" from dawn to dusk. Each contestant deposited his birds in a special pile to be counted by the judges. I visited these lovely picnic grounds and saw in my mind's eye shocks of "chickens" here and there, and busy judges, all bloody-handed, counting and neatly restacking the "kill" of each competitor.

It proved burdensome to have to bring in the whole bird, so sometimes contestants were permitted under the rules to be credited with heads only. Then the hunter shot his birds down, whacked off the head, stuffed it in the bag, and threw the body away.

My informant remembered seeing piles of putrefying prairie chickens waist-high, left to vultures and other scavengers after the competition was over, prizes awarded, and the participants happily dispersed to their respective homes. This kind of thing went on for years, he said.

I scented here one of those Texas "tall tales," and took occasion to check up on it among citizens old enough to remember the good old

161

days. I became convinced that the tourist-court proprietor was guilty of no exaggeration. Later I found on page 6 of Valgene W. Lehmann's study,[1] the same gory recital with this further detail: "These encampments began about July 4 and continued through the fall and winter."

Maybe July 4, being a patriotic holiday, "the *glorious* Fourth," was chosen as a suitable date for initiating the grand, free-for-all competition in killing prairie chickens. Contempt for wild life on the frontier is almost beyond belief. It lasted well into the memory of the present generation, and still persists in somewhat modified form in wide areas of public opinion. I note in the Gainesville (Texas) *Hesperion* of July 30, 1878, that "one hundred and fifty mocking-birds were carried to Chicago this week from Gainesville"!

It was my good fortune to be introduced to *Tympanuchus cupido attwateri* by a man who probably knows more about this particular subspecies than any other person now alive. Mr. Waddell has lived with Attwater prairie chickens and taken a particular and professional interest in them for twenty-five years. It was Sunday morning after church on March 26 when we made our first visit to "courting grounds" in the ranching and rice-farming country around Eagle Lake. He began instructing me from the very beginning, and continued talking little except prairie chickens the whole time I was with him.

He retold the story of pioneer slaughter substantially as I had heard it the night before, and added, "Of course, many birds have been killed in late years by poisoning."

"You see," he said, "these chickens are fond of the cotton-worm moth and so invade cotton fields in early fall." But the farmers are impatient and hire airplanes to dust their fields with poison. Waddell said he once found a hundred dead prairie chickens in the course of a mile near Egypt, Texas. He traced their route from the regular grassland range to the cotton field by birds dead in their tracks from eating moths dusty with arsenic. I sensed a little irony in

[1]*Attwater's Prairie Chicken, Its Life History and Management*, U.S. Department of Interior, Fish and Wildlife Service, North American Fauna 57, 1941.

this, feeling that the birds were not, like crows, on a destructive mission, but were really acting as the farmer's friends.

I found that "cow crowds," that is, the force of men who "worked cattle" on the open range, got their fresh meat principally from prairie chickens. Killing them for this purpose was not sport at all but a menial chore which was assigned to the camp cook as a part of his daily grind of duties. Thus a curious psychology: killing to eat is work, while killing wild life to no purpose is "sport." On the democratic frontier we find this survival of an aristocratic scale of values.

"But," said Mr. Waddell, "it's mainly rice that's reducing the prairie chicken population."

Ten or so years ago a series of big dams were built on the Colorado River which guarantee a dependable supply of water for rice farming; and that, together with a general rise in price of foodstuffs, makes rice farming profitable here. The native sod is broken up. During the three or four years in which this prairie land must lie fallow between rice plantings weeds move in, and generally only a remnant of the native prairie growths remains. Native grass, especially the bluestem, is favored by prairie chickens for nesting material and nesting sites. The hen scratches out a little hollow under a natural roof of this tall grass, pulls down some stems of it, arranges a few bits of grass, leaves, and feathers as a lining, and calls it a nest.

"It is the destruction of this native cover," said Waddell, "which is extinguishing the prairie chicken. The burning over of grasslands, overgrazing, and agriculture, principally rice, are restricting this bird's range to the vanishing point."

"Weedy rice fields," observes Lehmann (op. cit., p. 41), "ostensibly provide satisfactory grouse range; actually, however, they lack suitable courtship grounds and safe nesting cover, and, furthermore, the levees collect water that floods nests. Prairie chickens in fallow rice land apparently are doomed, even though they are hunted lightly or not at all."

Knowing something of those unadaptable species which have to have a certain environment and certain materials for nesting, I can easily believe that this is a true statement. In a natural habitat which

163

is being changed radically by man with his machines, high speciali-
zation in food requirements and nesting facilities is practically a
death warrant. It's the more unspecialized species which adapt
themselves best to the changes wrought by man. Nonmigratory
birds—and the prairie chicken is one—suffer most.

Drought in early spring, followed by wet weather during the nesting period, destroys many of these birds, since they seek out low
places for nesting which are flooded when the rains come. If, on the
other hand, the early season is wet, hens are driven to locate nests in
higher places and hence have a better chance to rear their broods.
This particular season—January, February, and March—had been
dry, and many nests were already built in low places subject to overflow. Although the farmers were anxious for rain, I was hoping that
it might be delayed at least long enough for the early birds to bring
off their chicks.

Mr. Waddell recalled many other natural hazards, including
hawks, but returned always to rice. He said a six-thousand-acre
refuge of native prairie, with plenty of bluestem, carefully guarded
from hunters and undergrazed, would save the prairie chicken from
extinction. This is an excellent idea for a state park along the borders of the historic Bernard River. While I am at it, I'll name the Reserve "Attwater State Park" in honor of H. P. Attwater, in belated
recognition of a notable Texas naturalist of the last generation. And
why not also make a complete job of it by naming the donors: The
Southern Pacific Railway Company, a corporation which Attwater
served long and faithfully.

The prairie chickens that Sunday morning had not, for our convenience, postponed their activities until after church services were
over. The booming grounds were sparsely occupied; some, not at all.
Finally, we ran across a pair of males drumming, fighting, or pre-
tending to fight, right in the middle of the road. We stopped at a
distance of about two hundred yards, and Mr. Waddell amused himself by imitating the boom and cackles of the parading cocks.

These two males, scenting battle from afar, at once lost interest in
their own quarrel and advanced side by side as comrades in arms to

dispute the ground with a hated intruder. The bolder one of the two came up strutting and booming to within fifty feet of the car, as Waddell continued his impersonation. Here I got my first view of that brilliant orange neck sac, which the booming bird inflates until it is tight as a drum and big as a turkey egg. He charges forward a few yards, pats his feet rapidly, throws up his neck tufts, and booms (I would call it more of a "woo" than a "boom"), while holding his tail upright and strutting, wings held rigidly, with tips of primaries almost touching the ground. He makes a proud and gallant figure.

I must here confess that a few days later, out alone, I attempted to imitate Mr. Waddell's imitation of the prairie chicken cock, but instead of advancing to the fray as his birds had done, mine all flew away.

This drumming business begins in January and goes on until June. The females gradually quit attending the concerts, go off, make nests, lay eggs, hatch them out, and take care of the broods. But the males, with fewer and fewer females to look on, continue their absurd performance.

The next day we found a male booming all by himself, pitty-patting his feet, inflating his sac almost to bursting, hopping high in air, flapping his wings, cavorting, cackling, and taking on generally. We decided to see just how long this solo performance would last. He continued forty-three minutes by the watch. How long he had been at it before we sighted him, I can not say. Neither do I know whether he was a victor in a tournament, having routed and driven off all opposition, or whether he was a challenger whose blasts thrown out to the winds were so threatening that none dared respond. He finally moved from the center of the road, crossed an irrigation ditch, climbed the spoil bank, and remained there in a listening attitude for some time.

The dispersion of the males over the booming ground is curious indeed. Each one seems to have a certain space which he is willing to defend with his life from any other male. In this area he struts, hops, flaps his wings, cackles, erects his ear tufts (pinnae), charges this way or that for a short distance, stops, pitty-pats his feet so hard against the ground that you can hear the tattoo fifteen or twenty yards away, booms with head and neck stretched out on a level with the plane of his body, while half a dozen other apparently intoxicated males, each with a "territory" of about equal extent, are performing in exactly the same fashion. The whole courting area may be an acre or more of level ground with short cover, and any trespassing of one cock upon the ground of another brings on a conflict, especially among the older birds.

These are not deadly encounters. They fly up and strike each other in mid-air like roosters, but, having no spurs, little blood is spilt. There's much bluffing, bragging, strutting, swaggering about, and vicious-looking feints, so that the engagements take on more of the character of a tournament than of serious, knock-down-and-drag-out combat. Occasionally two cocks get really angry and fight to exhaustion. Then a Krider hawk may sail in and make away with one of the helpless combatants.

Females are utterly passive. They stand around in the tall grass bordering the booming ground with heads sticking up, languidly looking at all the fuss and furore of the males. Presently one of them leaves her cover, advances upon the open space to a point about equidistant from two or three males, indicating acquiescence by her posture, when the favored cocks mate with her in quick succession. Then, as if disdaining any coquettish dallying about, she flies away.

In the early season no female comes near the booming grounds. The late-season concourses and cavortings of the males are also carried on with few if any females in attendance, since they are away absorbed in the serious business of brooding the eggs and taking care of the young. So the whole elaborate show in late season seems to be much ado about very little; that is, a kind of art for art's sake performance. If we consider the further fact that each male shares a female with several others, we must give the prairie chicken cock a place among the most assiduous and considerate of wooers to be found anywhere in the bird world. The young males, especially, are models of constancy. Mr. Waddell tells me that the perverse female never chooses a young male. All in all, it would seem that promiscuity, not monogamy, produces the authentic chivalric ideal—at least, among birds.

166

I was primed to see this proud male wallowing in the muck before the female, for I had read Schwartz's description of the "nuptial bow" of the Greater Prairie Chicken, and had studied his excellent photographs with amused interest. "The cock," says Schwartz, "prostrates himself with breast, bill and outer primaries touching the ground, the wings being fully extended" . . . holding "this position for from two to eight seconds."[2] Photograph 13 of the bulletin shows him sprawled out, tail spread, pinnae erect, rubbing his distended air sac in the dirt.

This pantomime of submission to a higher power goes beyond mere gallantry in the human view, or any seemly acknowledgment of the greater importance of the female in life's complicated scheme of things. By man's standards it is not a "bow" but a prostration; not a compliment, but an abasement, a paroxysm of self-abnegation. The cock apparently seeks to blend himself with the dust under the hen's golden feet, and to glory in a feeling of wormishness beneath the serene and indifferent eye of the creator and ruler of his little prairie chicken world.

I didn't see our own coastal cock in this oriental attitude of abject surrender. I wrote Tom Waddell, asking if he had. "No," he answered, "neither the bill nor the outer primaries touch the ground." Lehmann's description tallies with this. Also E. P. Haddon's colored movie of courting prairie chickens on Bernard Prairie fails to show this groveling posture. So far as my own observations go, the Attwater male impresses me as a warm wooer, but decent and dignified. Driven to human analogy, I should class him as medieval chivalric rather than cinema modern—that is, earnest, courtly and controlled, rather than impetuous and abandoned.

It was only after I was camped out in the middle of good prairie chicken country that the glory of the boom came upon me in full force. I had been hunting these birds for three days in a car; now I was in among them from morning until night.

---

[2]*The Ecology of the Prairie Chicken in Missouri*, by Charles W. Schwartz, Vol. XX, The University of Missouri Studies No. 1, University of Missouri, Columbia, 1945, p. 52.

The booming is best heard about sunrise on a still, clear morning. It swells out over the prairie like an even and insistent note from some deep-toned wind instrument. Under favorable conditions it may be heard a mile or even farther. Since I was camped within hearing of several courting grounds, the booming from them mixed and mingled, making a continuous resonance, rising and dying away in long waves of pleasing sound.

There was a booming ground near my camp. I awoke the first morning about daybreak to the clatter of five males cackling and booming with splendid enthusiasm. I sneaked along an immense shed built for a windbreak, hoping to use it as a blind to get a close-up view of the birds as soon as it was light enough to see. Unluckily the windbreak was full of cattle. On my stealthy approach, they stampeded right across the booming ground and frightened the birds away.

After the cattle were dispersed and grazing quietly, three of the cocks returned and stationed themselves about fifty feet apart. They cackled, boomed, strutted, fluffed up their ear tufts, and went on as if they expected all the females on the prairie to come running. No female appeared. I could hear booming from other grounds, but I couldn't tell by ear whether the sound was coming from nearby or far away, except by watching the birds, who make unmistakable gestures with neck and head whenever they utter this curious sound. The head comes down with the first "woo"; then there is a slight jerk, as of a singer struggling for a difficult note, and the head comes down farther with a greatly emphasized "woo," and then comes another "woo." They utter usually only three "woos," with the middle one accented.

The three cocks were lined up in front of me, the middle one about equidistant from the other two. The central bird proved to be an aggressor, charging alternately left and right into the respective "territories" of his two neighbors. The cock to his left at first resented the intrusion fiercely, and I thought they would surely come to blows. But as they approached each other more nearly they cooled down, and the prospective battle petered out in a little neighborly gossiping.

Following this invasion or, as it turned out, peaceful penetration, the central bird returned to his original position and forthwith began strutting and booming as if he had indeed subjugated a rival. Back on his own stamping ground, he indulged in a short period of self-glorification and then moved belligerently into the domain of the cock to his right. Here he was met with threats which he returned with interest. The two birds actually sparred a little, but shortly became chummy, conciliating and appeasing each other with low clucks and subdued cackles. Presently the restless one returned again to his home ground and proceeded to celebrate his second "victory" in much the same fashion as he had celebrated the first.

In the course of an hour this center bird swung back and forth four times, each time apparently in angry, fighting mood, only to become suddenly mollified as he got within striking distance of his antagonist.

Once I raised my binoculars to see a marsh hawk come sailing low over the booming ground. Then I looked again for my birds and none was to be seen. It was as if they had suddenly vanished into thin air. I spent about two minutes scanning the ground. For the first time I noticed that the booming ground was dotted here and there with dried-out droppings of cattle, little piles of dung that are called, locally, "cow chips." Presently I saw one of these chips rise and become a full-grown prairie chicken; then another, and another. My three birds were back again. Squatting down among these gray mounds, they were perfectly camouflaged. I think the hawk, also, was fooled, for he didn't check his speed as he swept over. Before the cattle came, with their convenient droppings, buffalo droppings doubtless served the prairie chicken as well. The size, color, and shape of a cow chip, seen from above, almost exactly corresponds to the size, shape, and color of a prairie chicken squatting on the ground.

These three birds tired of their performance about seven o'clock and flew away, one following the other at about minute intervals.

There was a dilapidated salt hopper standing in the center of this booming ground. Before daylight next morning, with blanket and flashlight, I secreted myself in it, under the illusion that I would now outwit the cattle who had rudely disturbed the birds the morning before. Venus was up and Jupiter was just peering above the horizon prepared to chase her up the eastern sky. There was little wind, and the temperature was about forty. I had time to twist and turn myself about to find out just which twists and turns might make a noise. There was a constant flapping of a loose piece of corrugated iron, once a part of the roof, as the breeze freshened a bit, but I knew the birds were used to this noise. I wanted to be careful not to introduce any *new* noises.

Just as a little red streak began showing along the eastern horizon I heard the first boom or "woo," deep and resonant. This was followed by cackling and flapping, which increased in intensity until I thought there must be a genuine fight going on just outside my blind. It was still too dark to see, so I had to content myself with trying to identify various sounds the combatants were making. Lehmann (op. cit., p. 12) lists sixteen distinct calls uttered on the courtship grounds; and he attempts to represent these calls by syllables, along with a description of how the syllables are pronounced. I stretched out in as comfortable a position as the salt hopper permitted and tried to disentangle one call from another. I made small progress.

The easily distinguishable *wooing*, or *booming*, is not represented by either of these two words. It is hardly suggested by them. What syllables or words on the printed page represent musical notes? None that I have ever seen. One may suggest ordinary cackling this way, but there are many different kinds of cackling; and the prairie chicken seems to be a master of each kind. As I listened to these birds fighting, I was, at times, reminded of a brown Leghorn hen who has stolen off to nest in the weeds, gone half wild, and is suddenly routed out from her cover. She screams as well as cackles. So do these birds, besides interspersing clucks, clacks, and curious whinings. While listening to them at close quarters you are in a veritable shower of sound.

I lay there in profound disappointment, feeling that I was missing a famous fight. I was sure that one or the other of the cocks would give up and run away before it was light enough for me to see them. But the intolerable clatter continued. Finally I screwed myself carefully around and got my eye to a peephole, and beheld the dim outline of a solitary cock engaging an imaginary enemy!

This was the central bird of the morning before. The other two were in their respective places also. Since it was not light enough for them to see each other, each was making himself as dreadful as possible by the vigor and variety of his flaps and cackles.

Besides sharp squeaks, cackles, clucks, and clacks, the prairie chicken, in mating excitement, utters other henlike sounds. There comes out now and then a querulous note, which seems to indicate caution, and a joyous cackle, like that of a hoarse pullet announcing her first egg. Then there is a series of quick, cackling calls which do not duplicate but remind one of laughing gulls gathered for a powwow on some lonesome beach. There were a few "pwoiks" mixed in, which, Lehmann says, always indicate the presence of females. The boom is the only musical note they utter. It has little variation in pitch, but is rhythmical.

It is a slander of our language, to which we owe so much, to say that any sound, sight, odor, or other impingement of the physical world upon the senses is "indescribable." And yet when I tried to set down my first impression of the boom of the prairie chicken I found that the word "indescribable," and none other, offered itself. What shall you say of a sound which slips in upon you so "silently" that you know not when it arrives nor when it fades away and is no more. I was aware of this sound before I ever heard it, or rather before I was thoroughly conscious of it. Waddell called my attention to it several times and I listened. Then, suddenly, I realized that the sound had been present—a faint ringing or humming, all-pervasive, an undertone arising like an odor from many flowers, and serving as a background for all other sounds. This you hear in the early morning far away from any booming ground. I knew that there was an unusual element of happiness in the morning air before the source of it broke through the film of consciousness. Then, with Waddell's constant prodding, I identified it.

This morning I found that one bird alone, close up, does not make an especially pleasing impression with his single boom. But when the air is filled with this background of sound, and, in addition, as was the case this morning, two or three cocks nearby suddenly break in with their challenging each other back and forth, not only with boomings but with flaps, cackles, and tattoos, it is like hearing savages going about their weird festivals in a forest, using concussion and wind instruments of which we have no knowledge, but producing altogether a wild, strange harmony.

One courting ground is in evident competition with another, each trying its community best to attract females. Meantime, the individual cock on each ground is making other than booming sounds, and sounds which, compared with the booming, carry but a short distance. He is trying to attract to himself the lion's share of the community "take." This is another strenuous competition. The Big Tent has its way of attracting the crowd; but, once the crowd is gathered, a competition ensues between and among the barkers for the sideshows.

Really, the attracting of the females to the grounds in the first place by means of concerted booming that is heard far and wide over the prairies for a mile or more is a kind of co-operative as opposed to individualistic or free-enterprise wooing—something analogous to the Platonic hymeneal festival which the great philosopher envisioned for the "guardians" of his Utopia. Of course, he eliminated all *individual* rivalries.

The vocal apparatus of the prairie chicken is so complicated that it takes a first-class anatomist with the assistance of an acoustical engineer to unravel and explain the unbelievable carrying power of the sound which issues from it and the ventriloquial qualities of the same, and why the intricate mechanism works at all. As it grew lighter I could see only three small henlike birds, charging forward, stopping suddenly to beat a tattoo on the ground with their feet, stretching their necks out with an enormous orange-colored ball swelling and deflating at the throat, as, without opening their beaks, the mysterious booming sound came forth.

Arthur Cleveland Bent, following Gross (1928)—to whose work

172

he refers—calls attention to the fact[3] that the air sac of the prairie chicken does not make but merely modifies the booming sound, which is produced by "air forced from the lungs which vibrates specialized membranes of the syrinx. . . . While the air sac is filling, the sound waves produced by the syrinx beat against these tense, drumlike membranes which serve as resonators," and give the booming its great carrying power. Listening, I marveled at the voice mechanism of the human being, simple by comparison, yet capable, as Mr. Waddell had demonstrated for me a dozen times, of fooling these birds completely.

As it grew lighter, cattle from the windbreak began dribbling out to graze. I congratulated myself on my cleverness in avoiding such a stampede as occurred the morning before. Presently, however, a rangy old cow with a crumpled horn, plodding along down the wind about fifty yards from my blind, suddenly lifted her head and turned her distended nostrils in my direction. Gradually she turned toward me like a weather vane and cautiously came a bit nearer. It was clear that she smelt something wrong with the salt hopper. Seeing her uneasiness, other cattle gathered about her, until there were forty or fifty, all slowly advancing and sniffing suspiciously. This cattle mob grew larger, and soon the salt hopper was surrounded, with all members of the mob alerted for instant flight. Fifty pairs of ears were funneled right on my hiding place. I didn't dare stir for fear of giving the listening, sniffing creatures fright. The birds were still carrying on undisturbed, since the cattle had gathered about very quietly. Presently a Brahma steer snorted and took off, and the whole herd followed helter-skelter down the slope. The chickens flew away and didn't return. I had succeeded in making myself invisible but not unsmellable.

This interference by the cattle caused me to transfer my attentions to another booming ground. John Coronal, a Mexican ranch-hand, called my attention to one about a mile away from my camp, in the middle of which an old rice bundle wagon had been parked for three years. This conveyance I thought might make a good blind.

[3]*Life Histories of North American Birds*, Bulletin 162, 1932, p. 272.

The "bundle wagon" is a huge, two-wheeled affair, built to trail a powered vehicle with bundles of rice from the field to the thresher. Since the general introduction of the combine into the rice country, it has fallen into disuse; and this one had been left to decay in the grassy corner of an old rice field. The bed of the wagon is at least 10 × 14 feet, with sides three feet high of solid material, except for a few knotholes, which I found convenient, and small cracks in the siding through which I could get a view of the grounds around it. There was a short grass area of about an acre on which, John told me, the cocks drummed every morning. I found this better hiding and much more comfortable than in the salt hopper.

On my way from camp to this blind long before daylight next morning, I was impressed with the fullness or completeness of the prairie sky. It is a hemisphere from which no hill takes any toll. There are no punctures in the horizon, no ragged edges. Venus rises here half an hour earlier than at home, and rests momentarily like a resplendent jewel couched on the horizon's utmost rim. There was no fog or mist. The air was so transparent that stars seemed to pop up rather than rise, coming to full brilliance the moment they were visible at all. The level prairie and the sea each has a generous apportionment of sky.

Approaching the blind, I flushed a prairie chicken, which uttered a sharp cackle as he made off. This forehanded bird was perhaps trying to outwit his rivals by spending the whole night on the courting grounds in order to take care of early customers.

I rolled up in a blanket and lay flat on my back in the bed of the bundle wagon, and had a spell of pure stargazing. I didn't hear the birds come in, but as soon as the booming from distant grounds was audible, my birds began booming too, and presently started hopping and flapping. As daylight came, I got an excellent view of two cocks approaching each other. Their necks were extended along the line of their backs, and their ear tufts thrown forward at about the angle a mule adjusts his ears to hear a suspicious sound about ten steps in front of him. The tails of these birds were upright or maybe tilted a bit from the perpendicular toward the head. Creeping toward each other, they looked like small rabbits, but rabbits with cheek pouches, and the pouches stuffed and bulging. The birds stood a long time facing each other, with heads down, like two roosters. But they didn't come to blows.

By sunup five males were at their stations, and several females were sitting around in the weeds. Three males gathered near a female at the edge of the short-grass area and engaged in some downright fisticuffing. Presently, one drove the other two away. He now paraded himself in front of the female, hopped high in the air, but did not approach nearer than ten or fifteen feet. He seemed waiting for her to come up on the booming ground, but he waited in vain. She did not choose to come.

As he walked away, he threw up his head with ear tufts partially raised and nearly touching the tail which was proudly tilted toward the head. He had the outline of a small basket: neck, head, ear tufts, and tail forming the handle of it.

I was surprised to see the cocks stop in the course of their wooing and take a bite to eat. This would seem to derogate from their famed gallantry. Even the commonest rooster eats with some hesitancy in front of his hungry hens. I have seen game roosters nearly starve themselves to death from pure gallantry. A number of years ago I kept one for a friend of mine in my chicken pen and found that I had to feed him in solitude to get him to take any nourishment at all. The prairie chicken cock is down-to-earth in this matter, and eats weed seeds and nips off tender sprouts of grass right in the presence of the females.

My attention now became distracted from the prairie chickens by two small insectivorous mammals—a skunk and an opossum. Far up the fence row I saw an animal moving toward me. He stopped a moment at every fence post, and I soon identified him as an opossum. I couldn't account, however, for his brief pauses. Soon I decided that he was looking for insects; and later investigation proved that in the long drought the earth had drawn away, leaving cracks around the posts half an inch to an inch in width, thus furnishing harborage for crickets, beetles, myriapods, and other luscious morsels.

Then I spotted a skunk. He had so much white from tip to tail that I thought he was surely an albino, but not so. He was a variety which the natives call the "broad-striped" skunk. He was loping about, tail hoisted straight up, busy with insects also; but hunting legitimately, being more of a sportsman than the opossum, who was taking his prey after it had been trapped in a crack. I think the skunk's white-striped bushy tail, hoisted and blowing in the wind with the additional up-and-down motion imparted to it by his loping gait, serves to scare insects out of their hiding places. One may question whether a small animal may thus without danger advertise himself to his enemies out on an open prairie. However, the tail advertises not only the skunk, but the skunk's defense. Perhaps his enemies see in that tail not so much an invitation as a warning. I had a dog once that killed every skunk he found running about in the open, but he did it at the heavy cost of a painful gagging spell, and violent sickness which lasted for hours. The security which the skunk enjoys is evidenced in his every action. He dares even man. I have been made to step aside and let him pass down a narrow path in the woods. He carries himself with an air, a kind of go-to-hell-if-you-don't-like-me style.

This little fellow came pretty near my blind, turning, twisting, loping about in thin weeds—nothing sly or sneaking about him.

The male prairie chickens now have two more months of rather futile courting to do before they may begin associating with each other on a more peaceable basis, in pairs or trios. From June on through the summer, while the females are taking care of the young, they enjoy this chummy sociability, with larger groups forming in the fall. In December males and females congregate in flocks, large and small, sexes separate. Charles W. Schwartz[4] says the greater prairie chickens gather during severe winter weather in large bisexual flocks. In the coast country this is the period of club life for both the males and females. But with the first hint of spring, even in January, the prairies begin ringing again with their far-heard booming. This continues for nearly a month before the first females hear

[4]Op. cit., pp. 44, 83.

176

the call and are moved to respond. Perhaps 90 per cent of the mating occurs in February and March. Then follow another two months of strenuous but ill-paid wooing, and the year has been rounded out.

The day, as well as the year, is pleasantly divided. From daylight until about 9 A.M., during the season, the males give over to "community" and individual wooing, with time out now and then for light refreshments. Then they are off idling or feeding until near sunset, when, on clear, still days, they repair again to the courting grounds for an afternoon session which lasts until nearly dark. As darkness falls on the prairie they sneak away into the tall grass for rest and sleep.

12   SWIFTS AND SCISSORTAILS

Early morning, as all bird lovers will agree, is the best time o' day to see birds. They are active then—courting, fighting, seeking food, or, in the exuberance of awakening from a good night's rest, simply showing off—calling, singing, letting themselves be seen and heard. The quality of the morning light is best for distinguishing their marks—black, white, or neutral—and for enjoying color and color contrasts, livelier, even, than may be found on butterflies or flowers. So from dawn until ten o'clock, in the latitudes of the Texas coast, is the golden period. Bird lovers find late afternoon excursions profitable also.

This leaves the middle of the day for "reading up," settling disputed points—or trying to, recording, et cetera; and for a midday nap in order to be fresh for a night hike with flashlight, for there is night life in the woods. Of course this is all too easygoing for the enthusiast who is appeased with nothing less than a dawn-to-dark schedule even in the summer months, from "kin-to-kaint"; from the time you "kin" see to the time you "kaint," in the southern Negro's talk. I envy these devotees their energy and their zest, but I prefer to take field trips in more philosophical and recreational mood; and, on occasion, I have found myself, fortified by a nap at midday, ready for night adventures, while my "kin-to-kainter" takes to his cot. In northern latitudes the middle of the day may not be so unattractive, but here the direct rays of the sun dazzle and tend to reduce the whole picture to dead black and white. Even a tall man at noon can step on the shadow of his head; and long before noon the intense light has robbed the flat landscape of its charm.

On this particular morning I was out betimes, and it was well I was. Invaders had slipped in during the night, and sky and ground forces had taken over this stretch of coast. Migrations of both chimney swifts and scissortailed flycatchers had arrived during the night. For a week I had been scanning the far reaches of the sky to find the first swift of the season, for he was already overdue. It had not occurred to me, however, to look for the scissortail, probably because you don't have to look for him. He makes himself so conspicuous that you can't miss him if he is about at all.

I had been out about half an hour when the haze lifted, uncovering a quadrant of pale blue northeastern sky, and there, disporting themselves, the swifts! Under cover of night and fog the aerial forces had arrived, while ground detachments of a co-operating species had slipped in and were occupying the more strategic lookouts in the vicinity of my camp—the matchless scissortails.

Now this was no gradual infiltration and diffusion of a species arriving by scouts first followed by small groups of the more adventurous individuals and finally by the rank and file trailing along until the woods were full, such as the term migration in this latitude usually implies. No, this invasion was evidently the result of a conspiracy nicely adjusted between two species; a *putsch*, sudden and decisive, with earth awarded to one of the allies and the heavens to the other. With no intimation of the impending attack, even though I had been on guard for a week, I strolled out innocently

179

that morning to be confronted by a *fait accompli;* the pugnacious flycatchers had taken over down below, the swifts above, and I could do nothing about it. I was at heart a fifth columnist anyway and didn't want to do anything about it.

Swifts and scissortails make a profound contrast: one, stumpy, dirty-looking as soot, with long, scythe-shaped wings and short, spiny-tipped tail, from every angle (and the bird is all angles!) strictly utilitarian; the other species, his co-conspirator, short winged, a five-inch bird with a ten-inch tail, very ornamental, dressed in pearl gray with dark edgings, a vivid black line through the eye, and flashes of salmon pink as he lifts his wings. He is of the leisure class, and shows no deep concern about anything—certainly no such intensity of purpose as the swift does, no bourgeois busyness, no indomitable rushing to and fro, as if life itself depended upon meeting an insect on the dot in some faraway corner of the sky. The scissortail has the philosophic self-assurance of an elite, the aplomb of a settled and unchallenged aristocracy whose ancient privileges it is bad form even to question. He takes his lumbersome prey on the wing in playful mood, and fights as if he were breaking a lance more in sport than in anger. He simply devils hawks, vultures, and crows—especially crows, enjoying mildly the impotence of their anger.

On the contrary, the lexicon of the swift contains only one word, *hurry.* He doesn't run—he dashes no matter if it's a marathon race. He throws into his every activity the burning concentration of a monomaniac.

The simultaneous appearance of these two species at seven o'clock on a morning in middle March forced these and other comparisons upon me. I turned from one to the other and back again, finally centering my attention upon a scissortail sitting calmly upon the most exalted twig of a dead treetop. He sat not in arrogance, exactly, nor "making his high place the lawless perch of winged ambitions"; but still he seemed to say "beware" with equal emphasis to the bald eagle that sailed past and to a grasshopper whose last hop failed to reach the level at which it suited the bird's royal pleasure to feed at this particular time. Flycatchers rarely dart down upon prey; they like to feed on the level of their perch, or a little above the level. This particular individual darted out only occasionally for a morsel, flying at a suitable height and at a convenient distance, returning after each sally to his station to consume his catch with delicacy and deliberation. All this assumption of easy superiority is characteristic of the species.

The swift, on the other hand, flies, with mouth agape or snapping like a turtle, at breakneck speed through swarms of buzzing gnats, gulping down those that happen to stick in his mouth or throat in true goatsucker fashion. While both these birds feed on the wing and are strictly insectivorous, there is a charming divergence of manner and way of life between the cultured elegance of our finest flycatcher and the speed and hurry of that intense, voracious, never-lighting little comber of the upper air.

I have seen this elegant member of the ruling class also in sharp contrast with the plebeian manners of our hoggish jays and grackles. In 1898 the city of Austin, Texas, installed a wasteful but quite effective lighting system, consisting of thirty-one light towers, each 165 feet high, on top of which powerful lights throw their beams earthward, creating a kind of artificial moonlight upon the city streets. These steel towers make a hazard for birds in migration, especially for the low-flying finches. I have found many dead birds around the base of one or another of these towers in the morning after rainstorms or high winds. On one occasion the ground was littered around the base of a tower with more than a hundred indigo buntings. This was, indeed, a "ghastly dew."

But in the fall of the year these towers provide a spread of fat, juicy insects, either dead or crippled, which have run afoul of the obstruction in darkness. This manna is for those hardy species which do not gag at a sour cricket or mutilated moth. Three different species of grackles and our one and only jay are the main beneficiaries. As soon as the ground has been cleaned up, these lazy birds begin climbing the tower to gorge on other insects which have bruised, scorched, or killed themselves by dashing against the powerful lights at the top and have fallen upon the platform built up there for workmen to stand on who have the care and repair of the lights.

I say these birds "climb," for they ascend by short hops and flutters from crossbar to crossbar, stopping and peering into crevices and scanning projections of the structure for any cripple taking refuge, or for any of the dead that happen to have been caught in falling. Each morning of early September one may see this gleaning of the towers.

To the filthy feast the scissortail comes not to participate, but merely for sport. Perched along the upper reaches of a guy wire, he looks at the spectacle in disgust. As one of the greedy ones, filled to repletion, flies earthward, taking an easy angle of about forty-five degrees, the alert scissortail literally rides him down, trouncing him most of the way, strewing the route with feathers. Then he flies back to his high perch to await another victim. I have seen one thus amuse himself for an hour; and I have gone from tower to tower and often found the same comedy in progress. Our border Mexicans say with some reason that the scissortail lives on the brains of other birds.

The scissortail is gentle, spectacular in action, conspicuous in repose. These splendid birds retreat gradually from their summer home. They dwindle away, usually by family groups; and even the rare large migrations leave a few rebellious stragglers. The bird lister begins to miss him from central Texas sometime in October, sensing a loss but at first unconscious of what it is. The vacancy questions but does not answer. His usual haunts have become impoverished by degrees, and even autumn color and breath of the first norther do not satisfy. Then, suddenly, the explanation: the scissortails are gone.

I try nearly every fall to record my farewell sight of this migrant, and of course make many entries before the final one. In a notebook dated October 29, 1946, I find as a final note the following: "Three scissortails (certainly the last or nearly the last of this season) feed from the top of a tall pecan just at sundown. They dash upward forty or fifty feet for small butterflies in migration. They maneuver above their prey and swoop down upon it. The sides of these birds are afire in the setting sun. Never before have I felt the real glory of pink."

They "gang up" in migration, but not in close formation, usually from fifty to a hundred individuals, loosely confederated, traveling southward by easy stages. The largest migrating group of which I have any record was furnished me by R. G. Hollingsworth, of Coleman, Texas, whose letter follows:

"On Saturday evening [September 17, 1949] just before sundown I was coming into Coleman from Santa Anna. There were several of us in the car. We noticed hundreds of birds passing across the road ahead of us from north to south. These birds were generally pretty high and we mistook them at first for bats. But later we ran into a large bunch of them nearer the ground and discovered that they were scissortails. None of us had ever observed scissortails in numbers of more than two or three in a place. I would say that there were at least a thousand of them in the one bunch which were near enough to the earth for us to distinguish them. I believe there must have been that many or more crossing the road in the two, three, or four miles previously traversed."

Mr. Hollingsworth, himself an accurate observer, has taken the trouble to secure confirmation of this statement from those who were with him at the time.

Late in October 1947 Mr. and Mrs. Charles W. Hamilton saw a similar migration of scissortails between Edinburg and Falfurrias in the neck of that famous funnel of migrations inclosed in the angle made by the lower course of the Rio Grande with the Texas coast. The Hamiltons report "at least 5,000 scissortails crossing the highway in a stretch of fifty miles." Mr. Hamilton is vice-president and trust officer of the National Bank of Commerce, Houston.

By the time I returned home from the coast in April, chattering notes were falling from the sky in driblets, announcing that the swift, most impetuous of all birds, was beginning his ethereal mating. In the early stages of this important activity, most species of birds become involved by degrees, the male slightly aggressive,

183

and the female coy. They appear to taste and savor the new relationship, dallying a bit and enjoying invitations and rebuffs—flirtatious, in fact. There is a considerable "warming-up period," as the athletic trainer says. Not so the swift. He is the most nondilatory, sudden, and fervent of all avian wooers. The evasions of the female are devoid of coquetry. Here is no sham race staged in a mood of make-believe. This pursuer is in deadly earnest, while the flight of the pursued proclaims a life-or-death effort to make a getaway. If the measure of her initial repugnance may be taken by the rate of speed at which she flees, we may call it "loathing," for it is easily a mile a minute. By the same token, of course, the ardor of the pursuers must be blazing in a hurricane of desire, since they stay in level flight only a few feet behind her, and it is only by ducking and dodging here and there in the roomy three-dimensional space of the heavens that she evades them at all.

In the swift's courtship flight, Nature provides a spectacular exhibition of triangular love, favorite theme of the fiction writers of all time: desire inflaming the hearts of two suitors for a third individual of the opposite sex at one and the same moment. Hour after hour in the warm days of early April, two (sometimes three) aerial rivals may be seen dashing after the "one and only" other swift in all the world, apprising you of their approach with little squeaky, ecstatic notes as, at jet-plane speed, they flash by and are lost in the blue almost before you can lift your head to get a look. Round and round in broadening circles miles wide, now plunging, now darting toward the zenith, or sliding along endless slopes of sky only to wheel again and climb at the same incredible speed, go these tiny creatures, cousins of the hummingbird and of the egregious goatsuckers, in a sky marathon which often ends only with the approach of night. As the sun vanishes even from their superior vantage point, darkness, closing in, drives them earthward and eventually into the double darkness of their sooty sleeping quarters. Pursuers and pursued now cling to the same wall, perhaps within a few inches of each other, but desire is dead. It will flame again only in tomorrow's sun as they rise into the dawn-tinted sky on rested and love-exhilarated wing.

The curiosity of everyone who has ever paid much attention to swifts has been piqued by seeing a few of them leave their chimney just before complete darkness and take off in a wide upward spiral. This has given rise to a legend that a few of them spend the short summer nights of northern latitudes soaring toward the stars.

An examination of authoritative sources convinces me that "the starlight flight of swifts" is folklore; yet they do fly high even after night has fallen on the face of the earth. The aviator, Harold Penrose,[1] encountered a chimney swift at 7,500 feet. It seems that when the air moves upward, taking along the swift's insect prey, the swifts follow far into the depths of the summer sky. When this upper current of air sets in at nightfall, the birds soar upward to again regain the sun, bask yet awhile in its golden gleams, and feed on insects of similar aspirations, perhaps sex-motivated. Similarly, in the early morning twilight: the early swift pursues his insect a mile high and catches him in sunbeams still invisible to all earthbound creatures. I would like to make the starlight flight of swifts a nightlong amorous madness, strictly consonant with his character; but our dull authorities say that they fly toward the stars only while the sun lasts at the peak of their evening flight and, in the morning, they but anticipate the sun; and that they fly for insects and not for love.

One October a friend of mine and I determined to get a "last date" on the swift. So each evening we watched the sky above our respective homes, and reported to each other over the telephone. He called me about sundown on October fifteenth to say that he could find no swift in the sky. I had found none, either, but decided, before giving them up for gone, to use my binoculars. Soon I found dozens of them feeding out of the range of natural vision. I called my friend and told him to use his field glasses. Soon he reported that he had found them, too, feeding at an immense height. This must have been one of those afternoons when the swift's insects had been borne aloft on upward currents of air.

I have estimated one afternoon's travel at five hundred miles, with yet no choice of suitors being made by this Atalanta of the avian

[1] *I Flew with the Birds*, Country Life Limited, Charles Scribner's Sons, New York, 1949.

world, whose lingering maidenhood extends far into the spring. Day after day the dizzy wooing continues before the courtship is consummated. How many miles are covered in the nuptial flights of a pair or trio of swifts has never to my knowledge been computed, but if these loops, swoops, spiralings, and elaborate curlicues of flight, as well as straightaways, were all disentangled and laid out end to end due west along the thirty-second parallel of latitude, the line would reach halfway around the world. Certainly the path of the more tenacious and enduring of these love-maddened triangles would, I am sure, stretch out that far. The swift beats the air with a mighty wing.

I suppose the purpose of all this is the same as that of the nuptial flight of the honeybee, that is, to protect the integrity of the wing power of the species, to see that no lame duck's genes get into circulation; for in no other species is survival so much dependent upon absolute mastery of the air. Here is a bird whose life is concentrated in his wings, and the true instinct of the female permits only the fastest flier and the most tireless to mate and reproduce his kind. Or if, as some believe, it is two females after one male—a Shavian triangle—the final result is the same.

In the nuptial race of these sky masters a selection occurs based on speed, endurance, and intensity of desire. In the summer days of this latitude these birds may course the air without lighting for fourteen hours on end—feeding, mating, and gathering nesting material in flight. Think of the number of insects it must require to power such incredible physical activity.

How far does a chimney swift fly in the course of a normal lifetime? That good bird columnist for the Nashville (Tennessee) *Banner* indulges[2] in speculations concerning the distance flown by a swift caught out of Fisk University Chapel chimney and banded by Mrs. Laskey. The banded bird was captured in a neighboring chimney nine years later.

"This swift," he says, "had made nine trips to northern South America and back, doubtless to Fisk campus, or nearby, for raising a family of little swifts. This annual pilgrimage to the Peruvian Andes

[2]Issue of May 8, 1949.

186

meant a distance of 50,000 miles, flown each round trip. Since this bird never lights from early morn to late evening, taking food and water and nesting material in full flight, we must add another 100,000 miles annually, which make a grand total of 1,350,000 miles flown during the nine years. If this creature was not born in the spring of 1939, then another 150,000 miles must be added for each additional previous year."

Doubtless a generous mileage allowance! But, as Dr. Mayfield points out, the captured swift may have been several years old when banded; and a contemplation of how much farther he flew after being released in good health encourages further speculations, involving astronomical distances.

In primitive America, chimney swifts nested only in hollow trees and were thus barred from extending their breeding range to the open country. With the settling of plain and prairie, and especially with the building of two-story brick or stone flues, their numbers have been multiplied and their breeding range has been greatly expanded. The more meticulous housewives are objecting to their free and unlimited use of chimneys. In my own home these birds have caused a domestic dispute of some causticity: to screen or not to screen is debated each spring as the happy chittering of the returning migrants begins to be heard around the place. The defense admits that they do fan a lot of soot down into the living room and that, in damp weather, the odor of their droppings is perceptible.

With wood now selling at $15 per cord, the chimney, more's the pity, is going out of fashion; and, as the old ones are closed, we shall have another victim of housing shortage on our hands. He cannot go back to the woods from whence he came, for the good reason that there are no more woods to go to. Destroy a forest and you destroy a bird; destroy a bird and you multiply vicious insects. Thus a chain reaction disastrous to conservation is set going. The swift, particularly, is a gobbler up of our own insect enemies; and his deletions, like those of the harmless, necessary bat, increase enormously the health and comfort of our environment.

In bird lists of the Austin region made twenty-five or thirty years ago, this bird is recorded as an "uncommon, irregular migrant, occasionally very common for a few days in spring."[3]

The earliest record of the swift's occurrence in Austin was made by Simmons of a single pair of migrants, March 26, 1915. Now (1950) these birds swarm over the whole region from early April to late September.

The first nesting swifts I ever saw in Austin were circling over the playing field of a new concrete million-dollar stadium, completed in 1924; and I am confident it was one of their first nesting sites here. If it took a million-dollar stadium to bring them, it is certainly not the least of the justifications for such a structure, and I say well and good. How thoughtful it is of these birds, in return for such prodigious expenditure, to clear the whole place of mosquitoes which bite readily through silk or nylon. I have seen them combing the playing field and skimming over vast tiers of empty seats in the early hours of a September morn, contributing their mite (and a mighty mite it is!) to the comfort of the fifty thousand or so spectators scheduled to assemble there at 2 P.M.

The mosquito is the worst curse of the low coastal prairies so far as camping comfort is concerned. I have seen important outdoor work suspended and workmen driven indoors behind the protection of screens by these minute pests. Sleeping under a bar, I have been awakened to find that a portion of my body, accidentally pushed against the netting, has been peppered through net and sleeping garment with bites, maybe a dozen punctures to the square inch. It takes a thick shirt to baffle this terrific insect, equipped as he is with a long, piercing proboscis. Thick shirts are impossible in the summer heat of this humid region, and I have never found a repellent that really repels a coast mosquito for any length of time. The Karánkaways, inhabiting this region when the first white settlers came, were found using rancid shark's oil to fend them off, which is the basis for the pioneer folklore that these savages had a racial odor which could be "smelt a mile."

[3]*Birds of the Austin Region*, by George Finlay Simmons, University of Texas Press, Austin, 1925.

One night I noticed a stalwart trapper of not less than two hundred pounds' weight, all bone and muscle, sitting near a wire screen indulging in occasional fits of laughter. I found that he had descended to trapping mosquitoes. He held the back of his hand near the screen to give the barred-out mosquito a whiff of heavenly human blood. The tantalized insects strode excitedly up and down on the outside, trying to get in to enjoy the feast. Some of the more impatient ones thrust their suck pumps through the screen in an effort to reach the man's hand. Then, with true trapper's instinct, he rubbed the inside of the screen gently with his thumb, thus catching his prey by the proboscis. He held the victims there gently for a moment and watched with delighted laughter their squirming and writhing before "dehorning" them, as he called it, by increasing the pressure until he mashed off the tip of the thirsty snout. He took an especial delight (and I did, too, after I was initiated into the sport) in catching three or four of the bloodsuckers at once. This professional trapper, one of the most successful in the whole Southwest, was accustomed, as a matter of daily routine, to taking wolves, bobcats, or pumas out of steel traps, and to devising snares for larger game; so there was the humor of incongruity in the sight of him intent upon and absorbed with this small quarry, so earnestly employing his trapper's ingenuity and with such evident satisfaction that small successes threw him into gales of laughter.

Seeing that swifts are "100 per centers," so far as the value to man of their food habits is concerned, living as they do on nothing except noxious insects, mosquitoes included, it would be worth while to build chimneys for them along the coastal bays, as Dr. Charles A. Campbell built his famous bat towers in the mosquito-infested bottoms of the San Antonio River near San Antonio, Texas.[4] All over their natural range swifts come readily in uncounted thousands wherever homes for them are provided. The rapacious lumber industry has destroyed their native nesting places in hollow trees, and now we are screening them out of our chimneys, which they readily accepted as a substitute. How better spend a little conservation

'For a description of Dr. Campbell's bat towers see *The Literary Digest,* April 17, 1915, p. 873.

money than by building breeding places for them? The same thing should be done for bats, which are an even deadlier enemy of the mosquito. The value of the guano would probably be sufficient to keep such structures in repair, especially in the coast country, where the soil is notably deficient in phosphates. At least it would be worth while to spend a little experimentally in an effort to stay the shedding of so much innocent blood—brute blood as well as human—for here flies and mosquitoes pester the stock outrageously.

Invasions of swifts seeking housing accommodations are sometimes quite dramatic. Louise M. Trueblood[5] describes vividly her struggle with swarms of these creatures while they were trying to take possession of her chimney. She heard their buzzing one night sounding like thunder, and undertook to dislodge them by building a fire in the hearth. "The beating of myriad wings," she says, "caused a breeze which made it impossible for any flame to live, and three times my kindled blaze was instantly fanned out." She finally got a fire started, and the hearth was immediately choked with singed birds, and the whole house was soon filled with the blinded and maddened creatures. A terrier ran amuck in the excitement, pawing the sooty birds and getting his feet daubed with the material, which he carried hither and yon, dabbling tablespreads and coverlets as he plunged about after his prey, tearing fine lace curtains to tatters, and marking the paper on the walls as he reared up with his forefeet trying to pull down birds out of his reach. The whole house was thrown into the utmost disorder. Laundry and repair bills were considerable. As a farmer friend of mine used to exclaim when Nemesis accorded with his own acute sense of justice, "Served her right—by Gum!"

In the spring of 1949 veritable clouds of swifts, estimated at ten thousand, invading Cotulla, Texas, new territory for them, took possession of a large chimney in the county courthouse. The local newspaper[6] recounts that "about dark every evening they would come in from all directions and pour down the chimney like bees going into

[5]*The Atlantic Monthly*, 158:657, November 1931.
[6]*The Cotulla Record*, April 29, 1949.

a beehive. Early every morning they would leave—evidently going in search of food."

Meantime, there were many complaints received by the county commissioners and suggestions as to what should be done about it. There was to be a community meeting in the courthouse one night and Deputy Sheriff Frank Newman was instructed to fire the intruders out. "But," the account continues, "they were packed in the chimney so tight that the flue would not draw, and all the smoke came back into the courthouse." I think the story is inaccurate here, since swifts do not "pack" in a chimney: they cling to its walls. The smoke was driven back by the beating of the wings, as anyone may find out who disturbs them at night. They simply fanned the smoke right back into the face of the law and drove the assembly from the courthouse, retaining possession of the sleeping quarters they had selected. Again, in the words of my farmer friend, "Served 'em right, by Gum!"

Answering an inquiry about this episode, Frank Newman, "Chief Deputy Sheriff," furnished me with further details. "I do not think," he says, "that the ten thousand figure was an exaggeration. . . . I really believe there were more. This was the first time I had ever seen these birds around here. . . . After I started the fire, someone came to the elevator and called to me downstairs, extremely excited, thinking the building was on fire. These birds stayed here several days, then disappeared as fast as they had come. It was quite an unusual sight for us. The birds would leave about daylight and we saw nothing more of them until about sundown, when they would really swarm in."

The *Record* erroneously concludes the episode thus: "Swifts spend their winter in tropical Central America, and at this time of year are returning to their nesting grounds around Labrador and the Hudson Bay region." No, they were not bound for arctic regions, but were going to nest and raise their young right in Cotulla and do away with uncounted millions of noxious insects in the Cotulla Country.

Swifts seem born to be the bone of many and diverse contentions. Perhaps no other species has caused so much puzzlement and dissension among ornithologists. The bird has been and remains a brain teaser. Here is a partial list of the queries he has inspired, which at one time or another have drawn eminent bird students into opposing camps:

1. After some length of wrangling, his classification was changed from the swallow family to that of the goatsuckers. Shifts from one species to another are common to this day. Occasionally new information and studies change the genus to which a bird has been assigned, and formerly families were often reconstituted, but a transfer from one *order* to another (as happened to the swift) was unusual even in the early days of serious taxonomy.[7]

2. Another ancient controversy concerned the migration or the "hibernation" of the swift. Even shrewd old Gilbert White was at times half inclined toward the hibernation theory, and on the point of accepting the contention that they disappeared in the fall by simply burrowing into the mud. Of course that went for swallows too, as the two species were classed together at that time. It is curious that a similar tradition hung for a while over the Carolina parakeet, the lovely little fellow our gun-toting ancestors exterminated.

3. They make a noise at night, ever so often, which various observers have compared to thunder. Just how do they "rumble" in this fashion? Discussion of this point rumbled through Volumes 62 and 63 of *The Auk* and has echoed off and on since. It is compared to "pipe-organ" vibrations, and is called by one writer a "rumbling noise." Ralph W. Dexter calls the chimney a "shaft, an open pipe with fundamental resonance frequency of 13, just in the range needed for perceptible overtone production."

---

[7]The swift is still sometimes confused with the swallow. It is unfortunate that one of his common names is "chimney swallow." In the spring of 1948 I read an AP dispatch from Kingfisher, Oklahoma, saying that "chimney swallows" had sealed over the vent of a furnace and flooded the house of Mrs. Howard Baldwin with poisonous gas, with near fatal results. I couldn't imagine a swift's nest sealing anything, much less anything as volatile as gas. I wrote the physician whose name appeared in the dispatch for confirmation of the details. He didn't identify the species but mentioned the fact that the birds made their nests with mud. Of course this exonerates the swift and places the blame for the "near tragedy" on one of the mud-daubing swallows.

4. The location of the winter home of the swift was long a matter of speculation. Multitudinous banding brought results. Only a few years ago natives of northeastern Peru began sending back bands which enabled Frederick C. Lincoln to place the winter home of our chimney swift "in the neighborhood of the Rio Napo in northeastern Peru."

5. It is agreed that they gather nesting material on the wing. But do they gather it with feet or with bill? This dispute once involved on opposite sides such eminent authorities as Coues and Fuertes. It was decided for Fuertes in favor of the feet.

6. "They invade some chimneys while other chimneys, for reasons best known to the swifts, have never been tenanted." I have not found the plans and specifications required by these birds. Before building experimental chimneys it would be well to make a comparative study of many occupied with unoccupied chimneys in an effort to determine the indispensable conditions for swift occupancy.

7. Composition of courting triangles. Opinion favors two males and one female.

8. It was formerly argued that these birds had no feet, since no one ever saw a swift perching. This has, of course, been disproved. They have feet, but not of the usual kind. They are clinging and climbing, not perching, feet.

9. Puzzling accounts are available giving the proportion of males to females. Audubon one July cut open 115 birds and found only six females, twenty-two of sex undetermined, and the remaining eighty-seven adult males. Not more than a month later he found many more females than males in the same hollow sycamore.

10. It was once almost universally the opinion of the authorities that the bird sometimes flew with alternate wing beats. The slow-motion picture says, "No, they fly as other birds do, with wings beating in unison."

11. Do they feed at night? This question has been settled also in favor of some night feeding. The proportion of night feeding depends, I should think, upon the latitude; hence, the comparative length of day and night. In this latitude, especially in early summer with daylight lasting twelve to fourteen hours, there is much late,

but little night, feeding. I have seen few birds leaving their chimney at nightfall; many leaving in early dawn. Observers have found the birds active at 10 P.M., at 12 midnight, and at 3 A.M., "with tenfold energy between dawn and 6 A.M." The romanticist reluctantly classes the "starlight flight of swifts" as legend.

12. Why, in certain sections of the country, do their migrations sometimes miss fire? Occasionally a prolonged storm crosses in front of a migration and delays it by destroying high-flying insects which they must have to live.

13. Do they carry bedbugs? No. At least not the kind human beings entertain. There is a parasite closely resembling our domestic bedbug which is found on them, but it requires a bird host. Man delights not them—no, nor woman either.

14. Do they complete the nest before laying the eggs? No, this bird is always in a hurry, and you may expect him to economize time in every possible way. With a partially completed nest the female lays the eggs, and the pair complete the nest as she and her mate hover over the eggs. It is said that the male and female change places on the nest every twenty minutes to three quarters of an hour.

15. Do they bathe? Yes. However, I doubt if it does much good. These chimney dwellers get oil of creosote from soot, thus waterproofing their feathers against direct downpours of rain in their nests.

16. In late summer and fall, when the birds congregate in certain chimneys by the hundreds, do the same birds occupy a given chimney each night? I know the same birds do not come to my own chimney, because there is such a wide variation in numbers during August, September, and October. One day there would be a hundred—other days only six or seven. I concluded that they roost in available chimneys near where they happen to be feeding when night comes on. Dr. G. R. Mayfield records a similar conclusion.

17. Three birds have been observed feeding nestlings.[8] Is it pos-

[8]Mary F. Day, "Home-Life in a Chimney," *Bird-Lore*, 1:78–81, 1899. Quoted in *The Birds of Minnesota*, The University of Minnesota Press, Minneapolis, 1936, Vol. I, p. 650.

sible that the courtship triangle persists after the eggs have been hatched? faithful suitor thus helping to take care of the family of the mated pair, or, perhaps, act as nursemaid, as Miss Day supposes. Or maybe it is straight-out polygamy, or polyandry, as Dr. Thomas S. Roberts suggests.[9]

Swifts are often mistaken for swallows, and are certainly not observed as generally as their numbers, neighborliness with man, and economic importance would seem to justify. They are quiet and unobtrusive. A neighbor of mine told me one day that he had never seen a swift. "You sleep," I told him, "within twenty feet of dozens of them every night from April to October." He would not believe me until I showed him a hundred or more dropping at nightfall into a chimney built through his upstairs apartment within twenty feet of his bed.

[9]*The Birds of Minnesota,* The University of Minnesota Press, Minneapolis, 1936, Vol. I, p. 650.

13 GOATS IN EXCESS

Little mohair is produced in the coast country, but, nevertheless, the mark of the goat is upon the land, especially in the coastal river bottoms. The results of herding too many of these browsers into eroding areas lying along the headwaters of certain rivers are clearly visible to the soil analyst in samples of alluvial deposits made as turbid waters, escaping the low channel banks, slush over lowlands and, partially relieved of their silt burden, discharge into coastal bays. The three counties around the mouth of the Guadalupe, for instance, support barely twelve hundred goats, while the three counties (little larger in area) in which the stream takes its rise, 250 miles northwest, pasture two hunderd and fifty thousand. So the silt and sludge of every headrise contains a percentage of the topsoil from goat-browsed slopes comprising the river's upper watershed.

There are other offenders here also—cattle, sheep, and—formerly—many horses; but the goat is convenient for illustration, having served man for many centuries, not only with meat, milk, and mohair, but as a "scapegoat."

Besides, this is one of the great goat-raising sections of the world. The Edwards Plateau (occupying roughly one eighth of Texas), in which the Guadalupe and the Nueces rise, and through which both the Brazos and the Colorado cut their ways to the Gulf of Mexico, produces 84 per cent of all the goats in Texas, the state being credited with 85 per cent of the production of the entire country.

On these rocky ridges of highly mineralized soil the nimble goat is up to his old tricks; but he is not yet doing his worst, except in spots. That "his worst" ruined much of the Holy Land and contiguous areas most authorities agree. It now appears that even while Pericles was flattering Athens with a glowing catalogue of her accomplishments, these browsers, following in the wake of ruthless lumbermen, were already beginning to gnaw away the glory that was Greece. Had the Grecian statesmen from about 500 B.C. on down been subjected in their youth to the discipline of a modern course in range management, our own poets might have been saved the trouble of composing so many elegies on that unhappy country. Where there is no vision of what is happening to basic resources, the people perish.

History teems with examples of retribution visited upon nations which consume their basic resources and try from then on to subsist on their own flesh and blood. "Northern Iraq and Syria," says Bayard Dodge,[1] "have been so neglected that malaria has become a curse, the sheep have created dust bowls, and only scattered groups of pioneers are living in places which were irrigated during the period of Abbasside caliphs as late as the twelfth century A.D." This case is typical. From all accounts, statesmen and rulers of ancient Greece were too much embroiled in political intrigue, too busy bargaining with faithless allies, or too taken up with placating the mob at home while waging desperate war abroad, to be concerned with

[1]"Palestine Refugees," autumn (1949), *Yale Review*, p. 72.

what the goats and sheep were doing to the topsoil, which was supplying life and vigor to the people.

Too many sheep are, in all conscience, bad enough, but the hungry goat is really a lethal browser. His neck, whose elastic reach rarely exceeds its grasp, his lithe lips, thin and tough for manipulating leafage and twigs into position for the scissoring, sharp teeth, have wrought in many lands a more permanent desolation than war itself. Our own goat ranchers, wishing to eradicate some noxious shrub, as, for instance, the lance-leaved sumac, sometimes turn their whiskered herds loose upon it, saying, "I'll *goat* it to death," a goat-country phrase for concentrating goats in an infested area until the offending shrub is destroyed, root and branch. Some ancient myth-maker, watching the hungry goat gnawing away in brushy rubble on an eroded hillside, perhaps got his inspiration for personifying Famine herself, crawling around in a stony field on a slope of Mount Parnassus, "pulling up with her teeth the scanty herbage. . . . Her hair was rough, her jaws covered with dust, and her skin drawn tight, so as to show all her bones."

The California nurseryman who uses sheep to strip leaves from his rosebushes before shipping them to market would probably find the goat destemming his stock as well as defoliating it. There is an old Rumanian legend to the effect that in the beginning goats had wings, and "used to fly about eating up the tops of trees. They did it so thoroughly that they left no leaf or bud, and never allowed a tree to grow up. When God saw what mischief they were doing and how they were destroying all the trees, he cursed them, and, taking away their wings, he said that henceforth they should only be able to climb up crooked trees, and so they do."[2]

The natural bent or talent of this browser for extracting the last bit of nourishment from a growing plant backfired beneficently in at least one instance in recent history by giving the world a new and valuable species of alfalfa, which should be named "The Goat's Gift to Agriculture." We should thank northern Turkey's hungry herds for this latest accession to our list of forage crops. The goat in the

[2]*Rumanian Bird and Beast Stories,* rendered into English by M. Gaster, Ph.D., London. Published for the Folk Lore Society by Sidgwick & Jackson, 1915, p. 86.

role of a natural scientist has been reported to the United Nations by Dr. P. V. Cardon, Administrator of Agricultural Research, United States Department of Agriculture.

In northern Turkey, American scouts found a single amazing alfalfa plant in a goat pasture. It covered several square feet. It grew like Bermuda grass, which no hitherto-discovered alfalfa had done. From a single root runners spread, putting down roots at intervals and sending up alfalfa leaves at these points. The plant had done this as a genetic change, in self-defense. The goats grazed so closely that the alfalfa could not produce seed. But instead of dying, the plant had developed runners which replaced seed as a means of propagation. It has proved adaptable to this country, and, concludes Dr. Cardon, its "potential value cannot be overestimated." Thus overgrazing should be given one white mark in the scorebook of conservation.

Many ancient instances occur in the Mediterranean Basin of highlands ruined and lowlands damaged by first cutting off timber and later browsing goats on the remnants of ruined forests. Plato, in the fifth century B.C., warns of the disasters which follow destruction of forests. The streams and springs of Greece were dried up, since rainfall quickly ran off slopes deprived of the vegetation which formerly slowed up the movement of the water and led it into underground channels. Ellen Churchill Semple[3] explains the process in detail.

"When the mountains were denuded of their forests," she says, "the violent autumn storms with their sudden downpour of rain scoured off the thin covering of earth from the steep declivities. The shield of foliage was no longer there to break the impact of the rain; the network of roots no longer held the light humus to the slopes. The *maqui* [chaparral], rooted in shallow pockets of earth, succeeded the denuded forests which formerly conserved and distributed moisture in the dry season, and preserved large areas for cultivation by irrigation. Under the assault of the goats, the *maqui* even

The Geography of the Mediterranean Region, Its Relation to Ancient History, by Ellen Churchill Semple, M.A., LL.D., Professor of Anthropogeography at Clark University, Constable & Co., Ltd. London, 1932, p. 291.

199

has grown shorter and thinner, exposing ever larger spaces to the scouring action of rain in winter and wind in summer, till mountains have become quite bare, as in parts of Greece and Spain. In many sections of the Mediterranean a single deforestation has meant denudation of the soil also and hence, the permanent destruction of the forests."

First the lumberman and then the goat! But the ancient lumberman was equipped only with axes of stone and bronze. If they accomplished with these primitive tools such ruin in a few centuries, the lover of the land must think with a shudder of what the modern and still more rapacious forest ravager of today can do equipped with power machinery.

Generally speaking, as the nomads conquered the city peoples of Asia Minor, their herds, largely goats, completed the desolation by skinning the land of its ancient vegetative protection; and, seeking shade at midday, these siesta-loving animals desecrated with their droppings the ruined temples of the dead. It was in some such desolated region of former grandeur that Shelley's "traveller from an antique land" saw "two vast and legless trunks of stone," still standing above a vaunting pedestal inscription, to which the poet subjoins:

> . . . Round the decay
> Of that colossal wreck, boundless and bare,
> The lone and level sands stretch far away.

A Spanish proverb says the goat never dies of hunger. Overgrazing by no other ungulate devastates a brushy slope so thoroughly as the goat does, for, hunger-pinched, he not only devours the foliage of a shrub, but "barks" it. Topsoil deprived of natural protection is at the mercy of torrential rains and off it goes, as it did in Greece and Spain, a thousand years' thickness in half an hour's downpour.

His greediness, however, as well as his marvelous gastronomical equipment, under intelligent control, are advantageous, as will appear later. But for the present, and however fond we are of the goat *per se*, we must admit that in excess he is a menace, and must be grown in moderation if he is to make his important material contributions to man and continue to divert our idle moments by his erratic behavior.

I had occasion lately to see the silt of the highlands arriving in the lowlands by the carload. I had arisen early—too early; and, while waiting for the fisherman's departure at sunup, beguiled the time by reading signs and by listening to brief, drowsy snatches of early morning conversation in a "hamburger joint" near the fisherman's landing. I noted a rudely printed warning hung up where all could see: "The manager of this place is not reliable for anything lost or stolen." Another notice pled, "Don't make fun of our coffee; you may be old and weak yourself sometime." A dozen of us were lined up on high stools fronting the steam-clouded mirror, plainly a faded relic of pre-Volstead days. A heavy voice at my side ordered a drink interrogatively: "Have you got an uxtry cup o' coffee, waiter?" I could see dingily reflected the row of customers, each one, chin in hand and elbow on counter, patiently awaiting service from the sweating factotum: boss, waiter, cook, and cashier—all in one.

Surely the saddest words of tongue or pen must be assembled and dipped in gloom to describe the highway "hamburger joint" in early morning hours when its first customers park trucks and stumble in on long-cramped legs for coffee and "Ham-and." As a double-convex lens focuses light rays, so this "joint" in the darkness before dawn brings together into compass of four smoke-begrimed walls the odors, sights, and sounds most depressing to the patriot. Dismal concentration!

"Why," I asked myself, "do they call this place a 'joint'? I shall see what Mr. Mencken says first time I am in a library"—a promise I have never fulfilled. But I know that the evil flavor of the term has warrant in history, for it clings like a bur and is current throughout the country.

I had heard the bawling of the juke box even before I entered. In beating ballad rhythm the singer was complaining, "It's a shame to love you like I do, I do." Then merely for the rhyme and not, I hope, to record any actual delinquency, the balladeer asserts that she has been "untrue, untrue." I was further advised in this song that a woman "is more than a man can stand" and "will drive almost any man mad." In addition, I found by listening closely, missing many words, that a man's only resort in this extremity is to "crawl into a hole and pull the ground over you." This "you" completed the rhyme scheme, jingling along with "do" and "untrue." The thing quit suddenly, ingesting the nickel with malicious click. "The rest is silence" —at least until another coin stimulates further bawling, rhymed and metered, to recount more misery of the next unlucky male in frustrated effort to get on with some woman who "is more than a man can stand." If, indeed, "architecture is frozen music," and this ballad or its like were solidified by cold, I wonder what sort of misshapen hut of brutish koo-boo, or hogan of degenerate savage would come out of the artistic deep freeze.

Listening were eight sleepy, sorrowful faces, rugged men in greasy jackets, each with a cigarette, sipping coffee between deep inhalations, gazing without greed at his "ham-and" or sausage and eggs, edged with grease now congealing from contact with the cold, thick oval dish in which it was served. All the while a young sailor with a dollar's worth of nickels stood punching a slot machine, puncturing the bawling ballad with the bolting, clicking clatter of that nerve-racking mechanism. There was one fat, blowsy girl at the end of the counter nearly asleep, who had a positively electric reaction when the young sailor cast a casual remark in her direction.

No blessing in the form of a twentieth-century Fred Harvey has as yet been conferred upon bus and truck drivers and upon the bus-traveling public. Maybe he was the great-grandfather of the "chains," ancestor of overlordship in retail business; but there are those still living to whom the name of Fred Harvey is a tender memory, since clustering about it are visions of brilliantly lighted and excellently serviced oases of good food, spaced at convenient intervals across a wide continent.

I drove on down to the fisherman's shack at the river's edge, leaving my coffee untouched since, besides being "weak and old," it had become chilled while I was bemoaning the fate of a nation which supports liberally such a wide variety of "joints." I think maybe the "joint" is evidence of an erosion more deadly and much more difficult to deal with than the simple material erosions of which I have been speaking.

At the river I was joined by a companion interested in finding what proved to be a nonexistent heronry twenty miles upstream. Dawn was breaking. The fragrant sweat of luxurious vegetation quickly routed out the sour odors which my nasal nerves were still registering with odious insistence. A blue grosbeak sang while the fisherman wrestled with his tangled tackle. It is a tiny voice to issue from so huge a throat and huger beak, and yet it added its mite of joy to the river-bottom chorus. The redbird, also of heavy throat and ponderous bill, began celebrating brilliantly the prospects of an open sunrise. Then with the first beams of the rising sun thrown across that forever level land, the peerless one, the mocker, began. White-eyed vireos uttered brisk, businesslike greetings from masses of wild grape; until, breaking in upon this concord of sweet sounds, came the sudden *put-put-put* of the fisherman's motorboat, and we climbed in.

The Guadalupe was up, crowding its low banks. My friend said the water was "soupy," and an ugly soup it was, limestone-tinctured, brewed in heavy rains on the steep slopes and tortuous gulches of the river's upper watershed—a "headrise," the fisherman called it. Drift swirled by, and my companion said that it was just such burdens of silt as this that had buried the finest oyster beds on the Texas coast. The crest of this particular rise had already passed. The fisherman pointed to the ribs of a wrecked boat half submerged, which showed a crust of mud recording the high-water mark of two days before. Limber-stemmed shrubs at the water's edge laved their leaves in the rushing stream, sucked under now and then, willy-nilly, and came up as if gasping for breath from their suffocating dip in the sludgy current. We made slow time, although the boat was amply powered.

I like fishermen who talk, and this one rattled away in a voice quite easy to understand above the noise of the engine. He gave us the field marks of the roseate spoonbill very well, and said he had never seen a picture that did the bird justice. For him it was a "fillamingo." We pressed him hard on this point, describing the flamingo, especially the bill. Finally, more from courtesy than from conviction, I think, he admitted that his was probably only a "Texas Fillamingo."[4]

Sensing in us an interest in birds, our host chattered on.

"Lookee," he said, "at them there two teeter birds. I flush 'em every trip. You kin drive 'em just so far, but no further. You wait."

We watched and waited. A pair of spotted sandpipers, with the spots on, flitted ahead. The channel was narrow and arched over with trees, so that they dared not come back by us, apparently afraid, also, to circle over our heads. So on they went up the river, alighting every hundred yards or so, as is their habit, and flushing again as the noise of the motor became to them unendurable. This went on for several miles. They must have gotten pretty tired, for their flights became shorter and shorter.

"Well, here we are," said the fisherman, as, rounding a curve, a

[4]So far as I know, the only identification of the flamingo on the Texas coast, generally accepted by ornithologists as indisputable, was made by my friend, Mrs. Jack Hagar, of Rockport, July 27, 1943, who knows more Gulf coast birds by sight than any other person in America, except Roger Tory Peterson, who knows as many, but no more.

On this historic occasion Mrs. Hagar's party consisted of the following: Fred C. Stark, San Antonio Zoological Park; F. E. Dietz, of San Antonio; Captain M. B. Mullinax; and pilot, Ben A. Earp. Mrs. Hagar reports the identification in *The Auk*, April 1944, Vol. 61, pp. 301–02, in part, as follows:

"While we were cruising along near Carroll Island of the Second Chain of Islands in lower San Antonio Bay, I saw a Flamingo standing in the water near the island. The observation was made through binoculars (Zeiss 8 × 40). I immediately asked Capt. Mullinax to stop the boat. Mr. Stark verified the identification and Mr. Earp, who has been a taxidermist for many years and who is acquainted with bird life, also concurred in the identification, as did Mr. Dietz, who is a student of birds. Capt. Mullinax was the last to view the bird with the glasses. The men then left the boat and I waded toward the bird, which had not moved from its original position near the marker of the National Audubon Preserve. I was able to approach within seventy-five feet of the Flamingo before it moved. Then it took several steps, rose and circled slowly about fifty feet over my head, showing the dark wing markings, with long neck fully extended and legs trailing behind. . . . The time spent in making this observation was half an hour. There were hundreds of roseate spoonbills standing near with which we could make comparison, and there was no possibility of confusing this red bird with the delicate, pinkish spoonbills."

Mrs. Hagar then suggests that the bird may have been driven in by a hurricane which on that day struck Galveston.

railroad bridge came into view. "Now you watch them little critters."

Sure enough, they changed their tactics. Fearful of flying under the bridge, although there was plenty of clearance—perhaps twenty feet—they flew right up to the bridge, became confused, crisscrossed the stream a time or two, and then rose and darted back over our heads.

"I ain't never been able to drive 'em under that bridge," the fisherman said. "And now you watch 'em when we go back." On our return at about triple the speed we had made upstream, we crowded these birds, and tired them down, since they barely had time to alight before we were on them again. When they were nearly exhausted, they rose and circled over us, going back upstream.

"Them birds can't fly over thirty miles an hour," the fisherman said.

"After passing Moore's Falls by means of locks, we again had recourse to our oars," says Thoreau, "and went merrily on our way, driving the small sand-piper from rock to rock before us." This I am sure was the spotted sandpiper, also. Who has not been charmed by this flitting little fairy of a bird, as, walking a lonely beach or skirting the river's edge, a pair keeps him company for miles, flying first ahead, then back, and then ahead of him again?

Now the banks became lower and lower, vegetation thicker and more tangled, the channel of the stream harder and harder to follow. The muddy waters were spreading, slipping away—now here, now there—reoccupying old channels, submerging thousands of acres and leaving everywhere an encrustation of mud. I was told that these waters were miles wide. Ages upon ages the rivers of the coast country have been building first marshes and then prairies from soil taken from the uplands; ages upon ages this process will continue. It is the acceleration of the process by plowing up and overgrazing the watersheds which is giving concern. As long as Nature had her way, the lowland was fed no faster than it could digest and absorb, while the highlands were robbed no faster than natural forces were replenishing them. Now lowlands are threatened with ruin from excess, especially of clays and coarser materials, while highlands, unable to recover losses, are being wasted away.

A student of previous cultures stumbled the other day on the ruins of a village in New Mexico which, he says, was probably inhabited five thousand years ago. There are no eroded slopes around this ancient site, no evidence of wasted resources, no telltale scars which will mark five thousand years hence—and forever—many sites of our own present-day communities. A gloomy view defines civilization as that arrangement of human affairs whereby people are enslaved and natural resources destroyed; and "the flowering of civilization" as a grand, drunken spree. Lights flash amid sounds of carousal, wine flows in rivers, human egotism rises to insane heights, Science boasts, and drunken poets vaunt the immortality of whatever regime happens to nourish them. But when the feast is finished and the lamps expire and the gray dawn comes, the spectres which attend waste and extravagance are found occupying the seats of the mighty. George Orwell[5] satirizes civilized destruction in its worst form, i.e., war, as a method of "using up the products of the Machine without raising the general standard of living." Under totalitarianism, the author says, equipped with the Machine, we shall destroy natural resources and then obliterate the products in war, since otherwise we can't keep people employed.

To call the present soil-saving program in this country a drop in the bucket is gross exaggeration. It's not even a tenth of a small drop in a good-sized barrel. It's too small to register in percentage, and to suggest its size in proportion to need, one must resort to weather-bureau language and call it merely a trace. It produces headlines aplenty, but it has not as yet influenced silt measurements in Texas rivers (except, of course, *below* the big dams), by the weight of a feather. Indeed, not at all.[6]

[5]*Nineteen Eighty-four*, Harcourt, Brace & Co., New York, 1949.

[6]This does not mean that erosion is not being checked on thousands of farms and ranches, but that it is beginning on thousands more. Present measures have not yet overtaken the spread of the disease, while already great areas are being abandoned as incurable. New sores appear faster than old ones are being healed, and, as will later appear, much "healing" goes to pot from subsequent neglect.

Its great value so far is educational. The idea of what soil is worth is gradually—only gradually—permeating the public mind. From this standpoint alone it is worth the effort and the money. But, as every conservationist points out, it's later than you think. Some believe it's too late. But in my opinion such men underestimate American genius for organization, executive power and American invention and production of dirt-moving machinery: steam shovels, terracers, ditchers, rippers, et cetera, which, as one writer says, place in the hands of this country a power never before entrusted to human beings, that is, the power of effecting geologic changes on a continental scale.

History, philosophy, archeology, myth, religion, formal science, and the informal science of common sense (which is supposed to unite the senses in an intuitive perception of truth)—all combine to urge one overwhelming lesson: soil is life, and a people uprooted from it die as a plant uprooted dies. Popular science claptrap, visions of magicmongers, or any comfort optimism extracts from the guarded statements of Science itself, hinting that man can and soon will achieve victory over Natural Law and lift himself by his own bootstraps, avoiding the wages of sin, is just so much unnerving illusion. One sound scientist, speculating in an off hour, as scientists should, suggests that wood may be eventually converted directly into animal food. Another suggests that there *may be* unlimited food supplies in the culture of microorganisms; still another, that sea water, chemically treated, *may* make the desert wastes of the world blossom as the rose, and so on. Each suggestion, fortified by a big name, is sensational enough to inspire big headlines, but headlines stripped of the "ifs" and "buts" of the pronouncement itself. Thus crumbs of comfort nourish illusions which point the anxious toward that secure harborage of "peace and plenty" existing only in the composite wishful thinking of a large section of humanity. It remained for France, most logical and realistic of nations, to build, by the plans and specifications of its best military engineers (most logical and realistic of professions), at enormous expense, a structure of steel and concrete along its eastern border, the proved futility of which has furnished our own language with a phrase for identifying the lie which hope invents to satisfy human yearning for security.

This easy optimism supplies the public mind with that inertia against which the conservationist pushes in vain. Generation after generation of our forebears moved west to virgin soil when land east was worn out. This ready relief has fortified our optimism by establishing a habit of mind which persists in the face of the fact that there is now no more virgin soil left "out west" or out in any other direction. If and when too many goats finally devastate the rich ranges of the Edwards Plateau, goat culture in Texas will probably decline to the Bedouin level.

Indeed, if one is determined to put more animals on a given area than its carrying capacity justifies, he should not do it with goats. Sheep are a little better, since they do leave the brush intact; and brush mistifies rain, while roots of it clutch the soil to hold it in place. Too many sheep are especially hard on open glades. They are driven to "mining" the grass; and, ceaselessly searching, ever on the move, they pulverize the surface with their sharp hoofs, opening the way for both wind and water erosion. Neat cattle are far easier on pasture lands, as any ranchman will tell you. Their broad, blunt hoofs do not cut up the soil. They are lazy grazers, and, when not actually feeding, "shade up" or trail off to water single file. More important still is the mouth: the big, moist, naked muzzle and thick immobile lips are fine for taking generous mouthfuls from baskets of plenty, but ill adapted to skinning browse plants, or burrowing for grass roots. Nor are neat cattle driven by hunger into ceaseless activity. They drift some, of course, but they have been known to starve quietly on ranges where sheep would eke out a pretty fair living. They do not tramp, tramp, tramp, as horses do, or race each other in mere frolic. The cowboy, suffering from fleas under his shirt, was thinking of horses when he complained, "It's not so much what they eat I mind, as what they tromp down."

There should be a penalty for overgrazing as well as the subsidy now in force for those who treat their ranges with some consideration. "The land," as Thomas Jefferson says, "belongs in usufruct to the living." But *only* in usufruct. No land title, guaranteed by the armed forces of the United States, grants an owner the right to destroy a basic resource, such as soil fertility.

"Land belongs in usufruct to the living." This principle permits taking from the land the *increase* and no more, and directs that its productive capacity remain unimpaired in trust for succeeding generations. Under this principle proved abuse of the soil is held to cancel the obligation of society to the owner. The land held by any nation is its only permanent investment. It may charge obsolescence against everything else, but not against this foundation of all its other wealth. Its people must be taught to live off the interest. Verily saith the Preacher, "One generation passeth away, and another generation cometh: but the earth abideth for ever."

Unless some such attitude as this is taken by organized society toward those whom choice and chance have entrusted with possession and control of the land, the nation itself will wither away as its resources diminish, just as hundreds of national units have already done within view of recorded time. The subsidy is justified only as a stopgap, or emergency device, since the principle of the subsidy has been proved parasitical—*cancerous*, in fact, and capable eventually of consuming its own host. Hence, there should begin at once education for a sounder theory of land use. Unfortunately, we do not have in this country the love of the land as land which has retained soil and sustained its fertility in parts of Europe, especially in the Scandinavian countries. We, as a people, love our cottage too little and our automobile too much ever to stay put long enough to develop a genuine Danish devotion to soil as soil.

Of course, all this deals with only a small corner in the great field of conservation. Cities use more water than Nature provides, and poison what they do use, so that it kills instead of nourishing; while to reap quick returns during a wet cycle power machinery scars up the face of Mother Earth in areas where Science says the touch of the plow is the kiss of death. "Smog" erodes the lungs of vast populations, and so on.

14 GOATS IN MODERATION

The goat is not to be dismissed as criminal: far from it. No doubt he has disrobed many a hillside, leaving its soil exposed to the bombardment of liquid bullets and to the wash and tear of runaway water violently seeking its level. But he has done this defensively, *in extremis*. Self-preservation is the first law of the animal world. Truth is, the sheer greed, or ignorance, or economic compulsion of the goat's master has often driven him to pasturing two goats where only one can be supported in decency.

It is not the use but the abuse of the animal that is at fault. Grown in moderation, he converts and holds for human use areas of waste or near-waste land. As a matter of fact, this superb browser fortifies man's diet by tapping mineral-rich strata lying below those drawn upon by grazing animals.

Grass and weeds are shallow feeders. Browse plants, on the other hand, send roots two, ten, fifteen feet deep to capture nutrients which the goat, with a tough digestive system, makes available in milk and meat.

In the early months of his life the kid demands weeds and grasses; but, as his insides mature, he transfers his attention to such hardy and forbidding shrubs as dwarf mesquite, low live oaks, scrub cedar elm, cat's-claw, and various species of buckthorn. Grasses degenerate in the fall. Rains leech them out, and sap goes back to the roots, carrying with it valuable minerals. Many shrubs and scrub trees, however, maintain throughout the year their rich, mineralized offerings for any stomach hardy enough to handle them.[1] Among our domestic animals the goat is the only answer. The main, all-year route over which certain sugars and proteins can reach the human stomach in usable form from plants of this type lies in the digestive apparatus of this browser. A trickle of these same processed food elements comes along on neighborhood roads from other animals, especially from game, but the alimentary tract of the goat is a highway.

It is no accident that some individuals who cannot digest cow's milk at all thrive on goat's milk; and it is no accident, either, that goat's meat is one of the most delicious of all meats. But this is true only if the animal has been nourished as his nature demands, that is, on plants themselves nourished in proper soil. A roast cut from the loin of a goat, or a glass of goat's milk, may contain nothing of these nutrients, or they may be rich in them, depending upon what the animal eats.

In the general business of food production—be it meat, fruits, vegetables, or whatnot—the ultimate consumer is too often the forgotten man. When you buy a cut of meat, a bottle of milk, a head of lettuce, or a basket of fruit, you have no way of knowing what it is worth as food, or whether it is worth much of anything at all. Its virtue is dependent upon the soil from which it comes. In the arithmetic of nutrition, also, two and two make not five but four. Special studies of teeth show the importance of this, and of diseases such as

---

[1]For greater detail, see *Grass, The Yearbook of Agriculture, 1948*, "Sheep, Goats, and Grasslands," by C. E. Holscher and D. A. Spencer, U.S. Department of Agriculture, U.S. Government Printing Office. Washington, 1948, pp. 96–97.

pellagra, goiter, et cetera. Indeed, there is coming to be catalogued a whole raft of "deficiency diseases," meaning that the patient's food lacks one or another of the elements essential for robust health. Some "deficiencies" are fatal; some merely weaken the body's defense, leaving it a prey to debilitating ailments of one kind or another. Only one who has been revolted by coffee made from the leavings in yesterday's coffeepot, or by tea from twice-steeped leaves, can appreciate the indignity offered the digestive system by feeding it food grown on leeched-out soils.

One day I was out in a pasture with I. V. Duncan, a pioneer ranchman of the coastal prairies, when we came upon a steer chewing a huge thigh bone. The animal was trying, apparently, to crush it in his jaws, and long streamers of frothy slobber flowed from his mouth. I was amazed at the spectacle, until Mr. Duncan informed me that the soil here failed to furnish the grass with certain chemical elements, absence of which induced the bone-chewing habit. From chewing infected bones, cattle thus contracted loin disease, so called because the afflicted animals became weak in the loins and, finally, unable to walk at all. He told me that a study had been made of this ailment, a remedy discovered, and the results issued in bulletin form. I found on the title page of the publication[2] the following summary:

"This Bulletin reports results obtained by feeding bone meal and salt mixtures and finely ground rock phosphate mixed with bone meal and salt to cattle in the Gulf Coast region of Texas. It was found that the bone-chewing habit exhibited by about 75 per cent of the range cattle in that region can be broken if each animal is fed daily about three ounces of bone meal mixed with salt. Animals getting this amount of bone meal make larger gains in weight than animals not so fed. Cows fed bone meal reared better calves. It effectually prevented creeps in range cattle, and greatly reduced losses from diseases other than those of an infectious character. It

[2]*Feeding Bone Meal to Range Cattle on the Coastal Plains of Texas* (Preliminary Report), Division of Veterinary Science, Texas Agricultural Experiment Station, Bulletin No. 344, July 1926.

was found that finely ground rock phosphate when fed alone, or when mixed with salt, or when mixed with salt and bone meal in equal parts did not give satisfactory results."

Now in the old days of the free range there was no bone chewing on these coastal prairies; and the explanation is simple. The bottom lands, as the country settled up, were fenced off into farms, leaving the cattle only the prairies upon which to graze. But it was these very bottoms, which were built up from silt brought down from mineralized uplands, and constantly replenished, which in turn supplied the forage in the bottom lands with the needed minerals.

Another ranchman (quite an experimenter, by the way) described to me the spectacular results he found in a fryingpan as a result of diet deficiency. Bacon from his hogs began foaming in the fryingpan, while withering away in the action of the heat to nearly nothing, like clipped lettuce in a blazing sun. This bacon, he said, was from hogs fattened exclusively on soybeans. When he "finished them off" for a few weeks on corn, the bacon ceased to foam itself away.

How many human beings go through life with the "creeps" from lack of some essential element in their food, there is no way of knowing. I have never seen any human being chewing bones, but I have observed in them an irrational craving for certain foods, on the one hand, and food phobias on the other, caused, in all probability, by lack of some essential element in their diet.

Nuts and fruits delve deep, also, as the goat does, for elements missing from topsoils, and so does the honeybee feeding on cat's-claw, huajillo (thornless acacia), and upon other species of mimosa in the brush country of southern Texas. This "Uvalde" honey is a product so delicious that most of it is marketed among discriminating people of sufficient means, the price being rather a drain on the average purse. Last time I wrote my honey man, a bee keeper, of Uvalde, for some, he replied, after several weeks, that he had "just located a few cases of cat's-claw and huajillo honey, all there is left in Uvalde County so far as I can find."

Our delight in wild meat, for example, is due to the fact that the wild animal is permitted to select what he wants, therefore what he needs, to eat. Domesticated animals are fed according to market fluctuations—now this, now that—according to which food is cheaper, just so long as weight is not impaired, for the animal is sold by weight. The very mention of a "wild" taste makes one's mouth water. Robert Frost's enthusiasm for blueberries and Thoreau's for huckleberries may be explained on the same theory, namely, that these berries have not as yet become nursery stock, bred and nurtured for looks rather than for nutrients. There's a folk simile, "as good as venison and honey," which expressed for the pioneer the superlative of gustatory delight. Both the deer and the bee have access to food elements found only in subsoils. Alfalfa, also a deep feeder, always tops the top of the hay market.

The goat has served man long, faithfully, and well. Among the earliest of ruminants domesticated, he provided warming skins, fiber for costly fabrics, guts for stringed musical instruments, choice meat, and milk that has always been considered a delicacy. The goat has done this on browse which our other domestic animals ate sparingly or refused to eat at all. He has devastated brushy slopes only when driven to it by his master's ignorance of conservation laws or by his greed.

Still, in the folklore of many lands, the goat is abused and derided. He is made out to be particularly contemptible in our own literature. So far as my own reading goes, no other animal (barring the snake, of course) is the subject of such slanderous insinuations, nor for a longer time in history. In the dawn period of western European culture, the stay-at-home slacker who seduced Agamemnon's wife while that great hero was away at war, and induced her to murder her husband on his return, was suckled in infancy, the tradition says, by a she-goat. What else, pray, may one expect from the milk of such a devilish wet nurse!

In the *Eumenides* Apollo addresses the hated crew of furies who are polluting his shrine as "wild goats unherded"; and Pan, in mood "ready to twitch the nymph's last garment off," is represented by sculptors of the period as having the legs, ears, and sometimes the horns of a goat. Although in early Christian tradition Pan died when the shepherds at Bethlehem were divinely informed of the birth of Christ, artists continued to use the goat god as a stock illustration of loose living, as they still employ the goat himself to externalize our conceptions of hilarious or cynical lapses from conventional morality.

The sheep, on the other hand, has been the darling of folk tales, religion, literature, and traditional lore generally. Just try the droll experiment of substituting "kid" for "lamb" and "goat" for "sheep" in either sacred or profane literature. Begin with the nursery rhyme *Mary Had a Little Lamb,* and go on to the highest flights of the tragic poets; you will find this amazing contrast maintained.

In medieval accusations against heretics for participating in the alleged orgies of witches, the records of the Inquisition present Satan worshiped in the guise of a goat; while, in the imagery of that period, the devil himself is identified by caprine hoof and horns.

Thus the "cloven hoof," in general use to this day as the sign of a devilish character, or malign intrigue, is the goat's hoof and none other; while the sheep has a "golden" hoof. Certainly the "golden fleece" which Jason obtained at such pains was not mohair. On Judgment Day the Lord "divides the sheep from the goats"—that is, the good from the wicked for purposes of resettlement and permanent residence. The custom among coastal Mexicans of herding a few goats in with flocks of sheep "to protect the sheep from disease," doesn't indicate a belief in the benign character of the goat. On the contrary, it is part and parcel of the superstition which attributes to the devil and his minions the ability to scare away the evil spirit which causes the disease, as the Karánkaway drank the most noxious potions to cure digestive ailments on the theory that the evil spirit's residence in the belly must be made just as uncomfortable for him as possible.

In medieval bestiary lore also, this wide-eyed, innocent creature —this goat—figures as "the animal type of lechery," whence Shakespeare's "thou damned and luxurious mountain goat." Iago implants in Othello's mind so vivid a simile of marital infidelity that it finally drives the noble Moor stark mad, muttering in his ravings, "prime as goats and hot as monkeys." When intoxication induces unseemly

215

amorousness, the person affected is said to be "goat drunk." The folk epithet "foxy grandpa" is humorously tolerant of the youthful pretensions of an elderly male; whereas "the old goat" is a lash of scathing severity rarely attached even to the whip of feminine scorn.

Thus literature, forever sensitive to folk beliefs,[3] is guilty of calumny in childishly judging the goat by standards of no validity except in human affairs, and in ignoring that much more general, as well as more generous, folk appraisal of animal behavior, "It's just the natur' o' the critter."

"We need another and a wiser and perhaps a more mystical concept of animals," says Henry Beston.[4] "Remote from universal nature and living by complicated artifice, man in civilization surveys the creature through the glass of his knowledge and sees thereby a feather magnified and the whole image in distortion. We patronize them for their incompleteness, for their tragic fate of having taken form so far below ourselves. And therein we err, and greatly err. For the animal shall not be measured by man. In a world older and more complete than ours they moved finished and complete, gifted with extensions of the senses we have lost or never attained, living by voices we shall never hear. They are not brethren, they are not underlings; they are other nations, caught with ourselves in the net of life and time, fellow prisoners of the splendor and travail of the earth."

When I read in Rousseau's *Confessions* (Part First, Book I) of his "pursuing or stoning a cock, a cow, a dog or any animal which I saw tormenting another, merely because it felt itself stronger," I see the natural, naïve reaction of a child; but feel that the aging philosopher, recalling the memory, should have added a note on the folly of thus measuring animal reactions by human standards. It is much like kicking a chair which you happen to stumble over in the dark.

Dictionaries and compendiums of folk sayings contain similar evidence of anti-caprine prejudice. The prefix "capri" carries in

---

[3]The scapegoat legend is world-wide, as Sir George James Frazer proves.
[4]*The Outermost House: A Year of Life on the Great Beach of Cape Cod*, Rinehart and Co., 1949, p. 25.

nearly every case a suggestion of quirk, whim, crotchet, or general irresponsibility; as in caprice, or in music, a wild, fantastic style. The English prefix "goat" is used more freely even than "dog" to slur the innocent as well as to designate obvious abominations. We have a disagreeable spiny shrub of bitter bark on Southwestern ranges, which folk call "goatbush" (*Castela texana*). In grisly voodoo ritual, the child victim sacrificed is called "a goat without horns." The wild fig bearing a tasteless fruit of little succulence is a caprifig, or goatfig. A stench-diffusing European moth (*Cossus ligniperda*) is a "goat moth." Crooked-legged people, knee-sprung, are goat-kneed in popular language, although the goat's leg is not unshapely. (There is a rich folklore, by the way, explaining why the goat's knees are bare.) A wild relative of wheat, having a sharp-pointed fruit injurious to livestock, is called "goat grass." Darlington's *Weeds and Plants* says of a European weed (*Aegopodium podagraria*): "It has made its appearance in some parts of Pennsylvania, and proves to be a nuisance not easily abated." It is called "goat's foot," or "goat weed."

One finds few goat-derived nicknames of favorable connotation in use among the people. On the other hand, a preponderance of words with the "sheep" prefix suggest pleasing attributes. The phrase to "cast sheep's eyes" brings up the image of maiden innocence receiving its first amatory advances. Sheepweed is the folkname for our lovely Indian mallow. "Sheep" words suggest meekness, innocence, ingenuousness, docility; and it is only the excess of these qualities which gives "sheepishness" a derogatory flavor. "Lamb" is used only to praise, sometimes even to glorify.

Like all other creatures, man or beast, against which there is established (from whatever cause) a popular prejudice, the goat becomes a sponge for soaking up further disreputable imputations. For instance, hardly a century ago, the seed of a species of caltrop came to this continent from southern Europe tangled in the wool of imported sheep.[5] Note that sheep brought this curse upon us. Came the

[5]A circumstantial account of the introduction and spread of this pernicious creeper is published in the *Scientific American*, issue of September 10, 1921, excerpt from which is quoted in *500 Wild Flowers of San Antonio and Vicinity*, by Ellen D. Schulz, M.S., 1922, pp. 115–16. Published by the author, now Mrs. Ellen Schulz Quillan, Curator of the Witte Museum, San Antonio, Texas.

automobile with tires less robust than the present product, which the bur of this plant punctured, since it is equipped with five needle-pointed stickers so distributed that, like a jackstone in repose, one point is always sticking up and ready for business. With this device for hitchhiking and with automobile traffic soon penetrating every nook and cranny of the country, the scourge spread, appearing simultaneously in a dozen states between the Rockies and the Alleghenies. Its scientific name suggests its wickedness: *Tribulus terrestris*. It has a number of common names, among which are "sandbur," "puncture plant," "bur nut," and, finally, "goat's head." I have asked a number of people why it is called so. In a goat country they say it's because it gets into mohair; but, ordinarily, I am told that the bur, held in a certain position, resembles the head of a goat. Frankly, I cannot see the resemblance, but the fact remains that the folk name for this nuisance weed is now in course of passing into the language as another reflection upon the goat. The sheep's participation in foisting it upon us is being quietly forgotten. Again, the goat "is made the goat."

The horns[6] of most of our domestic breeds of goat arch out of a narrow skull at an acute angle with the back. They are not shed annually, as the deer's horns are, nor do they cast off a shell like the antelope's. I have never seen how, even in feral state, they could be of much advantage to the animal in either attack or defense, or, indeed, put to any other serious use.

Once, however, I saw an Angora ram employing his horns with evident satisfaction, but in what seemed to me a ridiculous way, since so ponderous a mechanism was involved in an incidental, if not frivolous, operation. This stately male with patriarchal beard, monarch of a herd and conscious of his responsibilities, suddenly stopped browsing on the brink of a fifty-foot ledge. He paused as if considering a matter of great pith and moment. Presently, he tilted

---

[6]Evil superstitions, by the way, beset even the horns of the goat. The zodiacal constellation, Capricorn, literally, the horn of the goat, is significant in astrology as "nocturnal," which in the jargon of this "science" means an "unpropitious sign, movable, cardinal and melancholy, and in nature cold, dry, and earthy; the mansion of Saturn," et cetera.

his head at an angle to bring the tip of one horn into contact with a small space on his back, and scratched it by slowly nodding his head. This solemn, dignitarial itch made me laugh. I was conducted from grandeur to triviality in one short downward hop. I saw first the slight, sidewise tilting of the noble head, the sweep of the wide-spreading horns, the lower one of which my eye followed from brow to tip. I expected something significant, some clarification of the nature and outcome of this preparation, calculated and majestic; but my expectations collapsed as the ignoble purpose of the gesture was revealed.

I felt cheap as the monarch's stern eye encountered mine. The irritation mollified, the head had resumed its original posture, beard again in place, centered over the massive chest. He must have heard my titter, for the brute turned on me a look, as much as to say, "What, pray, are you giggling about? Why this ill-timed snickering?" Perhaps one should not try to pry into the private affairs of another species. "The look of the bay mare," says Whitman, "shames the silliness out of me." So did the quiet, tolerant gaze of this ram standing on a precipice, shame the silliness out of me. It is in such moments that animals, although reduced by our cleverness to subservience, seem to assume in our presence the dignity of an ancient superiority.

Shall one conclude that Nature produced the goat's horns merely that the animal might occasionally dislodge, or otherwise embarrass, a colony of parasites feeding around the roots of his straight-up tail? —which organ is itself the butt of a proverbial jest, "The goat cannot cover herself with her tail." These great horns surely have some other function, and still I have never seen one of our domestic goats put his horns to other than "scratching" use.

You rarely find them used ornamentally, either, as is the ram's horn of a kindred species, which, instead of merely twisting, opens out in a graceful spiral; nor are they dangerously set, as the Texas longhorn's, to frustrate and disperse a whole pack of wolves with one savage, sidewise sweep of the lowered head, or lift a newborn calf to his wobbly legs on icy ground. They are certainly not in any way as practical as the much shorter, much sharper, more perpendic-

219

ular horns of the Rocky Mountain goat (really not a goat at all), with which that animal has been known to stab fatally the grizzly bear, puncturing heart, lungs, or abdomen. Our goat's offense, on the other hand, is a butt, delivered with the upper forehead, and not involving the horns at all.

Man has found as little use for these appendages as the goat himself has. Biblical scholars say that they were rarely made into the shophar to sound the attack in battle or call the faithful into the synagogue on the Day of Atonement.[7] The sheep's horn was preferred for this purpose, as it was thousands of years later for fashioning those far-sounding hunting horns whose merry notes enliven tales of the chase in the Middle Ages—said or sung. Some say the wall of the goat's horn is too thick and the cavity too small to provide a sufficient volume of air for the required resonance; others say it's because the bell mouth is missing.

I asked Driscoe L. Bertillion, of Mineola, Texas, about this, since he has spent his life (as his father did before him) in the business of beautifying horns of various animals and mounting them for trophy lovers. He says he is rarely asked to mount goat horns, but is far from agreeing that they are not suitable for such treatment. The goat horn, in his opinion, "makes the finest dog-calling horn in the world." He admits that the processing is difficult and requires the skilled use of "modern tools and polishing compounds."[8]

Perhaps, then, it was not altogether baseless prejudice on the part of the ancients against the goat which caused them to avoid using the animal's horns, but maybe that they lacked the equipment necessary for converting a stubborn material to human use. Both goat and sheep horns should always be preserved, Mr. Bertillion says, as many beautiful and useful articles can be made from them, such as

---

[7]According to the *Jewish Encyclopedia* the standard shofar of the Old Testament was apparently the horn of a ram (male sheep), although on New Year (Rosh Hashana) it seems that the straight horn of a *wild* goat was used; at least some authorities think so. It was permissible to use the horn of any clean animal, except that of a cow or calf. The normal type seems to have been the horn of the male sheep.

[8]I am informed by another authority that no tool is better for this purpose than a simple piece of broken glass.

table legs, hat racks, wall flower holders, hunting horns, lamp stands, et cetera.

But, when all is said and done, functionally, as a part of the living animal, just what are the goat's horns for except to scratch with in areas inaccessible to lip, teeth, or hoof of hind leg? On the negative side, I have seen them as a menace to the life of the browsing animal. A goat gains his sustenance by sticking his neck out, often to its utmost limit, thrusting the whole head into tight places, especially into dark masses of tangled wildwood to nip tender shoots issuing from the inner branches. Ordinarily, if his horns become entangled, he can withdraw his head, breaking or tearing loose by sheer strength. But sometimes the gin holds, and so many a goat has died by his horns.

I spent a year on a goat ranch not so long ago where I had occasion to rescue goats caught in the forks of cedar trees, hackberry, and scrub oak; also from a division fence through the meshes of which the thieving creatures were stealing a few leaves from a neighbor. Ranchers tell me it is not unusual to find the skeleton of a goat hanging in a fence held by the horns. Once I discovered the back end of a goat protruding from a hole under an uptilted limestone slab. Here was a fine, fat ram held by his horns, which were firmly wedged between boulders of this miniature cave, the animal having been baited by some tender growths around the base of the stone. Goats graze underground if they can find an entrance. A few years ago some greedy goats led a couple of Bedouin goatherds into a small cave on a hillside where they made the most startling archeological discovery of the present century—nothing less than the scrolls of the Book of Isaiah complete, perfectly preserved in jars undisturbed for the last two thousand years.

Many years ago I had a friend—a quick-witted, enterprising man—who gathered goats far and wide with the avowed purpose of developing a hornless breed. He endured much bantering from his less imaginative acquaintances and finally gave up the enterprise; but I still believe that he had hold of an experiment noble in purpose, and that, with more time and money at his disposal, he might have succeeded. Certainly the country, among other things, needs a hornless goat with the long, soft, silky ringlets of the Angora.

It will be remembered that a goat got himself entangled at just the right moment in sacred history to save Isaac from being "offered up" by his priestly father; for, as Abraham was about to lay knife to the throat of his own son, an angel of the Lord said to him: "Lay not thine hand upon the lad, neither do thou anything unto him. . . . And Abraham lifted up his eyes, and looked, and behold behind him a ram caught in a thicket by his horns: and Abraham went and took the ram, and offered him up for a burnt offering in the stead of his son."[9]

Anthropologists rarely fail to cite this as a classic example of the transition in a culture from human to animal sacrifice. If so, we can afford to forgive the goat many transgressions.

Our goat is not so highly specialized for climbing as some of his distant kin, the Rocky Mountain goat of this country, for instance, or the chamois of Alpine fame. But he likes to climb, nevertheless, and is uneasy if left to his own devices on level land. He searches out high places, if any, thriving best on scattered brush naturally terraced along more or less rugged slopes. This is the real reason why he is the central figure in the most disastrous erosions of history.

It is pathetic to see the climbing instinct assert itself in those ani-

---

[9]Maybe a confirmation of this incident is found in an account of recent archaeological excavations on the site of the ancient city of Ur: "Mention may here be made of the curious 'Ram-in-the-Thicket' statuette of gold, lapis lazuli, and shell discovered at Ur. It represents a ram caught in a thicket, to the branches of which its legs are tied with silver chains—evidently a religious motif, for it is one oft repeated in similar situations. A possible connection between this figure and the Biblical story of Abraham's proffered sacrifice of Isaac has been suggested."—*The Bible and Spade*, by Stephen L. Caiger, B.D., Oxford University Press. London: Geoffrey Cumberledge, 1947, p. 38.

A doubt arises in my mind as to whether this statuette really represents "a ram caught in a thicket," since he is shown to be caught by the legs. I have never seen a goat caught in brush except by the horns. But perhaps the sculptor, city born and bred, merely *supposed* the goat was caught by the legs, as a man would be, failing to note that the sacred writer, familiar with the ways and wiles of goats, specifies that Abraham's ram was "caught by the horns." Or, perhaps, like so many modern illustrators, he didn't take the trouble to read the text he was employed to illustrate.

mals unfortunately transferred from a natural habitat to this coast country, generally as flat as a pancake. The sandy knolls, called dunes, offer the goat no relief, since his sharp hoofs sink into the sand and neutralize a natural springiness. He loves leaping from ledge to ledge, where the extent of footing is unimportant, if it is but solid and resistant. I have seen an individual poised like an inverted pyramid on a rocky promontory with all four feet occupying a space no larger than a man's two hands. Day-old kids engage in play on the brink of a precipice where a misstep, or any little dizziness, would plunge them to certain death, while their mammas browse nearby in unconcern. "Where the goat leaps, leaps that which sucks her," says the Spanish proverb.

Pastured in a flat country, they climb atop chicken coops, sheds, barns, rail fences—anything, in fact, that offers footing and provides a superior outlook. I was sitting on the front porch of a ranchman's home near Port O'Conner, Texas, one afternoon, observing a group of about fifty goats feeding a few hundred yards away, when suddenly the leaders threw up their heads, listened a moment, and then ran for the house with the whole herd following at their heels. They arrived just as the ranchman drove up in a small truck, over which they swarmed, covering the running board, fenders, bed, and roof of the cab. They were hungry for the only kind of exercise they really delight in—climbing. The ranchman told me they repeated this performance every time he stopped his truck in their little pasture. Moreover, they had learned, he said, to identify the sound of his truck as it approached from the highway and usually beat him to its parking place. On this particular occasion, there was no standing room left and competition ensued for the choicer lookouts, especially for the roof of the cab. They were lonesome for the high places: the goat aspires.

I remember a bearded patriarch who amused himself for a spell each afternoon with a seesaw which had been installed on the playground of an elementary school. The bell which dismissed school called this old goat up from level browsing to do his "daily dozen." He walked up the board past the middle until his weight tilted down the other end. Dismounting as he reached the ground, he

223

turned himself about and walked up until the balance was again upset, and so on, back and forth, up and down—until his climbing and descending muscles were satisfied. A teeterboard gives the goat the exercise his muscles most crave when exiled from his natural range. This is offered as a hint to goat raisers in a flat country.

15   SILT[1]

There's a green and growing island in one of the bays of the Karánkaway Country. It had an area of about four hundred acres in pioneer times. Now it is a respectable cattle ranch of four thousand acres. Silt built this island, and silt hasn't yet finished with the construction of it, or with that of dozens of other islands scattered along in the bays of the Texas coast.

Cattle now graze in places where, twenty years ago, there were producing oyster beds in eight feet of water. If these bays were suddenly drained, endless mud flats would appear, made up of sediments from the rice fields of the coastal prairie, and from the hills of the Edwards Plateau and on hundreds of miles northwest to

[1]The term "silt" is used in this and in following chapters in its popular sense. Technically, "silt" is a size classification, as "sand," or "gravel." Rock particles smaller than sand and larger than clay are "silt," regardless of composition, whether stationary or in transit.

225

farming areas just under the caprock. An east or northeast wind churns the San Antonio Bay into water so muddy that you can't see through a tumbler of it. Less than a generation ago there was good flounder fishing here in any kind of wind short of a hurricane. So it comes about that soil which should now be enriching the state with its contributions to farm and ranch products is smothering a once flourishing fish and oyster industry of the coastal bays: a double devastation.

Lake Corpus Christi, made by damming the Nueces, was hailed by some as a permanent solution of the water problem for the city of Corpus Christi a dozen years ago. In December 1948,[2] this permanence has dwindled to a "deficiency" of water supply for the city from this source in 1951 and 1952.

Certain enthusiasts for water conservation by way of big dams hailed the completion of the Possum Kingdom project on the Brazos (1941) as a permanent improvement; but the Reconnaissance Investigation of Sedimentation in Possum Kingdom Lake eight years after completion predicts that this big reservoir will be completely filled with silt ninety-eight years from its completion date. After a 70 per cent loss of storage capacity, engineers call the reservoir's "effective life" ended. So in this case "permanence" dwindles down to one year less than threescore years and ten; that is, the "effective life" of Possum Kingdom Lake under present conditions will end in the year 2009.

Paul Weaver, Chief Geophysicist of the Gulf Oil Corporation, told the Rockport Seminar, October 23, 1949, that dredging operations to clear channels for navigation, including the constant dredging and use of the great Houston Ship Canal, accelerates the movement of silt into the bays, only a fraction of which is carried on out and deposited upon the continental shelf through action of water induced by jetties.

Paul Walser, State Co-ordinator, Soil Conversation Service, speaking to the same Seminar, estimated that six thousand acres have been added to the delta of the Trinity River in forty years. How

[2]U.S. Department of Agriculture, Soil Conservation Service, Report on Sedimentation in Lake Corpus Christi and Water Supply of Corpus Christi, figured on basis of last thirteen and a half years.

many more thousands of acres will be built up in this delta by the time dredging operations now planned are finished, Mr. Walser did not venture to estimate. Mere acreage figures of delta do not tell the whole story. The weight of silt presses down the crust of the earth, so that at the mouths of certain rivers the silt deposits are a hundred or more feet deep.

F. E. Wehmeyer, Supervisor for the State Game, Fish, and Oyster Commission, called my attention to two small streams of the coastal prairie, one of which drains a ranching country of native sod; and the other, farming land, recently "improved" by construction of a system of drainage ditches. These two streams empty into adjoining bays less than twenty miles apart. One, the Tres Palacios, fed out of the farming area by way of drainage ditches, delivers into its bay loads of silt. The other, Karánkaway Creek, discharges into Karánkaway Bay its volume of water almost as clear as it was when it fell from the clouds upon its watershed of native sod.

One of these little rivers is functional, serving the purpose for which it was created. It is healthy and health-giving, blessing all life which comes within its influence—the land life along its shores as well as the life in its own waters, and also the life in the waters to which it finally surrenders its identity. It does its bit in the hydrologic cycle to which Nature assigned it.

The other little river is sick, preying upon the land at its source, eating it away, fouling itself and suffocating life in its waters and, at last, returning to its mother, the sea, evil for good. It is defeating the purpose for which it was created. It is a broken and corrupting arc in the hydrologic cycle.

Maybe these two little rivers should be endowed by public funds and left just as they are—one living joyously, the other dying miserably; since, taken together, side by side, they present visible, tangible evidence of a truth every citizen of this country needs to know—a demonstration so perfect that the wayfaring man, though a fool, cannot fail to get the point.

I'm allergic to silt, and with reason. I remember a rivulet we called a "branch" in the blackland prairies on the watershed of the Brazos

227

River where I spent my childhood. Across this "branch," where it cut off a corner of a little pasture, a neighbor built a dirt dam, which, much to his amazement, went on downstream with the first freshet.

Then he built another dam of dirt, but reinforced it with stone, and made a cobblestone spillway for flood waters. The new dam held, and much fun we had swimming in the little lake, and navigating a boat of crude construction. This lovely aquatic adventure lasted until the watershed of this "branch," comprising only a few square miles of bluestem sod, was broken up and planted to corn and cotton, after which the little lake was quickly filled with mud.

But our neighbor was a stubborn man. With mule-drawn scrapers during droughty seasons, he cleaned out the mud and thriftily distributed it over the thinner soil of his pasture, thus appropriating to his own use some of the good black land which his neighbors with unintentional largess had loosened and let go in their farming operations. But erosion redoubled, trebled, quadrupled as the years went on, until it took only one winter wet spell to refill his reservoir with silt. Eventually he permitted it to sod over with Bermuda grass.

How many years this little cache of fertility stayed put I do not know; but the last time I was by there the "branch" had again reclaimed its old channel. The limestone ledges of its banks had emerged from their burial and looked very much as I remember them before this pioneer settler tampered with the natural drainage sixty years ago.

On down Deer Creek, thence to the Brazos River and still on to the Gulf went this little pocket of the richest black waxy soil in the world. For this mutilation of the prairies and the muddying up of the streams we shed no tears, felt no concern, even had, indeed, no hint of what it meant. It was great fun during floods on small streams to wade waist-deep into the soupy water, grab fish as they came to the surface half suffocated, desperate, blinded, and sluggish.

Only a few months ago I found another silt incident which sticks in my memory. My own little gravelly hillside in the city needed dirt. Dirt haulers often supply their city customers with soil utterly dead from leached-out and worn-out fields in our vicinity. On occasion I have myself been a victim of this villainy. So I insist on seeing the dirt I buy *in situ*. My dirt dealer took me to a bottom of excellent soil which had been saved from the yawning bays of the Gulf coast purely by accident. A careless contractor many years ago built a highway across a little creek and failed to put in a culvert large enough to accommodate the flood water. With each freshet flood water is spread over twenty or twenty-five acres above the highway and is detained there for several days before the too-small culvert permits it to drain away. The wise farmer whose land was thus flooded didn't rush into court (as usual in such cases) with an action against the state for flood damage. On the contrary, this contrary man welcomed muddy water from his neighbors' fields on up the creek. He said it improved grazing for his dairy cows, since a film of silt was left after each flooding. It was his own idea. He knows nothing of the history of Egypt; and that magic name, "Nile," raises in his mind no vision of a thousand-mile ribbon of luxurious greenery hedged narrowly in by deserts on either side.

Years passed and deposits accumulated. Meantime, with the growth of the city at his door, demand for lawn dirt increased, and dirt dealers with their immense trucks kept dogging him for it at fifty cents a load. At the time I visited the place to inspect my load of dirt, an "open working" mining operation was in progress with a steam shovel loading up trucks as fast as they could drive by.

"Doesn't your conscience hurt you a little," I asked this farmer, "selling out this good soil from your neighbors' farms?"

"Ef'n they ain't got no more sense than to let it wash away," he replied with a shrewd twinkle in his eye, "I ain't got no more sense 'an to sell it."

In or about the center of the Karánkaway Country the Texas Colorado empties through an artificial mouth directly into the Gulf, and thereby hangs a tale. Early settlers here, besides feeding and fighting the Karánkaways, were deeply concerned with making the river, which then flowed into Matagorda Bay, navigable. Here begins the tortuous, century-long story of trying to make a river do man's instead of Nature's bidding; of trying to force burdens upon

229

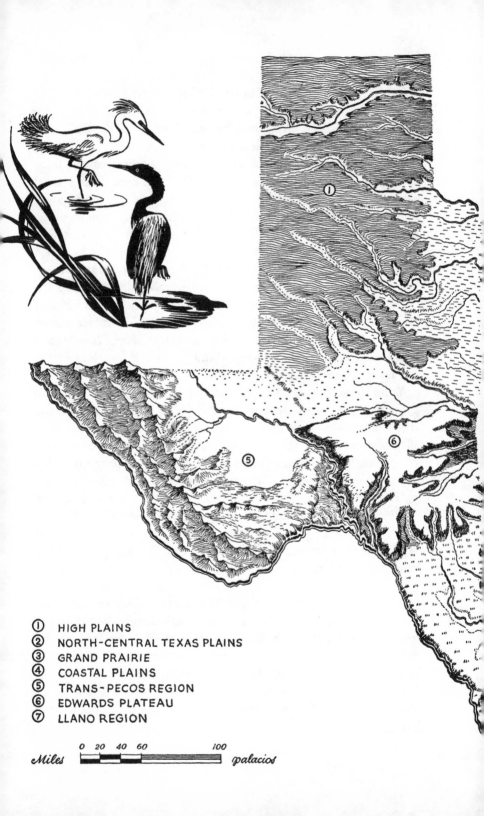

① HIGH PLAINS
② NORTH-CENTRAL TEXAS PLAINS
③ GRAND PRAIRIE
④ COASTAL PLAINS
⑤ TRANS-PECOS REGION
⑥ EDWARDS PLATEAU
⑦ LLANO REGION

Miles 0 20 40 60   100   palacios

TEXAS
MAJOR PHYSIOGRAPHIC FEATURES

"WEST" TEXAS   TRANSITION ZONE   "EAST" TEXAS

GULF OF MEXICO

it which it is in no wise equipped to carry; of making it sick and then trying to cure it with palliatives, hastily summoning a surgeon when it really requires only a sensible dietitian.

From earliest times the mouths of Texas streams were clogged with debris. But for such cloggings the coastal prairies would never have been brought to their present perfection, for cloggings changed channels, and natural deposits were distributed now here, now there, over wide areas, building up the level until gravity switched the stream to another place and then to another, back and forth for countless ages. If you don't believe in the beneficent work of cloggings, take Highway 35 at Houston and follow it to Corpus Christi, traversing this Karánkaway Country from end to end. But to get the full agricultural and stock-raising glory of this section of Texas, you should take a few short side trips northward along the route. Without robbing the highlands, as is now being done so disastrously, Texas rivers reclaimed from the Gulf a golden empire, at the same time establishing four hundred miles of littoral, rich in aquatic life, as a kind of compromise with the salt water which was all the time being gradually pushed back.

As settlements of whites pushed up these rivers, particularly up the Colorado and its tributaries, slashing the timber out of the bottoms, tearing from the banks of streams the retarding vegetation Nature had placed there for a purpose, leaving in their greed for more land only a turnrow between cultivated field and river brink— as these characteristic pioneer activities got well under way, an ancient and beneficent clogging of the river in its lower course, known as the "Colorado River Raft," became suddenly virulent. It began to extend itself five, ten, twenty miles up the river, not only further impeding navigation, but inundating settlements by throwing floods helter-skelter across the country, drowning stock and people, sweeping away cultivated fields, and playing havoc generally with man's puny installations.

For nearly a hundred years this raft played an important part in Texas politics.[3]

[3]For an excellent account, see "The Colorado River Raft," by Comer Clay, *The Southwestern Historical Quarterly*, Vol. III, No. 4, April 1949, pp. 410–26.

Enter here the corps of army engineers just a hundred years ago estimating the cost of clearing out the raft at fifty thousand dollars. On the basis of this estimate the Federal Government included in its Rivers and Harbors Act of 1852 an appropriation of twenty thousand dollars. I felt my prestige as a Texan a little lowered when I learned from Mr. Clay that far from the rugged individualists of that rugged era rejecting this Federal money, it was received with jubilation by communities all the way from Austin to the coast.

In the next seventy-five years, with cultivation of the Colorado watershed and the slashing out of the bottoms along the river, this raft grew to enormous proportions, the head of it in 1929 extending forty-five miles from the mouth. At a cost of more than a million dollars the raft was shoved down the river into Matagorda Bay, and then a channel two hundred feet wide and nine feet deep was cut from the natural mouth of the river through the raft (now in the bay), and on across Matagorda Island into the Gulf of Mexico. And all this century-long struggle failed to achieve its original purpose—navigation. It did relieve congestions and overflows, but that was largely a work of supererogation, since in a few years from the raft's removal a series of dams constructed a couple of hundred miles up the river reduced the danger of floods in the coastal area.

I think that ancient misnomer "mouth," which we use to designate the place where a river empties, has done the cause of conservation incalculable harm. Our river imagery is muddied at its source. We speak of the head of a river, but there is no mouth in the head. That orifice in our curious anatomy is at the other end. We speak of *the* source of a river, but a river has a thousand sources. In the long ages that rivers served as the main burden bearers of inland commerce, it became a habit to call the wrong end of a river its "mouth," because it swallowed vessels day after day and regurgitated them—an inelegant figure of speech, at that.

This topsy-turvy thinking about rivers, with its enormous overemphasis on their importance to transportation, persists in the popular mind to this good day, while great herds of cattle whiz along superhighways at fifty miles an hour, while Diesel-powered engineers haul a hundred monster freight cars at terrific speeds, and while the Berlin airlift provides on a world stage its revolutionary demonstration. And yet in the midst of these dizzy developments we permit the appearance of a battered old river barge at the sham wharf of an inland city to influence railroad freight rates. This is a lag in thinking comparable to turning off electric illumination to candlelight certain ceremonials; but it is not nearly so quaint and innocent. It is, indeed, responsible for the perversion and pollution of many a beautiful little river. Physical science outruns social science, as an automobile, an ox cart. Means multiply, while progress in their social application is arithmetical. Politicians are too often the "hireling Sophists" of our own day; and, as in the days of the Great Philosopher, they study only to give back to the people their own opinions. "They [now as then] are keepers of the monster, who know how to flatter or anger him, and observe the meaning of his inarticulate grunts." I am moved to say this after reading in the *Congressional Record* the late "debate" on the Rivers and Harbors Bill.

In the thinking of conservationists who have built up the conception of the hydrologic cycle, the many sources of a river are its mouths. What it takes in there is largely responsible for its healthful functioning. No one in the hundred years of arguments, pro and con, as well as in neutral analyses of the Colorado River raft problem, ever thought of this river as diseased, ever questioned the cause of the congestion, or ever suggested remedial measures of a radical nature.

There is no better place than at the so-called "mouth" of a diseased river to diagnose its ailment, for there we find out what it is being fed, whether it is digesting what it is taking in, the condition of its circulatory system, and whether or not its eliminations are normal. By the same token, there is generally no worse place to begin the treatment of the disease after its nature is discovered. Or so it was until the era of the big dams came on, of which more later.

I have an acquaintance steeped in the classical tradition. Ninety per cent of what he reads was written before the sixteenth century.

I was telling him something of the struggle modern society is having with its rivers, and he replied that it was no new problem.

"The struggle," he said, "of Achilles with the river Scamander, as told by Homer, is really an old conservation myth current long before Homer lived."

There is no new thing under the sun.

"You see," he said, warming up in this congenial field of making modern applications of ancient wisdom, "all the elements are there. Scamander first gives Achilles due warning against misusing the stream by turning it into a battlefield, but the impetuous hero disregards the caution. He underestimates the strength of the river, and smashes forward driving herds of Trojans into the torrent and follows them in, laying about with his sword, severing necks, running his victims through and through, cluttering up the stream with the debris of battle.

"Scamander is naturally indignant and puts on a terrific flood whose rage fails, however, to quell the ardor of the Myrmidons. Doubly infuriated, Scamander calls upon his brother river, Simois, to join him, crying above the thunder of the waters his curse upon Achilles: 'Deep under the flood let him be with mud and slime for his burial mound. I myself shall heap over him shells and pebbles and sand, so that the Argives shall not even find his bones.'

"Simois responds and the double flood below the confluence of the two rivers overwhelms the invader, slams him back and forth like a wisp of straw, until he has little breath left in him with which to implore his mother, Thetis, for help.

"Meantime, Hera has seen his predicament and dispatches her lame son, Hephaestus, to the rescue, who turns himself into flame, scorching the grass on Scamander's banks, withering the elms and tamarisks, blighting the flowers, and otherwise acting very much like a drought in a semiarid country.

"Thus barely did the greatest of all the Homeric heroes escape the river wrath by the skin of his teeth. Drought came just in the nick of time.

"And so," my classical friend concluded in mock-heroic style, "let this be a lesson to you: never, never, never corrupt a divine river or

235

put it to improper uses, degrade the purposes for which the gods leased it to man, filthy it up with oil wastes or sewage, or attempt with insufficient forces to curb its freedom; for even now at this moment are the river gods of America sitting in angry conclave, outraged at the indignities put upon them and very like plotting to rise in their wrath and spread pestilence and woe upon their tormentors."

16 MORE SILT

Some sixty years ago my home city of Austin, Texas, located on the middle course of this same Colorado River, went into the dam business, and has been in it almost continually since then.

Island or littoral peoples or inhabitants of other well-watered locations can hardly realize the intensity of the water longing of dwellers in arid, semiarid, or subhumid regions, where droughts scourge ever so often and stingy streams dry up and stink with air-suffocated dead. Man was meant to live an amphibious life; and only a desert poet could have written,

As the heart panteth after the water brooks,
So panteth my soul after thee, O God.

And only a city in a section of country subject to long dry spells could have been as enthusiastic as the capital city of Texas was when a

237

dam was completed across a stream which in dry periods was only by courtesy called a "river"—a dam providing fifty thousand acre-feet of lake water edging up to within four miles of the heart of the business district. That was sixty years ago.

A hard-headed geologist had warned the promoters against the site selected, saying it was exactly over a geologic fault, and that a secure foundation at that point was not only unlikely but impossible. Public sentiment, however, favored a location "close in." The lake should be within reach of the horse-drawn traffic of the day, so that pleasure seekers could get there after business hours. Citizens with boats available for week-end excursions liked to jump right into them and thus get away as quickly as possible from the madding crowd's ignoble strife. Fishermen, swimmers, promoters of regattas, and the simple lollers-about on lake shores—all preferred to have this body of water available by streetcar.

The geologist was ignored and forgotten. So was T. U. Taylor, Dean of Engineering, who warned that even if the dam held, the lake would soon fill up with silt. It just so happened that I was typing my way through college when Dean Taylor was preparing for the press the pioneer study on silt in Texas streams, and he gave me the job of transcribing the work. His handwriting was erratic and frequent conferences were necessary. He was a great and genial talker and, sensing my interest in river problems, those conferences for clarifying his writing often became a two-hour seminar on silt. By the time I finished the job, I could not look on Lake Austin any more with my original enthusiasm, for I knew what lay beneath the surface.

But, sure enough, just as its promoters predicted, the lake became at once a popular resort. There was boating, swimming, fishing, regattas, and presently a steamer called after a popular novel of the day, the *Ben Hur*, was launched and began the business of riding excursionists up and back for $1.50 per head, several hundred at a time. The *Ben Hur* even had a dance floor, and the society page in the Sunday paper often contained romantically phrased descriptions of social affairs, of music and dancing over "the moonlit waters" with the "changing skyline of the rugged hills ever in view," as the "stately steamer" navigated for fifteen or twenty miles "the placid, star-strewn bosom of the lake," returning usually about midnight.

Excursion trains brought throngs of people on week ends from distant places during "the season." This "outside money," as it was called, was graciously received by merchants, concessionaires, livery-stable proprietors, and the company operating a mule-car transportation system, which was soon electrified. One wealthy citizen placed in commission a private launch of an elegance that would have been a credit to any seaside resort.

Incidentally, a powerhouse was installed which was supposed to liquidate the bonded indebtedness in the course of half a century or so through sale of electric power.

This municipal dream lasted until one fine morning in April 1900, when a flood came roaring out of the hills, shoved a sixty-foot section out of the center of the dam through which the impounded water went raging on its way in one of the most fiendish floods of the river's history. The faulty foundation had been undermined, just as the geologist said it would be, and the dam broke, as he said it was bound to break; and, as soon as the water was drained out, it was apparent that the lake had been filling rapidly with silt, just as a professor of engineering said it would. The *Ben Hur*, by the way, was beached, and the magnificent private launch went over the dam and was never heard of more. Not much attention had been paid to the geologist or to the professor; the people had been given a seven-year water spree; mules again drew the streetcars; and the bonded indebtedness remained to threaten municipal credit. Thus ended the first lesson in damming up this little river. The dream so pleasantly nourished, along with the not-so-well-laid schemes of our engineers, was all at once a ghastly wreck. Verily, there it lay "deep under the flood . . . with mud and slime for its burial mound."

Years passed and people forgot what the place looked like. The whole thing was such an unsightly wreck that no one even wanted to be reminded of it. It was ten years before the municipality again took heart and began to think what might be done with the broken, disrupted, disordered and mud-encrusted remains of the once glorious vision.

Under an energetic mayor, engineers were found who thought the mistake could be remedied. Ways had been discovered to correct the faulty foundation; and, since the lake was filling so rapidly with silt, it was deemed advisable to raise the crest of the dam in order to secure a greater storage capacity. Masonry for this purpose was too expensive, so an elaborate system of gates was devised along the top of the stone structure which were nicely adjusted to tip at exactly the right moment to ease the pressure in exceptional floods, and tip back in time to impound the right amount of water. Blueprints of these intelligent contraptions covered many, many sheets of paper. I, along with other interested laymen, pored over them, and talked in hushed tones of their amazing ingenuity.

So construction proceeded. But on completion of the undertaking, the city refused acceptance on account of alleged defects. In due course floods came. Several gates were torn out; others stood firm but gagged, creating a drift jam of great acreage; water again found its way around one end of the dam and under its refortified foundation.

The mangled gates, the log jam, the roar of the torrent tearing under the structure, the delapidated powerhouse, beached boats and boathouses, silt deposits emerging as mud flats, first cracking in the sun and later covered with an impenetrable growth of pernicious weeds—these were the habiliments in which Nature chose to clothe this second costly encounter with a trick river god. The bondholders brought suit, a receiver was appointed, and the further financial contortions of the enterprise I have never followed out.

This second disaster revealed a still greater calamity: vast deposits of silt had practically filled the lake. It has been computed by engineers of competence and unquestioned integrity that in one flood of this river enough silt passed over the dam to have filled the reservoir level from intake twenty miles upstream clear to the top of the dam.

Engineers, like physicians, make mistakes—but they can't bury them. For instance, the first report on reclaiming the Everglades by means of drainage canals was made a century ago. Fifty years ago sixteen canals were dredged from marsh to ocean with disastrous results. Cost averaged about a million dollars per canal, and two million more was spent on locks, which exhausted the pot. Later, a sixty-eight-mile levee was built around the rim of Lake Okeechobee to keep hurricanes from blowing water out of it, and two extra canals were built at a cost of twenty-five million dollars; and then another twenty-five million was spent in ditches and pumps to induce the water to flow into the main canals. The measure of drainage success was registered in fires which swept hundreds of thousands of acres of dried-up muck, destroying soil fertility wholesale. Then the rains and hurricanes of 1947 proved this multimillion dollar drainage inadequate by dumping on the area fifteen thousand square miles of rain water which refused to drain away. Meantime, drainage had begun salting up the wells, since the original water level had been lowered and sea water sucked in to restore it (any kind of water seeks its level, salt water included).

Now, engineers in a different Federal service (Soil Conservation) have found out by survey that only six hundred thousand acres of the five million acres once claimed were any good for agriculture. So, having fought Nature for a century and gotten soundly beaten, man decided to compromise. At present, army engineers have the Everglades in tow with a far less ambitious plan which, it is estimated, will take ten years and two hundred and eight million dollars to complete, seventy million of which Congress has appropriated to cover cost of the "first unit."

By comparison with this Florida failure, our own little affair with the Colorado is minor if not minute. The second attempt to bridle this little stream rested softly in its silt until it was found that a dam could be built to withstand any flood.

The Tennessee Valley Authority has begotten "river authorities" all over this country. The main secret of its success is that in some measure it acknowledges to begin with the fact that a river is not a neighborhood affair, and that a municipality or other agency happening to be located on a river cannot bite out a piece of it and ignore the stream as a whole. The river is a living organism, or at

241

least it presents characteristics so similar to those of a living organism that to speak of it as such is more than a mere metaphor. A river system is one of Nature's units, and it must be dealt with as such if it is to be dealt with successfully for serving human needs.

Texas, with its thirteen major river systems (eight basins wholly within the state's borders, and the five others partly in), has proved to be an unusually favorable spawning ground for the TVA type of enterprise. There are now a dozen or more of these projects, either completed or under way, or in the promotion stage, between and including the Red River, which forms the state's northeastern border and the Rio Grande, which divides the state from Mexico along some twelve hundred miles of rough and thorny country.

It is unfortunate, however, that these children of the TVA have not all learned with sufficient thoroughness and acted upon the basic thesis of river unity. But of that, more later.

So it comes about that the third episode in the struggle to control the Texas Colorado River in the interests of humanity is the incorporation of the old wrecks of the two previous attempts in a much larger scheme, namely, reconstruction of the old dam along with other dams farther up the river.

Thus there emerges something like a system, with flood control in the foreground, electric power second, and recreational facilities taking a back seat as merely an incidental feature. At least dams are no longer located for the convenience of pleasure seekers, but at sites which meet engineering requirements, while pleasure seekers are forced to adapt themselves to these locations, as inconvenient as they may be. Meantime, the automobile and cheap gas have come to their rescue, and they no longer care whether a lake is ten, twenty, or even fifty miles away, provided the public builds wide, smooth, fairly straight, all-weather highways to the boat landings.

This system of dams impounds flood water and holds it in readiness for release as needed for power purposes and as required by farmers of the coastal area 150 miles to the southwest. It is a familiar story: flood control, irrigation, electric power. Rural areas for hundreds of miles are supplied electricity at low rates, while the lakes winding about, serpentine fashion among the hills, provide fishing, boating, camping, and nature enjoyment generally within easy reach of half a million people.

Buchanan Dam, first of the series, 150 feet high, stretches across a two-mile break in the limestone hills, creating a twenty-three-thousand-acre lake, seven or eight miles wide (in places), and thirty-two miles long as the crow flies. Its shore line of 192 miles indicates the meanderings, twistings, contortions, and doublings back of the old river channel. Three other dams—Inks, Marshall Ford, and the reconstructed one at Austin—follow, in the order named, down the river; and these four, along with two others now under construction, form a series designed to control and "civilize" a stream which has become increasingly more lawless as its watershed has been farmed, grazed and overgrazed, its wooded bottoms cleared, its banks denuded—all with too little attention to the rules in the conservationist's handbook.

Measurements of silt covering a seventeen-year period at the intake show that more that three thousand acre feet of silt from the uplands are dumped into Buchanan Lake every year. Engineers estimate that at this rate it will take about three hundred years to fill up; but, of course, long before it fills completely, its usefulness as a reservoir, constantly diminishing, will have ended.

Figures such as these have proved deceptive in calculating the life of a number of other reservoirs in various parts of the world. It should be pointed out that river records, especially in this country, do not cover a sufficient period to supply an absolutely reliable average. In the beginning, TVA engineers felt the need of more ancient records than were available of floods in the streams they were undertaking to control. They were driven to a search throughout the world for more ancient flood records of rivers; and from them based conclusions by analogy, since nothing better offered. But silt deposition is dependent upon so many different factors that studies of the world's river systems yield inadequate data for conclusive application to any particular situation.[1]

[1]Silt deposition is certainly a disease upon which the doctors disagree. In a recent Congressional hearing (April 1949) on bills to authorize construction of the Bridge Canyon Dam on Colorado River of the Far West, estimates by

A river is not a colt to be "broken," trained, stalled, and depended upon thereafter to do the will of his master. It is eccentric, unaccountable, either has no law of behavior or often keeps it secret from human investigators. Centuries, even, do not delimit its extremes.

There's a quiet little creek, stone-dry the greater part of the time, that rises a few miles west of my home city and flows east into the Colorado River which, at the point of this confluence, flows directly south. The creek thus makes an almost exact right angle with the larger stream. Old settlers tell me that once in the early history of the city there came a flood down this creek that pushed directly across the river and landed enough driftwood high on the opposite bank to supply the pioneer community for several years. I have found no written record of this flood, yet I know it occurred. The providential supply of a commodity as valuable in that period as wood, and one that lasted several years, could not be forgotten by the people enjoying its benefits. The fact that it stayed there for "several years" shows that it was deposited high on the riverbank, above the reach of the normal river floods which otherwise would have swept it away. Certainly no such flood in that little creek has occurred since. Yet it might occur again tonight, tomorrow, next day. It does not figure in the statistics of this stream whose flow has been measured only in recent years.

Silt is soil in suspension usually on its way to where it has no business. Part of it is topsoil, humus-laden; that is to say, stored by Nature with the rich leavings of life for purposes of reincarnation of life forms tomorrow, next year, next century. It is tinder ready to be kindled by that living Principle

Whose secret Presence, through Creation's veins
Running quicksilver-like eludes your pains.

Until the erosion of watersheds is under control, the big dam is only a stopgap, a short-term expedient, a "practical" solution to

engineers on the probable life of the reservoir—that is, length of time it will take to fill it with silt—ranged from fifty to three hundred years. "We don't know the answer to the silt problem," a reclamation engineer frankly told the committee.

serve until radical measures may be undertaken. Perhaps the worst thing about the big dam is that it obscures or covers up the real disease from the eyes of the great populous communities and relieves popular pressure for fundamental or systemic treatment of the diseased river. Certainly the patient is eased. It appeals to the person who thinks it a good joke to reply to long-distance considerations with, "What has posterity ever done for us?" Resorts to expedients by our overpraised pioneers certainly impoverished the land they found virgin and extinguished much of the beneficent life they found in a flourishing condition.

The investment in these Colorado dams has already paid for itself, for that matter, perhaps in flood control alone, if one counts the land value increment along the lower course of the river, say from Austin, Texas, to Matagorda Bay. But the diseased river is not cured, nor will it be cured until its watershed is cured. To impede the progress of silt from the point of its origin to the sea for even a hundred years or so is worth while. If that is the best that can be done, well and good. But in the long view, which the statesman in contradistinction to the mere political tinkerer is supposed to take, the solution of the problem is merely put off.

A situation has been set up which grows worse: the highlands deteriorate, the great reservoirs have a calculable life in terms of the short generations of man. It is true that the life of the coastal bays is given a lengthened lease, meaning that it is only to be more gradually smothered in mud.

This is not because our engineers do not know how to treat our diseased rivers, but because we are politically impotent. We can't apply remedies which Science prescribes and the Machine makes available because of the lag in political thinking as compared with technological thinking. Political thinking persists from an age antedating the Machine, which, like Frankenstein, has broken away from its creator, growing more lawless as he grows more powerful.

It would have taken machineless man a long time to have wrought the present havoc with soils. Without the Machine, our Great Plains would still be pastoral and stable. Our immense forests would have been renewing themselves almost as rapidly as a mere tool-using man could destroy them, although devastation by fire was a possibility even in that remote stone-ax age. With the free, unlimited, and unintelligent use of the Machine, we can accomplish (and at present rate will accomplish) a devastation in a few years which it would have taken our pre-machine ancestors ages to accomplish. The Machine accelerates, while political controls actually slow down, because the practical men, i.e., the after-us-the-deluge fellows, i.e., the why-worry-we'll-all-be-dead-anyway philosophers, are politically more powerful than those who propose radical remedies.

Well, maybe these dams we are now building so fervently, and, I think, so extravagantly, are at least putting soil fertility into safety-deposit boxes for exhumation by some later generation which, in its need, will rise up and call us blessed. There are parts of the world even today that have descended from an opulence comparable with ours to a "teaspoon" agriculture. Children are sent out with spoons to garner vest-pocket accumulations of humus stuck and hid away in cracks and crevices of rocks, to fertilize tiny terraces from which human beings are trying to wrest enough food to stay alive. What a bonanza one of our silt-filled reservoirs would be to future generations in this country if driven to such extremity.

Maybe, also, we shall gain the thanks of colonists of the coastal plain now being extended with our silt and sewage. And if this pleasing prospect is not enough to quiet twinges of conscience over our present prodigality with soil—letting the best of it slip away—let us find whatever solace there is in the thought of that immeasurably slow movement of earth's crust which will eventually lift up, as in the hand of God himself, plains and prairies from the vasty deep. Never fear, the buried lands will have their resurrection even before Judgment Day. They will be disinterred, refreshed, and revitalized with the sea's mysterious minerals, and perhaps for a wiser race of mortals to have and to hold but not to squander.

If, however, we are thinking more of the fortunes of our own children and grandchildren than we are of bequeathing a heritage to those shadowy forms which float before a mind's eye fixed on the vacancy of yawning ages—if we are thinking of our own near and dear kith and kin, we had better not be content with building colossal dams in the middle courses of our Texas rivers.

In the short-long view, it might be better to stop the soil before it starts away to find rest in a mud trap or on the bottom of the sea. Science now knows the devices by which this priceless topsoil can be made to stay put right where it is, but these devices involve conserving and using water as and where it falls from the gracious heavens. If and when these devices are fully employed, the silt-burdened runoff from watersheds may be so reduced as to make the extensive storage we are now providing for it seem quite irrational.

17   "LITTLE WATERS"

Following up the Colorado River another hundred miles, I ran across an enterprise which seemed to me to hold greater promise than all the big dams I had seen en route. Its name, Central Colorado River Authority, proved to be an alias. I expected to find plans under way for a big dam or maybe a series of them, hydroelectric power expansion, irrigation of arid acres, vast storage (including storage for anticipated silt), flood control, and so on. Instead, I found none of this, but a tiny project not concerned with Big Waters at all. Neither did I find any Big Money, but I did find a Big Idea. The economic interests of the whole county are harmonized in active and fruitful co-operation. Nature is being humored, not coerced; and results are accomplished with a minimum of outside financial assistance, in so far as the most important aspect of the work is concerned. It is being faithful first in little things.

While the success of this enterprise is due mainly to intelligent and energetic management, it seems to have been born under a lucky star, since Chance decreed that the preconditioning factors should be favorable. It is often remarked that one of the great advantages of a democracy is that it provides so wide a field for experimentation, tolerating even "fool experiments," as Darwin called them, approvingly.

Although this conservation program got its charter from the state under the pretentious name of the Central Colorado River Authority, the area in which it operates is confined to one county.

Fortunate circumstance number one is that Coleman County is a natural soil-water conservation unit. It looks, on the map, as if the person who drew the county lines deliberately marked off the upper reaches of the creek systems, all seven of them, and included no other drainage element to confuse the situation. Five of these creeks flow south and empty into the Colorado, which forms the county's southern boundary. The other two drain the northern portion of the county. Thus the political unit exactly fits the drainage unit. Since this county was organized in 1851, before soil-conservation plans were ever heard of in this part of the country, the conjunction of the geographic unit with a conservation unit is just one more of those happy accidents.

The next fortunate circumstance was the existence of legal machinery permitting the state to charter such an enterprise and endow it with the necessary authority as well as with a little cash. Really, the enabling legislation under which this authority is issued did not contemplate so small an enterprise: it had larger, but less scientific, projects in mind. So Chance, again, must get the credit.

Another preconditioning factor making for the success of the CCRA is that the inhabitants of Coleman County have experienced long periods of water scarcity. Often ranchmen had to "drive their stock to water," a phrase which must be enriched with actual experience before its depressing implications can be appreciated. One ranchman told me that during a drought some years ago he had to drive his cattle three miles to water for one hundred and eleven consecutive days. Villages and towns sometimes had to haul water for domestic use forty or fifty miles by rail or truck. In one village I visited, peddling water from door to door had been a recognized occupation for forty years: price, forty cents per barrel. Unsanitary conditions had been tolerated perforce, and typhoid had been common. In short, years of deprivation had already prepared the public mind for the reception of an ambitious program when the CCRA was created in 1935 by an act of the Forty-fourth Legislature.

The next fortunate circumstance is that there are no "Big Waters" here to bedazzle the public mind with grandiose schemes, but only "Little Waters."[1] For it must not be supposed that the "streams" all actually flow, except on occasion. The word "stream" in this context is a metaphor, naming dry channels where water, *if any*, may flow. The opportunity to flow is there whenever there is water present to take advantage of it. These small waterways are called gullies, or branches, ravines, or dry "cricks" in other sections of the country. We call them arroyos. They drain off flood water through wide-bottomed, U-shaped "draws," "swags," or "depressions." The county is credited with only 28.30 inches average annual rainfall, so most of the time the "streams" are streamless.

East and north, the surface of this conservation unit is generally rolling, but with considerable tableland; west and southwest, it is hilly, with wide valleys devoted to stock raising. The twenty thousand people live dispersed on farms, stock ranches, widely scattered villages and small towns. The largest town has only about eight thousand population. Until A- and H-bombs become much cheaper and delivery service greatly improved, it would hardly pay an enemy country to bother with Coleman County.

The time has come, like it or not, when one more criterion must be

[1]This term is taken from an eighty-two-page tract of the same title, the result of a co-operative study made by the Resettlement Administration, Soil Conservation Service, and the Rural Electrification Administration, under the sponsorship of Harold L. Ickes, Chairman of the National Resources Committee. The study was made by H. S. Person, Consulting Economist; E. Johnston Coil, Economist; and Robert T. Beall, Associate Economist. It has occurred to me that the fresh approach in this pamphlet (issued in 1935), and especially the "humanizing" of the problem, may be due to the fact that the authors of the study are all social scientists.

added to the list by which the wisdom of any given public policy may be judged: does it make for concentration or dispersion of the people over the face of the earth?

Since this is a land of "Little Waters," it is natural to find the program of the "Little Waters" people stated in so many words. "The solution," says Sam H. Cooper, Executive Manager of the Authority, "does not lie in spending all your money and toil on one great reservoir along some main stream; but it lies in *splitting up the pot*—building dozens of *small* reservoirs near the *sources* of tributary creeks leading into big rivers; in other words, storing up water near the source." (Italics supplied.) More specifically, Mr. Cooper says the general plan is "to control, conserve and distribute flood waters for all useful purposes as needed; to regulate the flow of flood waters from small ravines, small creeks, and the larger creeks. . . . This involves the construction of three classes of reservoirs: (1) small ponds and lakes [one thousand of which had been completed when I visited there]; (2) medium-sized reservoirs for community, municipal and small town use [six had been completed at the time of my visit and locations selected for ten more]; (3) larger reservoirs for flood control, irrigation, municipal, industrial, farm and ranch purposes." One such major project has been completed.

The larger installations have had WPA assistance, and the major one came in for the usual Federal appropriation. It is, however, in the smaller undertakings, tiny by comparison, that the real significance of the program lies. The Authority itself received an initial appropriation of five thousand dollars, nearly all of which was spent for dirt-moving machinery. It employed its own crews to man this machinery; and, by "contracting" with individual landowners and with village communities on cost basis with small per cent added to purchase new machinery, it has now eighty thousand dollars worth of efficient equipment and keeps several crews at work in the field continuously. This is conservation "at the grass roots," and opens up a field of almost unlimited extent, for there are thousands of square miles of upper watersheds in Texas—and, for that matter, throughout the Great Plains—which present similar opportunities for self-help in dealing with "Little Waters."

In this, as any but the most blurred vision can see, is the poetic simplicity of every Big Idea: catching the water where it falls, using it on or near the land of the just or of the unjust, as the nondiscriminatory bestowal suggests; obstructing and retarding runoff by every known means; trapping it by the cupful, barrel, or acre-foot, as the lay of the land offers the opportunity—thus making preventive war upon erosion. This is Nature's way—Karánkaway Creek vs. Tres Palacios. This is treating a water course as an organism instead of as a mechanism. This is a restoration of natural conditions, which, widely applied to a semiarid rolling or broken watershed, would soon make the more violent methods found along the lower courses of rivers—great drainage systems, levees, dredgings, gigantic mud traps, unnecessary—unnecessary, I mean, on so vast a scale.

It is only through these minute projects that old erosive wounds will be healed. It is only by the scientific management of Little Waters that we may hope to stop the gashing of new wounds in this suffering land. Here, at least, is hope of stabilizing soil, lifting the ground-water reservoirs back to near normal, replenishing dried-up springs, enticing wild life back, and nipping in the bud those disastrous floods now scourging the lowlands. Sociologically considered, it is a practical means of dispersing populations. True, it will not move seaboard cities to new locations back of our own "Urals"; but it does at least provide a "rooting" from which, in case the worst fears materialized, civilization could grow again. Concentrate water and you concentrate population; spread it and the scattering of population is automatic. This appeals not only to common sense, but with some force to those victims of fear who are now fearing something more substantial than "fear itself."

Even the most convinced conservationists often overlook the fact that a dispersed population conserves soil fertility while concentrated populations destroy it. The "wastes" of living on the farm go back into the soil. As communities grow in size, garbage, sewage, and other wastes become a more and more serious problem. Animal life, whose wastes are rich in life-giving elements, give place in the larger population centers to machine wastes, which are poisonous.

252

Rivers flowing through them are no longer rivers of life but rivers of death. The incinerator and the drain destroy the earth and the richness thereof. St. Edwards College, near Austin, Texas, has a keen professor of agriculture who contracts with the city to dump its mountainous garbage onto his compost heap, from which, after Nature's processing, it is fed into the impoverished soils of the college farm.

Another water-obstructing device, besides those already mentioned, widely used in Coleman County is the so-called detention dam, which holds up a flash flood for a day or two until its anger is softened, and then sends it purling on its way with all the roar removed. Meantime this "detained" water is irrigating and freshening up vegetation by spreading over acres of adjacent flats. This type of obstruction is like any other dam except that it is built to let the water leak out gradually. Half a dozen "detentions" may occur down a single draw, reminding one of the beaver dams of long ago, using one flood over and over again to moisten up marginal areas until the water is all used up. A ranchman told me that twenty acres which he had watered in this way at a cost of a thousand dollars now furnish stock more and better grazing than all the rest of the two hundred acres enclosed in that particular pasture. This is triple economy, for, while equalizing the flow of the stream, it enriches the overflow land with a slight deposition of silt and supplies needed moisture.

Villages co-operate. A convenient site is selected, and a dam is built usually with both storage and detention features, storing the water up to a certain level and then leaking it out after that level is reached. Boating, fishing, picnicking, athletic games and other recreational activities are provided. Wild life comes back to these "oases." The Goldbusk community, for instance, was surprised and delighted to find a flock of Canada geese spending the winter on their little lake immediately following its completion. None had been known in that community except in the memory of its pioneers. This charming goose courts domestication.

The CCRA also contracts on a cost basis the terracing of fields and pastures and "ripping" to open up to infiltration soils which have become sealed over by years of abuse, and the building of small ponds, called "tanks." In short, by all known devices applicable in this area, Little Waters are prevented from becoming Big Waters. Nature's way becomes man's way; the "pot is split up," and rain is made to bless instead of to threaten.

"As yet," says Mr. Cooper, "we have completed only about fifteen per cent of the 'must' part of our program, but gradually we are getting the job done."

The state of Oklahoma happens to be an enlarged edition of Coleman County, since it, also, is a land of Little Waters. It contains within its borders nearly all of the headwaters of its interior streams. It should cause no surprise, therefore, to find the Oklahoma Planning and Resource Board issuing a handsome pamphlet entitled, *Water in Oklahoma*, which presents the case for Little Waters convincingly, and gives the Little Waters program priority.

It seems to me a matter of first importance that the soil-water conservation district should be identical with the natural drainage unit. Unfortunately, most of these districts are formed on a county basis. A drainage unit should be carved out of a county, or out of two or more counties to form a soil-water conservation district. Then there is not only the opportunity but the inspiration to do something tangible toward using rain water where it falls and keeping topsoil in place.

The county is an expensive anachronism, anyway. The new edition of Rand McNally's "Cosmopolitan World Atlas" (first complete revision in fifty years) puts little emphasis on county borders any more. "In the old days," says a representative of that publisher, "the county was the basic unit of all maps. Now it has lost its importance. The city is practically everything." Quite so. Political units devised to meet horse-and-buggy transportation no longer fit auto-and-airplane transportation. It has been estimated by government scientists that the 250-odd counties of Texas could be reduced to sixteen units at tremendous saving of expense, as well as adding to the convenience of the people served by county administrations.

In short, the county is a "survival" in the anthropological sense, representing the usual "lag" in political thinking in our fast-moving machine age. It is kept in existence merely because of social inertia and fear by owners that land values may slip a little if the county courthouse is taken away. In all probability, this common-sense reform could be instituted or, rather, slipped in, only by some intelligent dictator in the topsy-turvy times of violent revolution. Just imagine the fight there would be now over so small a matter as *naming* the new political division: "Goliad" County to lose its identity in a "Victoria" administrative unit—"Only over our dead bodies!" People are just that way (perhaps wisely that way), and one had just as well make the best of it. But it is no reason why conservation agencies need be forced into this antique mold.

In Coleman County and in many other counties of the Colorado watershed, there are hillside seeps that seep no more; wet-weather springs that have been inactive for years; and many "permanent" springs of pioneer times now dry as a bone. I was shown mesquite flats bare of vegetation between the scraggly trees, with soil tightly sealed by seasons of pelting rains—flats once porous and absorbent with the sod of that choicest of native grasses, the curly mesquite, from which there was little or no runoff except in heaviest downpours. Before the white man fell upon this land with ax and plow and with his multitudinous herds of grazing animals, small quantities of water were trapped by innumerable devices—a drop here, a cupful there, a hidden trickle underground, a cache in an old animal burrow, minute particles held viselike in the clutches of particles of soil—reserves from minute to microscopic, but amounting in the aggregate to a gigantic "ever normal" reservoir to fend against those fearful droughts that occasionally curse the land.

It is a mistake to assume that the big dams catching water from eroded and still eroding watersheds store more than was stored in the days when natural forces detained rainfall in the highlands and let it gradually leak away. Compared with the original uses to which rainfall on Texas watersheds was put, big dams merely salvage rather than conserve. We have relocated the reservoir and changed its character, each for the worse.

Formerly, timbered bottoms, brushy hillsides, and wide grasslands, thickly sodded, soaked up rain water like a sponge. It seeped into the subsoil and eventually filled sandy underground strata from which it found its way by devious paths into bubbling springs at lower levels, trickling off to join other trickles to form (on still lower levels) streamlets whose confluence made streams—all moving unhurried in a widespread network toward the river channel. At every step this water was baffled, retarded, held up, so to speak, and made to deliver its toll to life. Nature was not interested in turning turbines or floating barges, but in producing just as much vigorous, varied, and abundant life as possible, dispersed along the way from the plains to the sea.

Some think this is a dream. Not so: the overwhelming proof lies in the land richness and life richness which we found here. Had not some such conservation by natural forces been in progress for countless ages, our early explorers would have found a desert quite as forbidding as may now be in the making. Throughout the eras of Nature's dominion over this land there were, of course, occasional disharmonies, violences, moments of madness, against which, however, precautionary measures had been taken to see that no irreparable damage was done.

Under natural conditions, the whole expansive watershed was a giant sponge which was pressed by gravity ever so gently, ever so steadily, to drain its life-giving contents without niggardliness and without excess. This was the heyday of the Little Waters. Floods came then as now—ten, fifteen inches of rainfall in a day over limited space—but the soil, well covered, took no pounding, and waterways were lined with vegetation which cushioned the assaults and tamed the rage of plunging waters.

The Little Waters people simply propose to reinstate Nature's plan in so far as it can now be re-established. They seek to rebuild the ravaged land, detain water where it falls, re-enact a toll system, utilize ancient storage facilities, reconstruct the old defenses, gouge out here and there innumerable pockets in hillsides to catch runoff. They plan to re-moisten the dried-out sponge, unseal the pores of embittered crust, re-water the watershed, and encourage it in every way to hold rather than shed the water which the heavens bestow.

Maybe water-nervous people find a sedative in the knowledge that only a puny trickle of the water that falls on the United States is diverted at all. "Figuring an average thirty-inch rainfall," says one such statement from an authoritative source, "the total yearly precipitation on our country would be around five billion acre-feet. Our total diverted use involves only a little more than two per cent of the supply thus made available from the clouds." There are millions living in the water-scanted West, however, who refuse to be comforted. It is not the amount of water in the country or in the world that interests them so much as its availability. Available water comes to them in little splatters of rain averaging anywhere from ten to thirty inches per year. To have and to hold this scanty apportionment right where it is delivered is the big problem of the Little Waters people. And it is not stated in this comforting bit of statistic exactly what is meant by "diverted." Is the water which now pours in such torrents off plowed fields, off denuded pasture lands, down the drainage ditches of highways and railways, on down the brush-cleared bottoms and scoured channels of creeks and rivers—is all this counted as "diverted" water? I doubt it. But an immense diversion has occurred, nevertheless.

I found Mr. Cooper sensitive to this type of diversion. His jealous eye was fixed on highway drainage as we rode along.

"Look at the map," he said. "This county, which needs every drop of water that falls, is gridironed with the drainage systems of highways and railways."

The drain is not inconsiderable, either. Any observant person who has traveled by auto or train in the semiarid West has seen bankfull ditches conducting torrents of water out and away from pastures dry as dust, as if in mockery of the grass withered to the roots. Nothing could better illustrate the unintegrated character of a community which suffers this folly and has suffered it for a quarter or even half a century. I have seen villages, through which highways and railroads have constructed their drainage systems, buy water back, hauled by truck or railway tank car at a fabulous price—not in an emergency, but year after year!

It would seem logical in a land of water scarcity that every agency whose work altered in any way the "lay of the land" would be placed under obligation to alter it only in such a way as to retard runoff and save the precious rainfall for the use of the inhabitants upon whom Providence attempts to bestow it. But exactly the reverse policy is pursued in the construction of railroads and highways. The dominating thought here is to get rid of the water and conduct it out of the country just as rapidly as possible. Engineers learned their drainage lessons in lands of excess water and now apply these lessons rigorously in areas of insufficient rainfall. Highway departments and railway companies have been haled into court so often on account of *flooding* adjacent lands that they have grown tender on this point, and naturally so. There is no case on record that I can find where either of these agencies has been sued, even in droughty sections, for depriving the land of the benefits of rainfall.

Still, one can scarcely fail to note the damage that is done to fields and pastures lying on slopes below transverse railroad or highway drainage ditches. However, in these same droughty sections, if the landowner can show any flood damage from a drainage system, he has a good case in court. So conservative is law! The lawmakers and the people generally got to thinking of flood damage first, and they can't seem to get their thinking around in reverse and consider the damage that may be done by taking water out of the country before it has had time or opportunity to confer its full blessings upon the people in the immediate vicinity of where it falls.

It is curious to note that the Great Khan, visited by Marco Polo in the latter part of the thirteenth century, considered this point: "The roads across them," [the pastures] says Marco Polo, "being raised three feet above the level, and paved, no mud collects upon them, nor rainwater settles, but contrary runs off and *contributes to improve the vegetation.*" (Italics supplied.)

I have talked with highway engineers whose work lies in areas of insufficient rainfall, and find them sympathetic but unconvinced that anything can be done about it.

Says one: "An ideal case can readily be assumed where water collected by highway drainage ditches could be used to irrigate adjoining land. This is not generally practical, however, for most of the land is cultivated and level." He is thinking of his own particular district. Again, "Erosion of road ditches is almost unknown in this area. Ditches are more often filled with sand blown off of adjoining fields."

He says further that most complaints about drainage have to do with land that is flooded. Moreover, "When the drainage is toward the road, the owner wants the road kept low so that the water can run across it, but the owner on the low side wants the road kept high to act as a dam or levee to prevent the water from reaching his land. If we had some way," he said, "to control the rainfall then the ideal situation of designing highways to keep the water on the land might be realized."

The more one goes into the matter of highway drainage systems, the more complicated it becomes. In one district in Texas a community requested the highway engineer to build an embankment across a small creek and place the drainage outlet high enough to create a small lake which was used for a year or two as a recreation center. Then a boy was drowned in it, and immediately the community about-faced and demanded that the lake be drained, which the highway department did at considerable expense. Another engineer recalled an embankment constructed to serve the double purpose of the highway and the impounding of water. Soon, however, the impounded water softened the embankment and ruined the concrete roadway on top of it. Railways have been more successful in this double-purpose type of construction.

The highway engineer whose attention is called to this matter usually points out that it is the business of highway drainage to humor "natural" drainage. "Whenever," he says, "a highway is constructed across even the smallest creek or ravine, care is taken to leave ample room for the highest water on record to pass unimpeded under the bridge or through the culvert. Thus 'natural' drainage is preserved."

This, however, is true only in so far as natural drainage is obviously indicated—that is, in places where water has cut into the surface and left a mark which we call a ditch, arroyo, ravine, gully, creek, or what have you. And it must be remembered that modern highways were begun after generations of land abuse, and hence everything that now appears on the surface of the land as drainage is not "natural" drainage at all. Thus the highway is often only emphasizing unnatural drainage.

But granting that veins and arteries are permitted free circulation, how about the "capillaries" of runoff, which spill by devious, percolating routes into these more obvious drainage ways provided by Nature? Examine a slope covered with natural vegetation during a rainy spell. Every weed, shrub, tuft of grass—every prostrate culm, fallen leaf, twig, or animal dropping—diverts water this way or that. Every drop that falls is entrapped in a maze of obstructions and must fight its way to the more visible runoff channels of the "natural" drainage system. Many are lost, that is, become entangled and detained in the soil itself, and follow down worm holes, down the outside surfaces of roots away from which the drying soil has parted, down crevices left by rotting roots or into bug burrowings, and into the very pores of the soil itself opened up by tiny, almost microscopic rootlets, alive or dead.

Whenever athwart this spongelike hillside a modern highway is built, the slow, downhill percolation of life-giving water is suddenly halted. The meandering little streams, the "capillary" circulation, spills into a ditch and is whisked away into what the engineer calls the "natural" drainage.

Certainly no blame attaches to a highway department operating under specific rules and regulations founded on laws which in a democracy are supposed to express the people's will. But that the people not only permit but direct such procedure is another instance of the public's attitude of ruthlessness in dealing with natural forces. It is an evidence of the psychology of dominance and barbarian swagger instead of a civilized attitude toward nature—that is, an attitude of accommodation, humoring, and co-operation.

The legal department of any state highway system offers many striking instances of entanglements with laws made long before the machine arrived to alter radically our way of life. A farmer with a field abutting on a highway asked permission to so construct his terraces that they might empty their water into a highway ditch. This terracing, however, reversed the natural drainage of the water. A farmer whose land abutted the highway a half mile away threatened suit against the state for turning more than the natural drainage onto his land. The state thereupon threatened cross action against the farmer up the ditch who did the terracing and thus unloaded the extra water. The second farmer objected that he didn't want to drag a neighbor into a lawsuit, and so the matter stands.

Another engineer suggests that if detention dams are installed at the behest of an individual owner, some means must be taken to keep that owner from overgrazing, since water detained on land from which natural cover has been removed is wasted by increased evaporation. Hence we might have the owner above the detention dam wasting water which another owner downstream could be putting to economic use.

After all, the state appropriates money for highways, not for building private irrigation systems, and no alteration in present policy is possible without legislation. Legislation comes from public demand, which can only follow upon public conviction of the vital importance of so managing Little Waters that they may make their full contribution to the life and happiness of the people to whom they are given.

This is only a special case of the maze of legal obstructions in which the soil-water conservationist finds himself as he attempts to apply the methods Science approves to areas cut up into tiny holdings, each holder standing belligerently on his legal right to do what he will with his own. Many other laws besides those affecting highways and railroad drainage systems need attention before soil-water conservation plans may be transferred from paper to the land itself. Indeed, gains in this program already (made largely at public expense) cannot be retained by any law now on the statute books.

H. W. Hannah[2] tackled this problem head-on in an address before a recent meeting of the American Association for the Advancement

---

[2]Professor of Agricultural Law, Department of Agricultural Economics, University of Illinois College of Agriculture.

of Science. I can quote here only a few sentences from the introduction and from the conclusion of his remarkable address:

"Progress in checking wasteful soil usage in the United States is gratifying—but not great. Though there may be areas in which substantial numbers of individual farmers have done about all they can do on their own farms, their soil maintenance and erosion-control problems are still not completely solved. Two major causes are responsible for this inability to finish the job: one is the lack of initiative and procedural machinery for bringing group action to bear on group problems; the other is the presence of certain legal road blocks inherent in our common-law system, and to some extent in our state statutes."

Professor Hannah then proceeds to specify legal road blocks with impressive emphasis. He does not enter into any detail concerning the "problem of group concern to the soil conservationist," that is, "how do we go about preventing the dissipation of creditable accomplishment?"[8]

"For the most part," continues Professor Hannah, "the rules of law within or in spite of which soil conservation activity must be pursued were designed to satisfy a set of human desires and to promote an economic expediency which regarded land as simply another item for sale, barter, use, and speculation. We are apt to feel that these rules, because of their long standing and because they have in the public mind become associated with the democratic processes, are unassailable, and that to suggest any change or revision is to suggest a modification of our form of government. In my opinion the relationship does not run that deep.

"It is more than likely that a retention of certain controls by the

---

[8]In grazing areas of Texas, for instance, an owner may be subsidized by the Federal Government for observing over a term of years proper soil-water conservation practices. At the end of the term he sells the land to another who proceeds immediately to cash in on subsidy-built reserve he finds there. Or the owner may turn tail on his own conservation work and cash in on it either himself or by lease. Presently the land is reduced to the same degenerated condition it was in before the first subsidy was paid.

Other means of euchring the government out of incentive money are in use, "dissipating creditable accomplishment," in Professor Hannah's polite academic phrase.

Federal Government at the time it was making a wholesale disposition of public lands could have supplied the needed protective element, and had that been done we today might never have guessed but what that was the democratic way to balance the interests of the individual and the interests of the public. In lieu of this retained control we have witnessed the spectacle of the Federal Government attempting to buy soil conservation from any farmer who will voluntarily make the assumed sacrifice, using as a yardstick no better guide than acres taken out of depleting crops or evidence that some limestone was spread or a terrace constructed."

If we are to have soil-water conservation in time and on a scale commensurate with the disasters present and in immediate prospect, political thinking must in some way manage to overtake the Machine and regain control of it.

18 DISEASED RIVERS

We hear a lot about "East Texas" and "West Texas," each with its Chamber of Commerce, and each represented by other voluntary organizations; but no north-south line can be drawn to separate the two. Much is made of the ninety-eighth or one hundredth meridian, "where the West begins," based on the assumption that Texas is set up with deference to the cardinal points of the compass. It is true that most of the twelve "climates" of Texas do have a north-south orientation, but geology, geomorphology, natural resources, population, and the human interests and occupations determined by these factors face each other not across meridians but rather across a zone running from southwest bearing northeast, cutting meridians at a slight angle. Lines connecting Montague County on the Red River with Starr County on the Rio Grande would enclose a transition strip indicating more accurately than any meridian "where the West begins."

The more important rivers of Texas, except the far eastern ones, all cross this diagonal; and the two longest of them (Brazos and Colorado) are almost exactly bisected by it. "Little waters" are found mostly north and west; "big waters," generally south and east. Particularly, the great spreading watersheds of the Brazos and Colorado, draining about a third of the area marked out above as "West Texas," lie northwest, while the middle and lower courses fall to the southeast. The area southeast of the zone, less in extent, contains easily four times the population. All cities of more than one hundred thousand population (except El Paso) are included in the coastward section.

Thus drainage is northwest to southeast, and the major river systems (except the Red River, Rio Grande, Canadian, and Pecos) lie, for all practical purposes, wholly within the borders of the state. If the accidents of history had made the systems of the Red River and of the Rio Grande the state's boundaries, the whole political unit would lie within the arms of these two great rivers, providing an ideal situation for a really scientific soil-water conservation plan.

Although somewhat short of the ideal, still Texas has a river unity hardly to be found in any other state in the Union and in few foreign countries. This river unity invites a unified treatment of Texas rivers if the end and aim is truly (as is always claimed) to attain the best land and water use. There is only one legislature to deal with, and talk of dividing the state is no longer taken seriously. "Texas, One and Indivisible," by the late Joseph Weldon Bailey, is still the most popular oration ever delivered in the state.

The time was when some Texas streams ran northwest, but that was long, long ago. A bulging of the earth's crust tilted the land from an altitude of around four thousand feet down to the coast. The dip is gentle enough, since it is fairly uniform throughout an extent of some seven hundred miles. It is an inclined plane, the northwest section of which receives too little moisture while the southeast is generally humid—too little above our zone and too much below it. With practically no other political units to fuss and dicker with

265

over water—no Arizona-California feud—a common-sense conservation plan would seem made to order, as obvious as the lay of the land.

The Balcones fault line, the state's longest and most distinctive physiographic feature, dividing lowland from upland, parallels roughly the Montague-Starr county zone. Beginning a little west of San Antonio, this fault swings northeast, bellying out a bit to include Austin and Waco before veering back to Dallas, where it becomes indistinguishable to the un-geologic eye, but really spreads fanwise underground from there in a northwesterly direction. Highway 81, San Antonio to Dallas, edges the escarpment, while Highway 77, Dallas to the Oklahoma line, follows a ray of the "fan." This fault separates the Edwards Plateau from the Rio Grande Embayment (see footnote, p. 91) at the south end and from the blackland prairies at the north end.

Surely northwest and southeast are strategic directions in Texas. The land tilts, the rivers run from northwest to southeast. Northwest is upland; southeast is lowland, set off from each other by an escarpment for hundreds of miles; northwest is dry, southeast is wet. Southeast is populous, northwest is not. Soil-and-water conservation is the big problem northwest; silt and flood control the big problem southeast.

But unco-ordinated "river authorities" are developing along all the important rivers—"lower," "central," "upper," for the main stem, and occasionally the same for the principal tributaries. Hydroelectric power, irrigation, flood control, and navigation each has demands which may be only partially harmonized. Navigation, for illustration, entails dredging; and in Texas rivers dredging usually means simply dumping into coastal bays (burying oyster beds, shrimp fields, and killing fish), since the streams near their outlets have become congested with silt.[1]

---

[1]The conditions described in the following news item are becoming of more frequent occurrence at the mouths of the larger Texas rivers:

"Army engineers at the Galveston district office have been asked to clear the Anahuac navigation channel in Trinity Bay of a silting condition which has all but blocked barge traffic into and out of the local slip. Silting has been especially bad near No. 9 light, and a section 1,000 feet south to 500 feet north

There is no end to this alternate constipation and purgation to give temporary relief as long as the soil of the watersheds, rudely disturbed by man's assaults upon it, remains unstabilized. Essential conflicts between and among interests, methods, and timing are becoming more and more apparent. There are too many cats in the bag.

So far as Texas is concerned, a unified soil-water saving and flood-control plan on a comprehensive scale within one geographic unit would seem to be directed by original nature and confirmed by man's political arrangements. The whole problem is intrastate. No Federal authority to impose unified development need be created, since the major river systems are already under one central authority. And unless the state assumes and discharges this obligation, natural unity will be split and the Legislature will become an arena for a battle of those blocs now foreshadowed by voluntary organizations.

Next to its harbors, the rivers of North America have had more to do with the distribution of its present population than any other natural feature. Often a harbor is at the mouth of a river, so the two work together. Inland, a ford, or a little falls to turn a water wheel, a damsite, a junction of two streams, head of navigation, or just water available for domestic use—any one, two, or more of these conveniences gathered up little clots of settlers which tended to grow into larger clots, and finally, in especially favorable locations, into those swarming conglomerations called cities.

It would seem that so essential an element in the life of a people as its rivers, and so obvious a one, would have been guarded as the nation's most sacred possession; and, when the Machine multiplied the uses and demands for water and for more water, increasing in a comparatively few years the per capita consumption ten- to a

---

of the light is filled in to a very shallow level, averaging around 5½ feet, it is reported.

"Barge tows coming into Anahuac are being delayed, since passage through the shallow area is possible only with high tide and good conditions. Rises in the Trinity River upstream discharge tons of silt into the bay and the channel must be dredged periodically so traffic can continue in the waterway."

hundredfold, we should expect every citizen to set the care of rivers first among problems of conservation—at least until smog began smothering city populations, at which point attention to the air we breathe becomes important also.

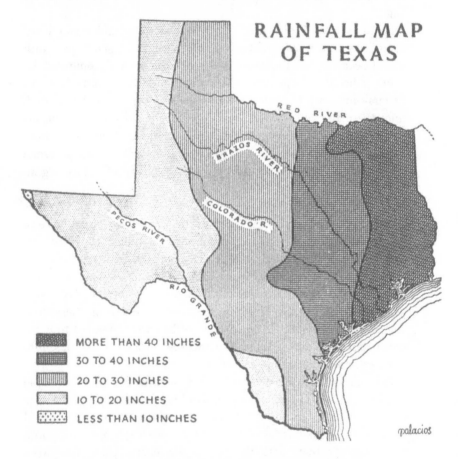

RAINFALL MAP
OF TEXAS

RED RIVER

BRAZOS RIVER

COLORADO R.

PECOS RIVER

RIO GRANDE

MORE THAN 40 INCHES
30 TO 40 INCHES
20 TO 30 INCHES
10 TO 20 INCHES
LESS THAN 10 INCHES

palacios

Pioneer America knew its Scripture. Could it not have taken hints from the words of the Hebrew prophets concerning the value of rivers? The visions of these desert seers had been intensified by experience, born and bred as they were in a land of water scarcity. The river as imagery in scriptural writing (see especially Psalms and

Isaiah) means life, abundance, salvation, here and hereafter, a blessing beyond price from the hand of Jehovah in his more lenient moods. Set first and foremost among the Seven Plagues of Egypt is the corruption of its principal stream. Fish died "and the river stank, and the Egyptians could not drink the water." In Genesis "a river went out of Eden"; and, in Revelations, John, in a state of ecstasy, was shown "a pure river of water of life, clear as crystal, proceeding out of the throne of God and of the Lamb." And he beheld "in the midst of the street of it, and on either side of the river . . . the tree of life" . . . In the factual record of a desert people, struggling for generations against a stingy water supply, lies the basis of much of this imagery.

But scriptural-minded as it was, pioneer America failed to grasp the true importance of its rivers. Too much stress, perhaps, was put on metaphorical, too little on their materialistic, aspects. The "hereafter" of interpretative sermons obscured the factual basis of the imagery and sucked much of the meaning out of the "here," as is evident if one cares to read critically the hymns of the period. Grouped in bareheaded reverence on the bank of a river already being contaminated by preventable pollutions, congregations witnessed the rite of baptism, a symbolic purging of the soul, singing of a heavenly river in words that imputed to it a purity they would have done well to demand of those earthly ones which were supplying their daily needs.

There has come lately into the language a phrase which should give every citizen a sense of nausea—"raw river water." For "raw" read sewage, machine poisons, dirt, disease, presently "radioactive waste" (deadly beyond belief), and unspeakable filth of a thousand kinds. In the more populous sections of this country, reservoirs for domestic use are often guarded from gulls and from other wading birds, since their feet, dabbled in the filth of rivers, may start a plague. There is, of course, no knowing how much contamination those still unguarded reservoirs receive from this source. Gulls fly a long way and love to feed in noisome places and then, being decent birds, wash their feet in cleaner water.

The desolation of our waters, although less apparent than that of the land, is deadlier. The price we have paid for concentration and mechanization is beyond all price. Science and technology change and convert, but creation remains a function of the Almighty.

Our political system is proving inadequate. It cannot seem to deal with rivers intelligently. There's too much "pull," pressure, and bargaining. Settlements were made first along the lower courses of rivers, for here water transportation was possible. Presently, inland cities arose, usually along the middle or upper courses of the more considerable streams. Railroads found it expedient to establish lower rates for cities at "the head of navigation" than for those vigorous communities which had taken their stand farther up the river. A fight ensued which usually took the form of moving heaven and earth (especially the legislative bodies of the latter) to advance "the head of navigation" upstream—not always navigation worthy the name, but any kind of phony navigation by which the railroads could be made to lower rates. Here began a perversion of the natural function of many streams, and soon the pork-barrel aspects of this competition stunk up politics with an odor similar to that arising from the streams into which the cities began dumping their filth: a double pollution.

Into the melee come other conflicting interests: hydroelectric power, irrigation, flood control, recreation—one or more camps pulling, hauling, lobbying for the lifeblood of one little stream or for that of larger rivers, and, finally, for that of the "great spinal river," involving the lives and fortunes of fifty million people. The "Big River" of the Ojibways, along with its main tributary, the "Big Muddy" of the Illinois Indians (really *one* river and overlord of America's waterways), even the great "Father of Waters," the majestic Mississippi itself, has been and is now being torn in the strife between rival interests. It is being treated as a mechanism that can be taken apart and pieces of it assigned here and there, rather than as an organism whose physicians should prescribe systemic treatment since its degeneration is systemic.

The only way to have a healthy river is to find out what it was like before it was corrupted by man and his machines, and base treatment on restoring, rather than on further corruption of it. A river diseased is much the same as any other diseased organism, and the doctor should first be taught to recognize the organism's normal state before being permitted to make a diagnosis and prescribe his remedies.

Consider the essential conflict of interests between navigation and soil conservation for the waters of the Missouri, a great part of whose watershed lies in a semiarid section. The Pick-Sloan Plan, under way since 1945, contemplates spending eight and a half billion dollars principally for big dams, irrigation, hydroelectric power, navigation, and flood control. But now comes the Department of Agriculture with its own plan for spending eight billion dollars in the next thirty years to "tie down the Missouri River Basin's soil and stabilize its forest and farm resources."

Dr. R. R. Renne, President of Montana State College, addressing the American Farm Economic Association, meeting in Laramie, Wyoming, September 1949, points out a conflict between these two plans. "To carry out the agricultural project concurrently with the Pick-Sloan construction may result in our discovering that a basically sound program will leave us with many large dams that will never operate as now planned." He raises the question of who has first call on the water that falls on the watershed. "Water is very precious and the program will be of very little local and national avail unless the resulting water is put to the most important and best uses." He proceeds to discount navigation's claims to *any* water, and concludes, "Agriculture should demand a position of priority rather than second or third place. It is high time we got first things first in the Missouri Basin." The line seems here to be drawn quite sharply.

Maybe a layman should not presume to discuss so technical a matter, but I can see in it nothing more complicated or difficult to understand than this:

Jones owns a mile of land along the big end of a little creek. Smith owns the upper five miles of it, or a few thousand acres which include the watershed of insufficient rainfall. When this land was first occupied by white settlers, the uplands were well grassed, soil stable,

271

and the creek bottoms plentifully timbered. Accommodating beavers had engineered free of charge a few low-water dams. The stream had a regular flow of clear water which no one thought to measure, and such floods as there were, although occasionally as violent as we have today, were not so very destructive.

Later occupants cleared off the timber, overgrazed the uplands, killed out the beavers and sold their hides, and practiced row cultivation up and down the more fertile slopes. These lands were in this unstable condition when Jones and Smith came into possession of their respective holdings.

Any heavy rain now lifted the creek out of its banks, overflowing Jones's farm, and deposited here and there bedloads of clays and gravel washed down from the gullied hillsides upstream. Floods tore down fences, drowned stock, wrecked crops, and otherwise played havoc along the lower course of the creek.

In order to curb this devastation, secure for himself a supply of irrigation water, and furnish power for his little mill, Jones builds a reservoir at a natural damsite of a size to impound current runoff. He knows the silt problem, so he enlarges his reservoir to a capacity which will take care not only of the water, but of the sand, gravel, and silt which the freshets bring down from the eroding uplands.

About the time this work on the Jones's holding is completed, Smith, fortified with a generous subsidy, begins a conservation plan which results in stopping erosion and curbing the runoff almost to the vanishing point. Old, dried-up springs begin to flow again, and there is a rise of some feet in the water level of the wells. The creek now has a pleasant little flow of water the year round, but certainly not enough, even reinforced by occasional freshets, to keep the Jones reservoir full, or run the mill or irrigate the farms.

Now, whose water is this, anyway? Should Jones be able to stop Smith's conservation program? Or does the court hold that the rain which falls on Smith's place is his to do with as he pleases, so long as he builds no big reservoir, capable of storing, say, more than fifty acre-feet? Jones complains that his investment is largely wasted if he can't get more water. Smith replies, "You had no business building such a big reservoir." Jones retorts, "Was I to wait until the abuse of your land ruined my land also, without trying to protect myself?"

It seems to me that the mistake was made in attempting an un-co-ordinated development. The creek is a unity designed to serve the land along its borders, and there should be an analogous unity in its management. A central authority, sympathetic with both projects, should have been set up to direct the reclamation of Smith's holdings—certainly in the interest of society—and then to determine the size and character of the downstream development, also in the public's interest.

My old Sunday-school teacher, J. B. Cranfill, a prohibition stalwart of the last part of the last century, used to deprecate the local option campaigns then in progress, saying, "The trouble with local option in dealing with the liquor traffic is that it is too local and too optional." The same may be said of our soil-water conservation plans—they are too local and too optional.

It doesn't take engineering training or any great scientific intuition to see that an eroding hillside fills with mud the fishpond into which it drains. It is unnecessary to have elaborate plans, studies, graphs, contour lines, and all that to decide that the Smith conservation work should be carried out in advance of the construction of the Jones dam. As the saying goes, anyone with one eye and half sense can grasp that at a glance. Under one ownership, a man would be thought crazy who built a dam on the lower course of his creek before he took the pains to stabilize his soil on the watershed which was being swept away right under his nose with every flood.

Indeed, what is required here is *social* engineering. Opposing ownerships must be harmonized and made to see that their interests are, in the long run, identical. In the language of Professor Hannah (quoted p. 261), there must be "initiative and procedural machinery for bringing group action to bear on group problems." Before employing construction engineers to carry out some piecemeal project, much ground must be broken. The long-term view of reclamation projects must be established in the public mind. Jones and Smith must be shown that their true interests, far from being in conflict, are, in fact, identical. Their land may be divided, but its drainage system is one and indivisible, jointly owned, and therefore must be jointly developed and administered. The organic nature of river systems and the community of interest in them must be fully understood in order that public opinion will support such legislation as may guarantee river-basin improvements in logical order and prevent the "dissipation of creditable accomplishments" after such improvements have been completed. Physical science, technology, the Machine provide only the physical means for making effective the will of the community; they do not give that will intelligent direction. That must be done by the social scientists and politicians.

Elephant Butte Dam was long the pride of the country, and a generally accepted demonstration of scientific water management. Its storage capacity was 2,638,000 acre-feet in 1915. Now 450,000 acre-feet of silt have settled in it, and at present rate it will be filled level full of silt in ninety-eight years.

Something happened to the beautiful and historic valley lying between the dam and the Colorado line. For three centuries Indians and Spanish colonists occupied this truly wonderful valley, content to exact from the soil only what the soil was designed to yield. But in the middle of the nineteenth century an exploitative economy swept in with conquest by the United States. By 1890 there were 1,525,000 sheep and cattle grazing in the valley, from the dam to the northern boundary of New Mexico. At the present moment, two thirds of the land in this valley, irrigated for nine hundred years, is no longer irrigable on account of siltation and erosion.

Only 10 per cent of the water in the Rio Grande flows in from the Rio Puerco, but it brings along with it 60 per cent of the Rio Grande's total silt burden. This diseased tributary, draining 5,860 square miles, belches a terrific slime into the larger river which, at the point of confluence, becomes ten times as muddy as the Mississippi at its muddiest.

In its upper reaches this diseased river is devouring indigestible lumps of a great plain once heavily sodded and considered by stock-

274

men one of the finest ranges for grazing herds in New Mexico. The Bureau of Land Management has been at work on the Piedra Lumbre, one of the worst subdrainages of the Rio Puerco, building detention dams and dikes, regrassing and planting trees on eighty square miles. When this work is completed, water flowing from the Piedra Lumbre, we are told, will be "clear as it was the instant before hitting the earth." We may hope that once completed, the powers that be will not permit this "creditable accomplishment" to be "dissipated."

This is a small drop in the big bucket of the Rio Grande watershed, but it doesn't take a reclamation engineer to see that it is a step in the right direction, and one that should have been taken before the first mortar was poured on the Elephant Butte project.

Soil conservation means tying down the soil. That, in turn, means water conservation on the land where the water is received as rain. On the droughty watershed it means retarding the flow of the water as it falls, inducing it to take underground channels to refill failing ground-water reservoirs, and the creation of a multitude of small surface reservoirs, called "ground tanks" in the Southwest. This involves altering the face of the earth somewhat, introducing cover vegetation, often sodding plowed fields, terracing, installing gully blocks, detention dams, and restoring to the margins of streams vegetation known to retard current. In short, by every device known to science water is retained and runoff reduced. This is the procedure Science prescribes for these watersheds.

Now it takes water and lots of it in steady supply to float vessels or turn turbines; hence, great impounding reservoirs are built to receive this runoff, if any, and to equalize the flow of the stream. I say "if any," for no one knows what the normal runoff of any Texas stream is, and similar statistics are insufficient in many other parts of the country. How much water got away from Nature's own retarding devices—vegetation, beavers, soil whose porosity natural agencies preserved? And how much got away before drainage systems of railroads and highways, now gridironing the watersheds, were laid out? No one knows. Soil conservation requires that water from the skies be held as long as possible in all areas of insufficient rainfall. But without statistics on normal runoff, how are engineers to know how big to build the dams, or whether, in a given situation, it is worth while to build a dam at all?

A twenty-year experiment with closed terracing in Dickens County, Texas, just below the caprock on land typical of great areas of the upper watersheds of both the Colorado and the Brazos rivers resulted in stopping runoff completely. This is the Experiment Station's answer to the much debated question, "What to do with rainfall?" in those sections where soil and slopes co-operate in the utilization of it.[2] Although the average annual rainfall in Dickens County is only 18.75 inches, one year (1941) there was 42.85 inches—and still no runoff or erosion! Not a drop of water escaped by surface drainage during this twenty-year period from the fields in which closed terraces were constructed. Of course all slopes and all soils of this watershed are not susceptible to such radical treatment, but millions of acres are, and a large percentage of the water that falls can be retained on the greater part of the remaining areas.

Suppose the account of this twenty-year experiment escaped the dingy, mimeographed sheet where it is now recorded, along with other buried treasures of similar importance to the public welfare; and altogether they became something in the nature of a revelation during a long cycle of drought and desperation. Suppose the scientific experiments in this field along with the countless preachments of conservationists became emotionalized, generating a species of religious enthusiasm for "saving the soil." Stranger crusades have swept the country.

In short, what if all talk and headlines about soil conservation were transferred from maps and plans to the ground itself? What if all the villages and towns of those desiccated regions, thousands of them, began suddenly to impound runoff in ravines and creeks round about for domestic use and for the recreation of their youth—fishing, swimming, boating, et cetera—to keep these restless creatures

[2]1065 Progress Report, Texas Agricultural Experiment Station, A. & M. College of Texas, entitled *No Run-off and No Erosion for Twenty Years.*

from running off twenty or thirty miles to amuse themselves deleteriously?

If this were to happen, how much runoff would be left? Nobody knows. It is X, an unknown quantity, for which no serviceable equation has yet been devised. Such a program would start ancient springs running again, and would lift the water level in thousands of wells. There's little doubt about that. And the water that did reach the big reservoirs downstream would be largely *clear* water, and the lives of the reservoirs prolonged indefinitely.

How can all these apparently conflicting interests be handled in a democracy like ours? The larger part of the wealth and the great bulk of the voting population are generally found along the middle and lower reaches of any given river. Land values are concentrated, and those powerful forces interested in maintaining and increasing these values support further concentration of population right where the congestion has already occurred.

Population thins out progressively as you leave the huge aggregations along the lower courses of river systems, travel up tributaries, and climb out on plain and plateau. A different psychology prevails. The big city is divorced from Nature, so much so that the linkage between life and soil tends to become disjoined. Vegetables grow miraculously in the market. Giant elevators and limitless warehouses are filled from railroad cars. The sight of these fruits of the land raise in the mind of the average city dweller a dimmer and dimmer vision of golden harvests stretching away to the horizon, or of wide expanses of blooming orchards.

On the other hand, he is intensely aware of the importance of water, water, and more water. When, however, water turns its ugly face upon him, leaps his defenses and tears his city to pieces, he loudly demands its immediate control. He rarely considers the control of water where it falls, but turns his mind to dams and bigger dams, levees built higher and higher, and deeper and deeper drainage ditches.

The attack upon river systems embodied in some of these "conservation" plans represents the typical attitude of the white man toward his natural environment, hostile and arrogant rather than gen-

277

tle and co-operative. Nature, uncoerced, once exercised a benevolent influence over the waters that fell from the heavens. Nicely adjusted was Nature's balance. Soil, removed from the uplands in the gentlest of all "erosions," built terraces and prairies only as fast as soil could be manufactured by those natural agencies assigned to the problem. There was no "dumping" into coastal bays of silt, machine wastes, oil, and filth, impoverishing the natural life of these waters. Texas rivers were once truly "rivers of life." As long as Nature was in control, each river system was nourished as an organism, and its business was conducted for all, impartially, on a self-sustaining basis.

I am told that a lot of the land on these watersheds is really not worth saving. One may buy good land for less per acre than it would cost to save the land now being washed away. This is a partial statement of the situation, since no account is taken of the loss to society generally of the annihilation of a basic resource, and no estimate is made in this accounting of the damage done by the silt from this "worthless" land as it is deposited downstream. Of course, there are areas eroded now past redemption. The land is worthless. It is not even performing the function usually allowed in a western phrase to the most worthless of all land, since it no longer "holds the world together." However, this worthless subsoil is now being permitted to cover up good land downstream, or fill up costly reservoirs, or deaden the waters of rivers and of coastal bays. An eroding area of this kind is a running sore on the face of the earth, and must be healed if the stream which receives the suppuration from it is to be restored to health.

In spite of its cinema reputation, Texas is not tough, that is, ecologically. It is really a tender land, and cannot stand the buffetings that certain other areas of the world have endured and still support a human population in health and vigor. I have seen parts of the toughest part of it—the black waxy prairies—finally succumb to the assaults of a feckless generation, cotton dying in patches of such extent as to give whole fields, green-mantled in early spring, an appearance of some sort of dingy leprosy before bolls have had time to mature. I have seen in my boyhood days the crown and upper slopes of gentle hills, on which the black soil is mixed with fragmented limestone, produce ninety bushels of oats to the acre. Now many of these slopes are all bleached out, pale as death, and really dead in so far as ability to support vegetable life is concerned. Many old-timers have seen bale-to-the-acre[3] land in 1883 abandoned as worthless in 1903.

Generally, rainfall diminishes as you travel up Texas streams, ranging from forty or fifty inches annually along the lower courses to only twenty or fifteen in sections where the smaller tributaries thread out over the western uplands. If any part of the state needs more water, it is the watersheds—the roof of the house, not the gutter—but that is the very section which, more than any other, is shedding its water unused in the greatest volume. Its towns and villages suffer, its formerly abundant wild life grows scarcer year by year, its water table is being lowered, while soil losses in some areas border on the disastrous.

Dr. Bennett, Chief of the U.S. Bureau of Soils, says that the nation's annual average soil losses through erosion amount to three billion tons, including 92,172,300 of the five major plant food elements: nitrogen, potassium, phosphorus, magnesium, and calcium. It is no wonder nutritional diseases are on the march in a population whose food is being thus radically impoverished, year after year.

For every bale of cotton Texas has produced in the last hundred years, soil nutrients to the value of $322.90 have been lost by erosion, and a bale of cotton will do well to average in value $100 for the period. "While farmers have gone broke," says J. G. Burr, "the bays of Texas and oyster reefs have paid the penalty of being a dumping ground for this eroded soil."[4]

Finally, if there is not enough water to go around, to whom should it be awarded? And if it must be divided, on just what basis should the apportionment be made? The Texas Board of Water Engineers is called upon to make such decisions day after day. This board is

[3]The value of a "bale" in those days ranged from fifty to a hundred dollars.
[4]*Texas Game and Fish*, August 1948, pp. 15–16.

directed by the Legislature to give preference and priority to the following uses of water in the order named:

1. Domestic and municipal uses, including water for sustaining human life and the life of domestic animals.[5]

2. Water to be used in processes designed to convert materials of a lower order of value into forms having greater usability and commercial value, and to include water necessary for the development of electric power by means other than hydroelectric.

3. Irrigation.

4. Mining and the recovery of minerals.

5. Hydroelectric power.

6. Navigation.

7. Recreation and pleasure.

Thus the advantage of a political unit's coinciding in boundaries with a geographical one is already apparent. A legislative enactment provides rules of priority and sets up a board to administer the same. But this mechanism, valuable as it is, is far from sufficient. Further measures imposing the unified treatment of a river system are necessary, with successive steps in the development prescribed to insure that first things come first.

The Federal Government, through numerous grants, has recognized the financial inability of the average farmer or ranchman to treat his land right. A little extension of this principle, along with a single, efficient organization bent on securing the right use of the whole river, would effect prodigies of conservation. Such an organization could not fail to see in erosion a double menace, first to the watershed interests, whose land is being gradually taken away from them, and next to the hydroelectric, navigation, and, generally, the down-the-river interests in the vast burden of silt which the waters carry. Scientific flood control, therefore, would begin ordinarily in the higher reaches of a watershed and work down slopes, ravines, arroyos, and lesser tributaries to the main artery, for certainly there in the highlands is where the emergency is greatest, and there is where an ounce of prevention is worth a pound of the cure custom-

[5]It will be noted that this provision gives priority to every use of water by "uplanders," suggested in the chapter entitled "Little Waters."

arily applied along the lower reaches of the river system. It is easier to break a colt while his mouth is tender than it is, later, to conquer him as an outlaw.

At least this would seem to be the logical order for conservation measures to be arranged in any political unit divided about half-and-half between "Little Waters" and "Big Waters."

INDEX

283

285

Jackdaw, 103
Jaeger, Werner, ix
Jaques, Florence Page, 98
Jason, 215
Javelina, 51, 68, 145
Jefferson, Thomas, 208
Jeffries, Richard, x, xiii, 125
John, the apostle, 269
Juke box, 201

Kant, Immanuel, 116
Karánkaway Bay, 227
Karánkaway Campsite, 63
Karánkaway Creek, 227, 252
"Karánkaway," derivation, 8
Karánkaways, 4; location of, 8; canni-
    balism, 10–11; cruelty of children,
    11; missionaries' records, 10–13,
    153; and pioneers, 13–14; reject
    Christianity, 13; trance of, 14–16;
    eviction of, 14; place names, 17;
    fishermen, 21; gigantic size, 22;
    kitchen middens, 22; odor of, 188;
    drink of, 215
Keefer, C. A., 18, 24, 27, 30, 33
Keefer, Mrs. C. A., 30
Kennedy, William, 152
Killdeer, 65–66
Kilmer, Joyce, 59
Kitchen middens, 22
Kluckhohn, Clyde, 12
Kuechler, Jacob, 5
Kuykendall, J. H., 14

La Bahia, 4, 153
Laffite, Jean, 4, 129
Land, absentee ownership of, 108
Land ethic, 108, 209
Land, "worthless," 278
Lantana, 93, 100
La Salle, 3, 22
Lehmann, Valgene W., 162–63, 167,
    170–71
Leopold, Aldo, 114
Lewis, Alfred Henry, 80
Lincecum, Gideon, 4
Lincoln, Frederick C., 193
Linnaeus, 149
Live oak, 105–6, 142–43
Live Oak County, 92
"Loin disease," 212
Longhorn, 106, 219
287

Lotor, the washer, 81
Low plains, 55
Lumberman, 200
Lycaon, ix

Macaulay, T. B., 126
Machine, menace of, 245–46
"Maginot line" psychology, 207–8
Man-of-war bird, 24
Mantis, 104
Maqui, 92, 110, 199
Marco Polo, 46, 258
Martins, 98
Marvell, Andrew, 132
Marx, Olga, ix
Matagorda Bay, 22, 91, 229
Mayfield, G. R., 187, 194
McCarley, Mrs. Jack, 75, 76
Meadow lark, xi, xiii
Mechanists, the, vii
Mencken, H. L., 201
Mesquite, 56
Mesquite Bay, 27
Midwest, American, viii
Mirage, 123
Missionaries, 12
Mississippi River, 270
Missouri River, 271
Missouri, Kansas & Texas Railroad
    ("The Katy"), 1
Mockingbird, 98, 203
Montague County, 264
"Morality" in nature, 104
Morwitz, Ernst, ix
Mosquitoes, 150–53, 188–89
Muir, John, 107, 156
Mustang, 106
Mustang Bay, 61

"National" birds, xiii
"Naturalist," definition of, vi
"Nature faking," xiii
Nature "frames" her pictures, 148–49
Nature's "conservation," 205, 278
Nature's morality, 216
Nebraska Rod & Gun Club, 27
New Braunfels, Texas, 5, 6
Newman, Frank, 191
"Night soil," 116
Nile River, 229
Nudist cult, 139
Nueces River, 17, 92, 108, 197, 226

Rockport, Texas, 18
Rogers, Benjamin Bickley, 37
Rousseau, 149, 216
"Runoff" experiment, 276
Rutledge, R. H., 38

Sabine Pass, 3
Saint Charles Bay, 18
Saint Edwards College, 253
Saint Joseph's Island, 4, 21
San Antonio Bay, 18, 226
San Antonio River, 4
Sanctuaries, ancient, 36; modern, 38
Sand dunes, 62
Sandpiper, spotted, 204
San Jacinto, Battle of, 4
San Patricio County, 5
Scamander, 235
Schulz, Ellen D., 217
Schwab, Gustav, ix
Schwartz, Charles W., 167, 176
Schwarz, E. A., 99
Science and Sentimentalism, vii
Science, pure and applied, 57–58
Scienter, 85
Scissortailed flycatcher, contrasted
    with Swift, 180; feeding habits,
    180–81; migrations, 179, 183;
    "hazes" other species, 182
Selway Bitter Root Primitive area, 38
Semple, Ellen Churchill, 112–13, 199
Seton, Ernest Thompson, 81
Shakespeare, 215
Sheep, and erosion, 208; folklore, 215;
    prefixes, 217
Shelley, P. B., 200
Shofar, 220
Silt, defined, 225; builds island, 225;
    Houston Ship Canal accelerates
    movement, 226; in Lake Corpus
    Christi, Possum Kingdom Lake,
    Trinity River Delta, 226; in Tres
    Palacios and Karánkaway Creek,
    227; in a "black land" creek, 228;
    farmer sells, 229; "Colorado River
    Raft," 232–33; classical example,
    235; in Lake Austin, 239–40; in
    Lake Buchanan, 243; in storage,
    245–46; remedies, 246–47
Simmons, Geo. Finlay, 188
Simois, 235
"Sixth" sense, 49

Skin, as a cooling system, 133; expo-
    sure of, 133, 135; self-renewing,
    133; alters human types, 134; care
    of, 134; enduring nature of, 136;
    pleasures of, 137–39; and dress, 140
Skunk, 53, 176
Sky, 117; and architecture, 118; psy-
    chological influence of, 119; and
    animals, 120; and poets, 121; illu-
    sions of, 122–24; transformed by
    Copernicus, 124; of the moon, 125;
    horizons of childhood, 126; "travel-
    ing," 130–31; of the prairie, 174
Smith, Emmett, 53
Smith, John, 81
Social engineering, 273
Soil-water conservation, insufficiency
    of present program, 206; by control
    of "Little Waters," 250–51, 253;
    Nature's way, 252, 256; Oklahoma
    Plan, 254; an "ever-normal" reser-
    voir, 255; highway and railway
    drainage, 257–61; legal "road
    blocks," 261–62; subsidy gains dis-
    sipated, 261–62; unified plan, 267;
    political system inadequate, 270;
    "Pick-Sloan Plan," 271; Department
    of Agriculture Plan, 271; hypotheti-
    cal case, 271–73; Rio Grande Valley
    of New Mexico, 274–75; "no run-
    off, no erosion in 20 years," 276;
    who owns the rain?, 280
Solis, Father, 13
South, Rev. Robert, 137
Southern Pacific Railway Company,
    164
Sparrow, English, 138; lark, 103
Species creation and extinction, 34
Spencer, Herbert, xii
Spoonbill, roseate, 66
Sport, prestige of, 45
Squirrel, 131
Staats-Zeitung (Texas), 5
Starlings, xii
Starr County, 264
"State" birds, xiii
Steel trap, 74
Stilt, black-necked, 63
Sunlight, "filtering" of, 100–1
Swallows, violet-green, 98
Swallows confused with Swifts, 192
Swifts. *See* Chimney swifts

289

The KARANKAWAY COUNTRY
and ADJACENCIES

Miles

VICTORIA

GOLIAD

PORT LAVACA

Guadalupe River

San Antonio River

Garcitas Cr.

Lavaca River

East Karankaway Cr.

Karankawa Bay

Trespalacios

Matago

OLD INDIANOLA

PORT O'CONNOR

ARANSAS
NATIONAL WILDLIFE REFUGE

Coleto Cr.

REFUGIO

Aransas River

Copano Cr.

Copano Bay

Blackjack Peninsula

San Antonio Bay

MATAGORDA I.

50 miles to
Camp in the Brush

ROCKPORT

Nueces River

ARANSAS PASS

Aransas Bay

ST. JOSEPH I.

NORTH

WEST   EAST

SOUTH

CORPUS
CHRISTI

Corpus Christi
Bay

MUSTANG I.

Corpus Christi Pass

← PADRE I.

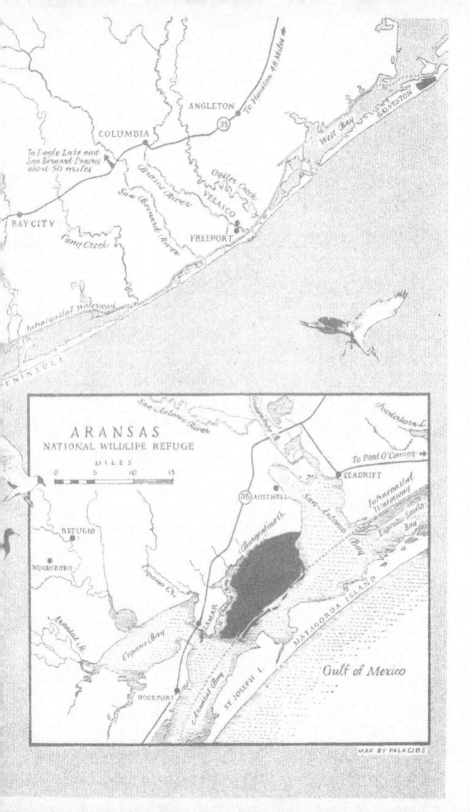

ANGLETON

To Houston 48 Miles →

35

COLUMBIA

To Eagle Lake and
San Bernard Prairie
about 50 miles

West Bay

GALVESTON

Brazos River

Oyster Creek

San Bernard River

VELASCO

BAY CITY

Cany Creek

FREEPORT

Intracoastal Waterway

PENINSULA

ARANSAS
NATIONAL WILDLIFE REFUGE

MILES
0   5   10   15

San Antonio River

Powderhorn L.

To Port O'Connor →

SEADRIFT

35 AUSTWELL

Intracoastal Waterway

REFUGIO

Burgentine Cr.

San Antonio Bay

Espiritu Santo Bay

WOODSBORO

Copano Cr.

LAMAR

St. Charles Bay

MATAGORDA ISLAND

Aransas Cr.

Copano Bay

Aransas Bay

ST. JOSEPH I.

Gulf of Mexico

ROCKPORT

MAP BY PALACIOS